© Copyright – J.C. Marco Ltd. 2022 – All rights reserved.

ISBN: 978-1-7778014-1-0

The content of this book may not be reproduced, duplicated, or transmitted without direct written permission from the author or the publisher.

Under no circumstances will any blame or legal responsibility be held against the publisher, or author, for any damages, reparation, or monetary loss due to the information contained within this book. Either directly or indirectly. You are responsible for your own choices, actions, and results.

Legal Notice:

This book is copyright protected. This book is only for personal use. You cannot amend, distribute, sell, use, quote, or paraphrase any part, or the content within this book, without the consent of the author or publisher.

Disclaimer Notice:

Please note the information contained within this document is for educational and entertainment purposes only. All effort has been executed to present accurate, up-to-date, reliable, and complete information. However, no warranties of any kind are declared or implied. Readers acknowledge that the author is not engaging in the rendering of legal, financial, medical, or professional advice. The content within this book has been derived from various sources. Please consult a licensed professional before attempting any techniques outlined in this book.

By reading this document, the reader agrees that under no circumstances is the author responsible for any losses, direct or indirect, which are incurred as a result of the use of the information contained within this document, including, but not limited to, — errors, omissions, or inaccuracies.

To Tiffany,

Having you as my best friend has meant the world to me.
I want to express my heartfelt love and gratitude for being there with me through everything. Thank you for listening to my excited ramblings when new ideas came rushing into my brain. Thank you for being my cheerleader when I was weak. This book would not be a reality without your input, collaboration and knowledge.

I appreciate you.
Much love as always

To Treva,

Thank you so much for your input and knowledge.
Your expertise and feedback has been an invaluable resource, and I am forever grateful.

Blessed Be my Friend
Light & Love

IMPORTANT
PLEASE READ

As you begin your magickal journey, you will quickly discover that the craft can be customized to your own specific preferences and needs. The content provided in this book is intended to be informational so you can make your own decision about what will be integrated into your own personal practice. The craft is beautiful in the sense that you decide what stays and what goes. It's all about research, learning, reading, understanding and confidently building a practice that is true to you.

Do not feel obligated to follow or adopt the practices written herein. Change them, alter them, make it your own. That's what the craft is all about.

Find YOU and your MAGICK, however that looks.

Though this book is inclusive of many different cultures, traditions and practices, it is imperative that we do our due diligence to research and understand the many aspects of the craft that typically fall into 'cultural appropriation.' The craft has been influenced by many other traditions throughout the decades, so we need to respect those cultures and traditions if we choose to utilize their practices in our own craft and magick. Please be respectful if you adopt a practice that is not from your own ancestral roots.

Blessed Be.

Topics

1. A Magickal Journey
2. Magick - The Truth
3. Magic or Magick?
4. What is a Book of Shadows?
5. Book of Shadows Blessing
6. To Summon your Book of Shadows
7. Witchcraft, Wiccan or Pagan?
8. Types of Witches
9. Budget Witch
10. Wiccan Rules & Laws
11. The Wiccan Rede
12. An ye harm none, do what ye will
13. Thirteen Goals of a Witch
14. Threefold Law - The Rule of Three
15. Pentagram and Pentacle
16. Intention
17. Tools of the Craft
18. The Altar
19. Casting a Circle
20. Consecrating
21. Cleansing
22. Centering & Grounding
23. Clearing & Charging
24. Banishing
25. Shielding & Warding
26. Sigils
27. Witchcraft Symbols
28. Alphabets & Writing
29. Animals & Familiars
30. The Elements
31. Candle Magick
32. Herb Magick
33. Crystal Magick
34. Number Magick & Numerology
35. Magick for the Days & Hours
36. Wheel of the Year - Sabbats
37. Esbats
38. Moon Magick
39. Deities & Spirit Guides
40. Divination Methods
41. Creating your own Spells
42. Sources

PLEASE NOTE: These topics are not listed by page numbers. They are in order from beginning to end. The better you are connected to your Book of Shadows, you will find that it is instinctive to get to where you need to go. You can also use colored ribbons to mark different chapters.

A Magickal Journey

Witchcraft cannot be described
in a single definition.

At its foundation, witchcraft is a way of life that
someone chooses if they want to connect with
the energy inside and around them.
Witchcraft is a very personal choice that requires
you to look at every part of your life, give your
craft your whole heart, and respect and value the
energy in everything.

If these are your goals and you want to master your
craft with love, light, and a good heart, then you
are a Witch.

Welcome home. Welcome to the Craft.

Magick - The Truth

When it comes to practicing the craft, or Magick, I feel that it is important to know a few things about how to practice, where to practice, what to practice, and the many rules and laws that are associated with being a Witch.

Truth is....there really are none. It is simply a personal preference.

Don't get me wrong, there are a lot of practitioners out there that like to 'follow the rules' and practice with a very stringent set of ideals and methods. There is nothing wrong with that at all. If you are someone who likes to follow instructions and rules, then go for it. I tend to see many new beginner witches asking questions like; "If I do a protection spell, can I use Rosemary?", "What is the best crystal for a wealth/abundance spell?"

Asking questions is great, I mean, how else are you going to learn what to do, and how to do it properly? Truth is though, the best and most effective magick that I have found, is when you just get your hands dirty and try different things. The power of your magick comes from within you, not from any outside mystical forces, and there is really no need to obtain or have all of the special tools, herbs, crystals or fancy books. These 'things' are helpful in boosting your spellwork and energy yes, but every single one of us have magick within ourselves, we only need to tap into the innate abilities we have had this entire time.

That's the really fun part about being a witch, you get to decide what works best for you and your practice. If you decide that stirring your coffee in a ritualistic manner in the morning is a good enough means for 'casting a spell,' then rock it!

You decide how you want to practice your magick, simple as that.

Just be mindful that there are many 'traditional' practitioners out there who practice their craft with strict rituals, rules, and a mindset of right and wrong. These individuals can be a great resource to learn from absolutely, just don't get too caught up or feeling down if someone were to tell you that you are doing it wrong, because you are not. Respect another Witch and their practices, but you do not need to make it your own practice. Be yourself and have fun.

The information that is provided in this book has worked for thousands of witches across the globe. These are merely 'guidelines' of information that will help you better understand the craft. Take the best and leave the rest. Create your own magick and be yourself. The best way to find your own witchy groove is to grow, learn as much as your can, experiment, try different things and ALWAYS record or write down everything.

Magic or Magick

The Oxford Dictionary defines the noun "magic" as "the power to supposedly change things by calling on unexplained or supernatural forces." But it goes on to say, "Mysterious tricks, like making things disappear and then show up again, are performed as entertainment."
Those who conduct witchcraft, understandably, do not regard their practice as a trick displayed for the enjoyment of others.

The word "magick" was thought up by Aleister Crowley, who was a controversial occultist and the founder of the religion Thelema (from the Greek word for "will") and the leader of the British esoteric movement and spiritual practice that is now known as Wicca. He added the 'K' to the end of the word for a number of reasons, one of which was to set his art apart from that of stage magicians and illusionists, who only work to entertain people.

Some argue that the distinct spelling is redundant, particularly when discussing the craft or old deities, because the distinction is apparent. Crowley's Thelema theory, on the other hand, meant that he used the term magick to represent any act that brought someone closer to their 'True Will,' or life's purpose.

Our 'will' is distinct from our 'desires.' You may want a larger house, more money, or for someone to quit gossiping about you, but all of these things are in the present moment and will pass. There are a lot of outside influences, including friends, family and even co-workers who will try to tell you what you should or shouldn't do, but according to Crowley's idea, you should not conform to the wishes of others.

Your eventual destiny is established by your True Will, and all magick you do should be in line with it. Magic does not have to be supernatural to work. Magick is anything you do that leads to your True Will, no matter how ordinary.

Many witches use these words interchangeably, and some steer clear from the word 'magick' all together. If you prefer to use it in your writings, then it's your choice.

What is a Book of Shadows

A Book of Shadows is your personal journal where you can record everything that you experience and do magickally. Your Book of Shadows will be your sacred and private place to record instructions for rituals and spells, your experiences, magickal information, and your personal magickal journey.

When Wicca was still very much dominated by covens (a group of witches), there was only one Book of Shadows kept for the entire group, typically in the care of the High Priestess or High Priest. This shared Book of Shadows would only be revealed when the coven met for rituals, spellwork, or any other magickal workings. When the book was not in use, it was typically covered with a soft cloth and placed in a secretive location only known to its caretaker.

Today, even though many covens still use one Book of Shadows, it is not uncommon for individual witches to have their own Book of Shadows. Nowadays, the term 'Book of Shadows' is more of a commonplace term to describe a personal journal, full of your own favorite spells, their results, rituals, and magickal information that you have gained throughout your practice and journey.

It is important to remember that your Book of Shadows is a sacred place that will hold all of your thoughts, desires, dreams, spellwork information, rituals, and anything else that you wish to record. Keep your Book of Shadows in a safe place, and don't forget to perform a book blessing and/or a protection spell to keep your Book of Shadows safe from prying eyes and any negative influences. Don't worry, there is a Book Blessing and a spell to find a lost Book of Shadows included for you to use.

Difference between a Book of Shadows and a Grimoire

BOOK OF SHADOWS: This is your personal journal or diary for your craft. This is where you write down all of your spells, your rituals, the outcomes and also your thoughts and feelings. This book should be of great importance to you and should be kept in a secret place away from prying eyes.

GRIMOIRE (gruhm-waar): This is a book that holds all of your magickal information. This includes all of your research, your correspondences and any other knowledge that you find essential to your craft. This book does not necessarily have to be kept private, but it's your choice.

The book that you have in your hands right now is essentially a
2-in-1 Book of Shadows and Grimoire in one.

Book of Shadows Blessing

Select a candle of your own choosing, and be mindful of the color in which you pick.

Try using a candle of your favorite color for an extra boost of power.

Clear your mind and focus your energies before continuing with the blessing.

Once you have centered yourself, light the candle and say the following:

Elements, protect this book

From wandering eyes and prying look.

Fill it with thine ancient power,

in this right and ready hour.

H. (2008, May 10). Book of Shadows Blessing. SpellsOfMagic. Retrieved July 1, 2022, from https://www.spellsofmagic.com/read_post.html?offset=0&post=32954

Book of Shadows Blessing

To Summon your Book of Shadows

Should your Book of Shadows fall into the wrong hands or be taken by evil, casting this spell will return the book to its rightful place. This spell will also help in locating your Book of Shadows should it become lost to you.
Feel free to use any herbs or crystals that you feel personally connected with to increase your energies and vibrations, and when you are ready, chant:

> I call upon the ancient power,
> to help me in this darkest hour...
> Let my book return to this space,
> claim haven in it's rightful place!
> So mote it be!

Witchcraft, Wiccan, or Pagan?

What's the difference?

Witchcraft, Wiccan or Pagan

As you explore magickal life and modern Paganism, you'll hear the terms Witchcraft, Wiccan, and Pagan a lot. They're not the same however. Paganism and Wicca are often discussed as independent concepts. Do they differ? In a nutshell, yes, but it's not that simple.

Gerald Gardner introduced the public to Wicca, a Witchcraft tradition, in the 1950s. The Pagan community is divided on whether Wicca is genuinely the same kind of Witchcraft that the ancients practiced. Regardless, the terms Wicca and Witchcraft are frequently used interchangeably. Paganism is an all-encompassing term for the multitude of different earth-based religions.. Even though not all Pagans are Wiccan, Wicca is in this group. So, here's what's going on to help you understand. Every Wiccan is a witch, yet not all witches are Wiccan. All Wiccans are Pagans, however, not all Pagans are necessarily Wiccans. Finally, some witches are Pagans, while others are not; some Pagans practice Witchcraft, and some don't.

Many people have a sense of "coming home" when they embrace an earth-based spirituality. People frequently comment that when they first encountered Wicca, they felt as though they had finally found their place. Some people see it as a way to get TO something new, not away from something else.

Please keep in mind that the term "Paganism" encompasses a wide range of diverse traditions. Even though one group may do something a certain way, not everyone will follow the same rules. Statements about Wiccans and Pagans typically relate to MOST Wiccans and Pagans, with the understanding that not all practices are the same.

Many witches who are not Wiccans exist. Some are Pagans, while others consider themselves to be something completely different. The name "Pagan" derives from the Latin word "Paganus," which roughly means "Hick from the Sticks." It was first used to describe individuals who resided in the country. As Christianity grew, the same country dwellers were sometimes the final holdouts sticking to their previous beliefs. As a result, the term "Pagan" came to refer to individuals who did not worship the 'typical' god of Abraham.

Gerald Gardner popularized Wicca in the 1950s, and many modern Pagans have adopted the discipline. Gardner did not invent Wicca, although he did base it on ancient traditions. Many Witches and Pagans, on the other hand, were perfectly content to continue on their own spiritual journey without converting to Wicca. So, "Pagan" is an encompassing, or umbrella term for a variety of spiritual beliefs, including Wicca, which is just one of them.

Witchcraft, Wiccan or Pagan

If you are still a little confused about the differences between Witchcraft, Wicca and Pagan, the below definitions formally describe each of their meanings. You can also do your own research and use the notes section on the next page to record your own findings.

Witchcraft [wich-kraft, -krahft]

noun

- the art or practices of a witch; sorcery; magic.
- magical influence; witchery.
- an irresistible influence or fascination.
- rituals and practices that incorporate belief in magic and that are associated especially with neo-pagan traditions and religions (such as Wicca)
- Practitioners of Wicca ... use the tools ... such as the broom (a purifying symbol), the wand, candles, crystals and the knife .... They refer to their practices as witchcraft ...— Lesley Wright
- Wicca, which emerged in the 1940s in England, is the original form of modern Pagan Witchcraft. — Meg Yardley

Wicca [wik-uh]

noun

- (sometimes initial capital letter) a nature-oriented religion having rituals and practices derived from pre-Christian religious beliefs and typically incorporating modern witchcraft of a benevolent kind.
- a religion influenced by pre-Christian beliefs and practices of western Europe that affirms the existence of supernatural power (such as magick) and of both male and female deities who inhere in nature and that emphasizes ritual observance of seasonal and life cycles.

Pagan [pey-guhn]

noun

- (no longer in technical use) one of a people or community observing a polytheistic religion, as the ancient Romans and Greeks.
- a member of a religious, spiritual, or cultural community based on the worship of nature or the earth; a neopagan.
- a person who worships many gods or goddesses or the earth or nature : a person whose religion is paganism.

Definitions of Witchcraft, Wicca and Pagan cited from www.merriam-webster.com

Witchcraft, Wiccan or Pagan

Types of Witches

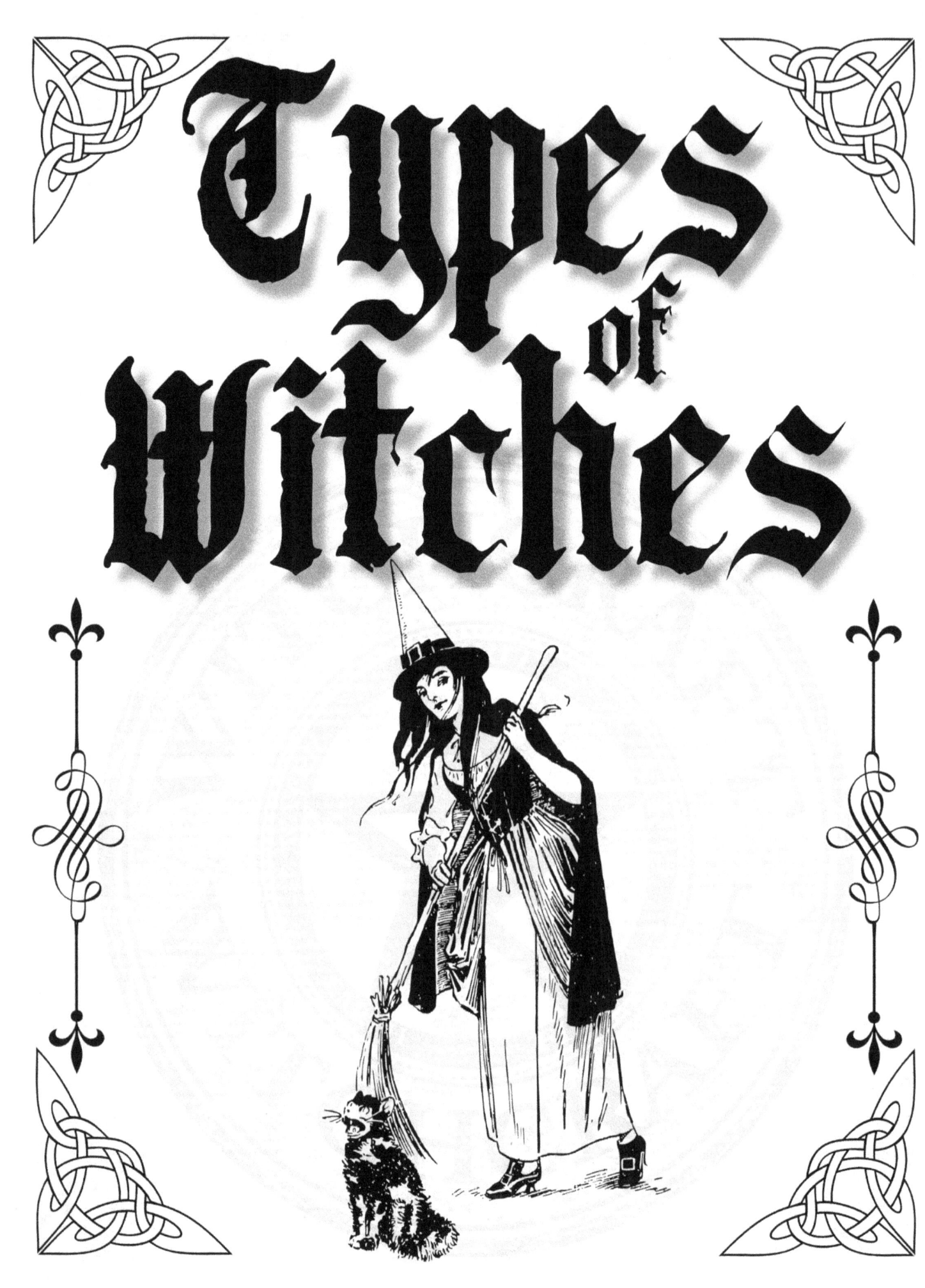

Which Witch is which?

Now that you have found your way home to the world of Witchcraft, you will most likely start to learn about certain practices and ideals that suit your personality, morals, style, and interests more than others.

Not to worry, because there are many different types of witches out there, and every one is unique in their own way. Each witch has their own way to practice their craft, and because of these individual practices, we have many different 'types' of witches in our community.

You will find a list of different witch types below. These examples are only a small portion of the many different types, and there is no limit as to how many types there can be. If you desire to be an electronic witch, then I say go for it.
Also, there is no rule stating that you have to identify with just one type, you can be multiple different types at the same time, or as we like to call it, an Eclectic Witch.

- Animal Witch
- Artistic Witch
- Baby Witch
- Broom Closet Witch
- Cosmic Witch
- Country Witch
- Coven Witch
- Crystal Witch
- Divination Witch
- Draconian Witch
- Eclectic Witch
- Elemental Witch
- Faerie Witch
- Garden Witch
- Glamour Witch
- Grey Witch
- Hereditary Witch
- Kitchen Witch
- Lunar Witch
- Religious Witch
- Sea Witch
- Secular Witch
- Solitary Witch
- Storm Witch
- Swamp Witch
- Traditional Witch

Which Witch is which?

Animal Witch

- A witch that respects and worships the animal kingdom in their practice.
- This witch will most likely have an animal familiar or a pet (typically a cat, but can be any animal of choosing).
- By having an animal familiar, these witch's are deeply connected to the energy of the animal kingdom.
- Usually can understand animal 'language' and speaks to their animal counterparts, are very in tune with animal signs and portents.
- Tends to relate to animals more than people.

Artistic Witch

- Tends to put magick into their art.
- Enjoys drawing, painting, instruments, writing.
- Hardworking and very creative.
- Enjoys doing their own DIY projects.
- Uses charged water, herbs and oils in their art.
- Likes to make their own candles and soaps.
- Typically has a fancy and ornate grimoire.
- Effortlessly writes their own chants and spells.
- Incorporates music into spellwork.
- Usually has an elaborate artistic altar setup.

Baby Witch

- Someone who is just beginning their journey with magick and the craft.
- Depending on who you ask, 'baby witch' is a debatable term as more experienced witches do not like to call their new recruits 'babies.'
- More commonly known as the 'Beginner Witch.'
- No, this is not a witch that sacrifices babies. LOL

Broom-Closet Witch

- This type of witch is exactly as it sounds. This is a term used for the many individuals in the witch community who have not revealed their path, journey, skill or religion to their friends or family. This could be due to their age, family religious beliefs pushing hatred toward the craft, or this could be a new witch who is scared to tell others, and by doing so, their path and journey in the craft is a hidden secret.
- Will typically practice in secret and discreetly.

Which Witch is which?

Cosmic Witch

- Uses planetary, celestial and zodiac energies.
- Studies astrology and astronomy.
- Includes supernovas, meteors, black holes, galaxies and eclipses in their craft.
- Uses astrology as a form of divination.
- Often skilled at astral travel.
- Worships the planets.
- Typically believes in aliens.
- Planetary alignments, lunar cycles, days of the week and planetary hours play a huge role.

Country Witch

- Typically has a home in the countryside.
- Has similarities to a cottage/green witch.
- Typically grew up on a farm.
- Deep love for all animals.
- Loves to be outside enjoying nature.
- Not afraid of physical labour; hard worker.
- Good at everything and quite the handyman/woman.
- Finds peace in the silence, does not like the city.
- Generally an eco-friendly individual.
- Practices everything a green witch does.

Coven Witch

- Works with a group of witches (the coven).
- All witches in the group typically work from one shared Book of Shadows.
- Dedicated to practicing rituals and spellwork with the other members, never alone.
- Believes that group magick is more powerful than solitary magick.
- The coven has a secret place where everyone meets to practice their spellwork, typically a ritual space.

Crystal Witch

- Prefers working with crystals and stones.
- Adept at crystal healing techniques.
- Usually interested in Reiki or energy work.
- Ability to channel balance in the Chakras.
- Meditates frequently.
- Enjoys working with the moon.
- Cleanses and cares for crystals regularly.
- Knowledgeable on all things pertaining to crystals, their properties and correspondences.
- Will usually use a crystal ball to scry.
- This type of witch is a branch of green witchcraft.

Which Witch is which?

Divination Witch

- Well versed in all forms of divination.
- Typically likes to use crystals.
- Enjoys using incense and smudge sticks.
- Tends to have a deeper connection to the spirit world and can read tarot cards proficiently.
- Can interpret signs and omens from the animal kingdom.
- Has the ability to pursue necromancy, but rarely.
- Can be clairvoyant or have prophetic visions.
- Intuition and perception is typically at higher levels, and this witch rarely needs to use any tools or additional items during practice.

Draconian Witch

- A witch who calls upon dragons to help aid in their magickal work.
- Tends to have dragon themed decor and imagery in their home and ritual space.
- Dragon deities, or deities resembling dragons are their primary worship.
- The fire element has a deep connection with this witch, and plays a vital role in the majority of their spells and rituals.
- Can practice astral travel with ease when conducting their spells and rituals.

Eclectic Witch

- Probably the most popular type of witch.
- Has a wide variety of like and interests.
- They can enjoy gardening and herbs.
- They can enjoy cooking and baking.
- They can enjoy astrology, the moon and stars.
- Can come from any religious background.
- Each eclectic witch is vastly different.
- Personalized magickal path, typically has their own journal or Book of Shadows.
- Eclectic; Pulling ideas and styles from many different sources.

Elemental Witch

- Power comes from one of the four elements; earth, air, water, or fire.
- Invokes elemental energy for magickal goals.
- Typically uses tools that correspond to the elements to enhance spellwork and rituals.
- Usually works with one element in which they are drawn or bonded to, and respects the other three elementals and their power.
- Can simultaneously work with all four elements at the same time.

Which Witch is which?

Faerie Witch

- Communicates well with the Fae.
- Leaves Fae folk offerings regularly.
- Rosemary and Thyme are common herbs.
- Learns and researches the Fae and spirit lore.
- Belief in mythological creatures.
- Enjoys building faery gardens and houses.
- Enjoys nature, especially forests and waterfalls.
- Likes to work with crystals.
- Environmentally friendly.
- Skilled and knowledgeable on Fae mannerism, tradition and greetings since they can be tricksters.

Garden Witch

- Also known as a Forest Witch, Green Witch or Hedge Witch.
- Highly connected to the energy from Earth.
- Typically has their own garden of herbs.
- Learns and studies local plant life.
- Uses the energy from the earth and universe.
- Connects with plants, trees and wildlife.
- Respects local land spirits and all things green.
- Often has a green thumb and enjoys plants in their home.
- Potions are made from flowers, herbs and plants.

Glamour Witch

- Works with beauty, love and self-love spells.
- Enjoys makeup and perfume.
- Often a fan of bath rituals.
- Works with deities such as Aphrodite.
- Loves roses and beautiful flowers.
- Makes DIY soaps and cosmetics.
- Has a love of Rose Quartz.
- Connects with delicate animals.
- Pink, Red and girly aesthetic.

Grey Witch

- Embraces light and dark magick.
- All about the balance in things: Yin & Yang.
- Often works with spirits.
- Often uses some form of divination.
- Tends to be a neutral force in the world.
- Not afraid to express opinions.
- Believes that nature is balanced.
- Often does not believe in karma.
- Tends to cast curses when it is needed.
- Directs bad energy back to where it should have gone.

Which Witch is which?

Hereditary Witch

- Comes from a family of witches.
- Family tradition is followed strictly.
- Typically has a wise ancestor in which they learn from.
- Learns magick from quite a young age.
- Family Book of Shadows was passed down.
- Balanced family life.
- Witchcraft is 'in their blood.'
- Aspires to have children so that they can also pass down the tradition.
- Outsiders are rarely included in rituals.

Kitchen Witch

- Loves to cook and bake.
- Use of herbs and spices in their cooking.
- Loves being with family; the caregiver.
- Purchases local in-season and organic goods.
- Most likely has a garden for herbs and veggies.
- Adept at herbal remedies.
- Maternal instincts and loving nature.
- Infuses magick with every meal they prepare.
- Housekeeping tends to become a magickal task.

Lunar Witch

- Can also be called a Moon Witch.
- Deeply connected with the cycles of the moon.
- Practices spellwork and rituals during important moon phases.
- Timing for spells is heavily reliant on what moon cycle is best for the magick.
- One who likes to make moon water.
- Worships the moon goddess.
- Will typically study astrology and astronomy.
- One who enjoys to meditate under the light of the moon and invoke its energy.

Religious Witch

- An individual that believes in magick and also still believes in their own standard religion as well (Christianity, Jewish, Orthodox, etc.).
- Can maintain an equal balance of beliefs and practices.
- There are a lot of new witches out there that ask the same question; Can I be a witch and still be religious? The answer is yes. Many witches still practice their traditional religion along with practicing the craft.

Which Witch is which?

Sea Witch

- Loves to be near a body of water.
- Works with the oceans and seas for their magick.
- Their magick and worship is water-based.
- Use of beach related items for magick.
- Worships sea deities and water creatures.
- Connected with tha phases of the moon.
- Enjoys the energy of thunderstorms.
- Works with a lot of salt for rituals and spells.
- Feels relaxed when at the beach or near water.
- Enjoys doing lots of bath rituals.

Secular Witch

- Secular Witchcraft is a philosophy that forgoes the worship of gods and goddesses in its practice. It is essentially a variation of the conventional style of ritual magick and spellwork, as many witches are secular or atheist.
Because there is no theological philosophy that defines witchcraft and magic, witchcraft has an open door policy when it comes to spiritual beliefs.
- Typically has their own belief surrounding the craft and what it entails.
- Create your own path that is right for you.

Solitary Witch

- Typically someone who likes to work alone.
- Usually prefers to practice in their own home or preferred space.
- Prefers a more one-on-one practice when worshipping deities.
- Usually more comfortable to practice alone and in private.
- Most new witches start as a solitary while they are learning to become more knowledgeable before reaching out to other practitioners.

Storm Witch

- Most of the time, they focus on storm crafting and magick that is tied to emotions.
- One of those people who would sit outside just to watch a tornado because they find peace in the chaos.
- Summoning storms takes careful time and consideration.
- Often are very artistic and expressive people.
- Loves all kinds of extreme weather.
- Will be loyal beyond measure if you are their friend.
- Great with animals.
- Loves to play in rain puddles.
- Finds peace when standing in the rain.

Which Witch is which?

Swamp Witch

- Tends to focus more on traditional folk magick.
- Lives near a swamp or lake.
- Knows the importance of the healing properties of mud and herbs found in and around their home.
- Likes the 'earthing' practice, and can typically be seen walking barefooted.
- Usually skilled herbalists and potion brewers.
- Very adept at poppet and spell jar magick.
- Values family above all else.
- Likes to sing rather loudly at times.

Traditional Witch

- One who studies their ancestors and other folklore attached to witchcraft.
- Also known as a Folk Witch.
- Will focus on their own local history and spirits in order to honor the 'traditional' manner of practicing magick.
- Old history and customs are usually held in the highest regard.
- If you follow the Traditional Wiccan Witch path, you are one who will most likely follow the Wiccan Rede, the laws and rules, and will not sway or practice anything that strays from the 'right' path.

As you can see, there are plenty of different types of witches that are out there in the world. The 26 examples that I have shown you here is just a short list of the many possibilities. If you feel that you identify to a type of witch that is completely different, there is absolutely nothing wrong with that, and I personally say you should just be you, and practice however you feel most comfortable. Being different or weird or strange is awesome, and we love and embrace each and every witch for who they are, no matter what they believe or how they practice.

It is encouraged that you learn and read as much as possible, and forge your own path.

When it comes to your own magickal journey, there is no right or wrong.

Which Witch is which?

Be your own type of Witch. Feel free to do some research and see what other types of witches are out there, or you can make a whole new type of witch that suits you and your personal style.

Type:

Characteristics:
_____
_____
_____
_____
_____
_____
_____
_____

Type:

Characteristics:
_____
_____
_____
_____
_____
_____
_____
_____

Type:

Characteristics:
_____
_____
_____
_____
_____
_____
_____
_____

Type:

Characteristics:
_____
_____
_____
_____
_____
_____
_____
_____

Which Witch is which?

Be your own type of Witch. Feel free to do some research and see what other types of witches are out there, or you can make a whole new type of witch that suits you and your personal style.

Type:

Characteristics:

Type:

Characteristics:

Type:

Characteristics:

Type:

Characteristics:

Which Witch is which?

Be your own type of Witch. Feel free to do some research and see what other types of witches are out there, or you can make a whole new type of witch that suits you and your personal style.

Type:

Characteristics:
_____
_____
_____
_____
_____
_____
_____
_____
_____

Type:

Characteristics:
_____
_____
_____
_____
_____
_____
_____
_____
_____

Type:

Characteristics:
_____
_____
_____
_____
_____
_____
_____
_____

Type:

Characteristics:
_____
_____
_____
_____
_____
_____
_____
_____

Which Witch is which?

Be your own type of Witch. Feel free to do some research and see what other types of witches are out there, or you can make a whole new type of witch that suits you and your personal style.

Type:

Characteristics:
_____
_____
_____
_____
_____
_____
_____
_____
_____

Type:

Characteristics:
_____
_____
_____
_____
_____
_____
_____
_____
_____

Type:

Characteristics:
_____
_____
_____
_____
_____
_____
_____
_____

Type:

Characteristics:
_____
_____
_____
_____
_____
_____
_____
_____

Budget Witch

Simple things you can do to save money and still be the best witch you can be!

Budget Witch Tips

It's been said before, and I will say it again: How you practice your craft is entirely up to you. There is no right or wrong, and contrary to what some hardcore traditional witches might tell you, there is no need to go out and spend a butt-load of money on all the witchy things you need to cast a spell or perform a ritual. This section is going to clarify that you most likely have everything you need already, and if not, creating the things you need is just as fun and budget friendly.

First things first, there is a substitution for EVERYTHING

If you are new to the craft, spellwork and rituals, it is most likely a daunting concept when you look at the item list to perform a spell or ritual properly. Most of the time, when you see another spell that someone else has written, it is most likely filled with items that THEY have at their disposal and have tried and succeeded with those items. That being said, you might think that in order for the spell to work, you will need those exact items, but it's not always about the 'ingredients.'

When you are working a spell or ritual, the best part is to try different things. Don't be afraid to mix and match herbs, try different crystals, learn about correspondences and just get your hands dirty. That's where the true magick comes from. Get the thought about 'what is right? what is wrong?' out of your head right now. Your magick comes from your intention, not from the items that you buy and use on your altar or ritual space. Yes, they do help, but that's not what magick is all about.

- Rosemary can be substituted for any herb
- Rose Petals can be substituted for any flower
- Clear Quartz can be substituted for any crystal
- White Candles can be substituted for any candle color
- Tobacco can be substituted for any poisonous herb
- Frankincense can be substituted for any oil
- Sage or Palo Santo can be substituted for any incense

Budget Witch Tips

When it comes to having the items you 'need' to perform magick, there is no easier place to start than in your own home. A lot of new witches don't realize that they have just about anything they need already.

- Don't have a chalice? Use a wine glass or a piece of china meant for fancy dinner parties.
- Hmmm, I don't have the correct candle for this spell, what can I do? Do you have any birthday candles laying around. Those will work just as fine as any other candle. You could even use the flameless candles that are run on batteries if you need to.
- I don't have a fancy silver or earthenware bowl to place my water and salt into? Just use any bowl. Heck, I've seen witches using Tupperware for ritual use, it's quite practical and won't break.
- I don't have a statue of the God and Goddess? Well, if you have internet, a computer and a printer, there is always the lovely Google to help you out there.
- What happens if I don't have an Athame? Do you have a letter opener? What about a butter knife?
- No wand? Go for a walk in the forest. Almost certain you will find a stick or twig that calls out to you, and you can carve or decorate it however you want, which will make it even more powerful for you.

Are you seeing where these examples are leading? It doesn't matter if you do not have the exact item needed, you can make substitutions and use whatever works for you, that's the beauty of being a witch. We make the most of what we have available to us. It shouldn't be about going and spending money, because the truth of the matter is that Witchcraft can be a very expensive practice, however it doesn't have to be, plain and simple.

Collecting items that may be passed down to you while you are learning your craft is a great thing. If there is an item that you cannot substitute with anything in your home, you can always try the dollar store, a thrift shop, or join a Witchy swap group online. You can find everything you need at budget friendly prices, plus you are recycling and saving the Earth. Sounds like a win-win to me.

Budget Witch Tips

Wiccan Rules & Laws

Don't worry, we don't have broomstick flying witchy police to enforce these. Or do we?

The Wiccan Rede

Bide the Wiccan Laws we must, In Perfect Love and Perfect Trust.
Live and let live. Fairly take and fairly give.
Cast the Circle thrice about to keep the evil spirits out.
To bind the spell every time, let the spell be spoke in rhyme.
Soft of eye and light of touch, speak little, listen much.
Deosil go by the waxing moon, chanting out the Witches Rune.
Widdershins go by the waning moon, chanting out the baneful rune.
When the Lady's moon is new, kiss the hand to her, times two.
When the moon rides at her peak, then your hearts desire seek.
Heed the North wind's mighty gale, lock the door and drop the sail.
When the wind comes from the South, love will kiss thee on the mouth.
When the wind blows from the West, departed souls will have no rest.
When the wind blows from the East, expect the new and set the feast.
Nine woods in the cauldron go, burn them fast and burn them slow.
Elder be the Lady's tree, burn it not or cursed you'll be.
When the Wheel begins to turn, let the Beltane fires burn.
When the Wheel has turned to Yule, light the log and the Horned One rules.
Heed ye flower, bush and tree, by the Lady, blessed be.
Where the rippling waters go, cast a stone and truth you'll know.
When ye have a true need, hearken not to others' greed.
With a fool no season spend, lest ye be counted as his friend.
Merry meet and merry part, bright the cheeks and warm the heart.
Mind the Threefold Law you should, three times bad and three times good.
When misfortune is enow, wear the blue star on thy brow.
True in love ever be, lest thy lover's false to thee.
Eight words the Wiccan Rede fulfill: An ye harm none, do what ye will.

The Wiccan Rede (5 versions) (wiccanhuntress.tripod.com)(2001)

The Wiccan Rede
SHORT VERSION

Bide the Wiccan Law Ye must
In Perfect Love and Perfect Trust
Eight words the Wiccan Rede fulfill
An it harm none, do what Ye will
What Ye sends forth comes back to thee
So ever mind the Rule of Three
Follow this with mind and Heart
And Merry Ye Meet,
and Merry Ye Part!

The Wiccan Rede (5 versions) (wiccanhuntress.tripod.com/thewiccanrede)(2001)

An ye harm none do what ye will

These last eight words of the Wiccan Rede are crucial to remember when practicing the craft.

Of all the information that is provided to you in this book, it is this very sentence that stands true for our community of witches.

Simply put, these eight words are stating that as long as we as witches are not bringing any harm to anyone, anything, or any creature through our spellwork or rituals, we can practice how we please.

For this very reason, the majority of witches choose not to practice or attempt to cast any curses or hexes as they are most likely formulated to bring harm to someone, something, or a creature through their wording or intention.

If you also follow or adopt the Threefold Law in your own practice, you will know that anything ill-willed is basically asking for a karmic kick in the ass.

Thirteen Goals of a Witch

- Know Yourself
- Know your Craft
- Learn and Grow
- Apply knowledge with wisdom
- Achieve balance
- Keep your words in good order
- Keep your thoughts in good order
- Celebrate life
- Attune with the cycles of the earth
- Breath and eat correctly
- Exercise the body
- Meditate
- Honor the Goddess and God

G. (2019, August 21). The Thirteen Goals Of A Witch. 3 Pagans and a Cat. Retrieved July 1, 2022, from https://www.patheos.com/blogs/3pagansandacat/2019/08/the-thirteen-goals-of-a-witch/

Thirteen Goals of a Witch

Threefold Law
The Rule of Three

*Ever mind the rule of Three
Three times your acts return to thee
This lesson well, thou must learn
Thou only gets what thee dost earn.*

This is the Threefold Law of the craft.
It has long been believed that this Law will protect us witches from harm if we only practice good magick. The theory behind the Rule of Three, is that whatever magick you perform, either good or bad, there will always be a karmic reward or consequence attached. For example; If you perform a spell to help someone, then the Law states that you will karmically receive 3 times the good energy in return, or 3 good things will happen to you.
On the flipside, if you do a spell that is meant to bring harm to someone, then alternatively, you will karmically receive 3 times the bad energy in return, or 3 bad things will happen to you.
Not all witches believe in this rule, so feel free to make your own decision as to whether or not you would like to adopt this as your own belief.

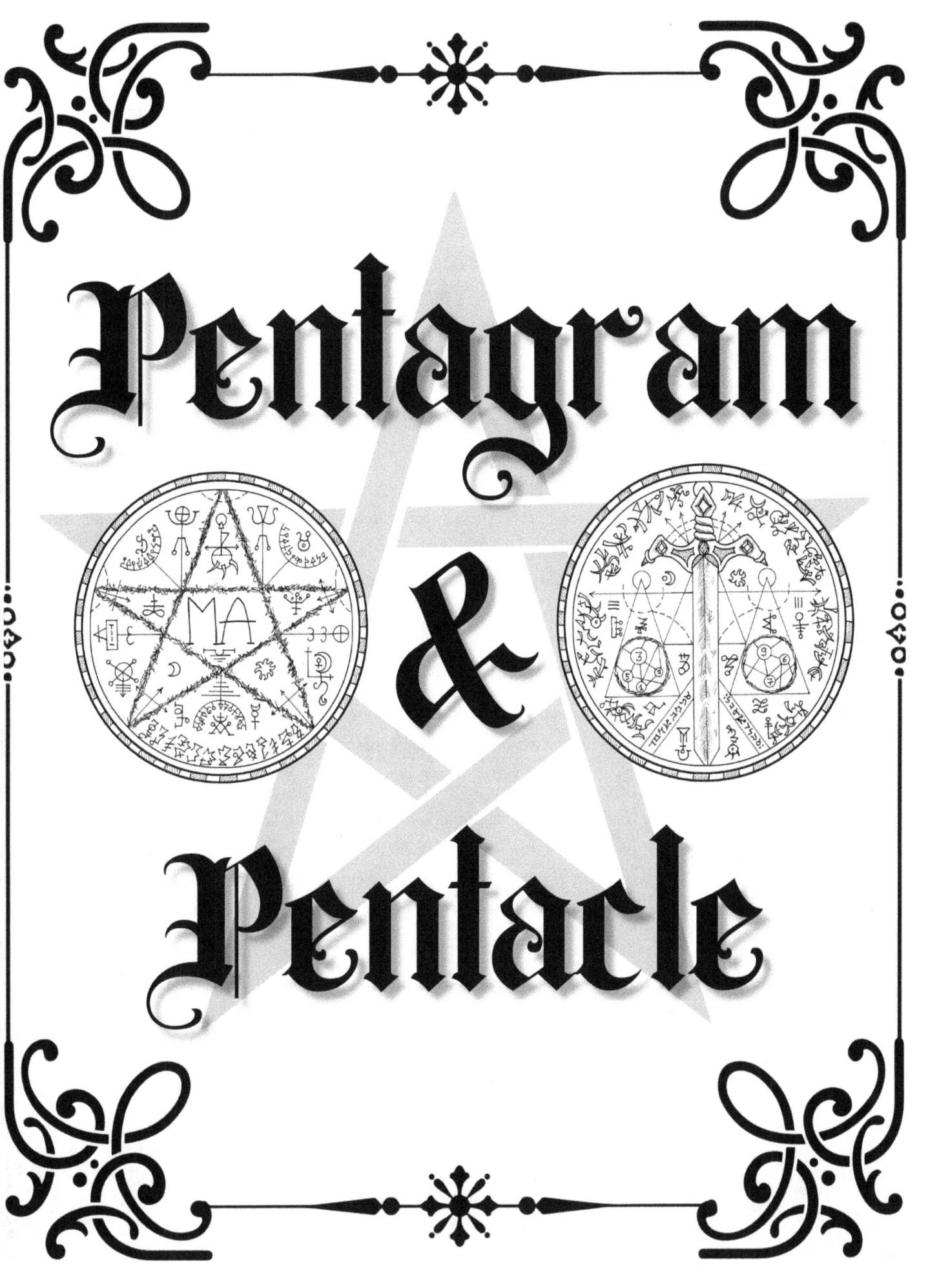

Pentagram & Pentacle

The Western world's relationship with the pentagram is controversial. It has long been regarded as a symbol of Satanism, and has only lately been recognized as an appropriate emblem of religious affiliation on the headstones of United States veterans. This stock symbol is frequently used in the horror and fantasy genres. Despite the vast amount of infographics, memes, and articles regarding the 'real' significance of the pentagram on the Internet, they are often omitting its use in general Western Esotericism and its history outside of current Wicca.

Is there a difference?

To begin, there is a significant distinction between a pentagram and a pentacle that should be addressed. Is there a way to find out? Since the two are so frequently interchangeable, what's the point in separating them? Honestly, it's not that difficult.

A pentagram can be used as a pentacle, and this is a common occurrence. But pentagrams are not present in every pentacle. The word "pentacle" first appears in the English language in The Heptameron by Pietro d'Abano and The Key of Solomon, which were both written in the 1600s. There is no mention in these books that pentacles are exclusively pentagrams, or that they even contain a pentagram at all.

The theory that the pentagram was a magickal symbol was popularized by Heinrich Cornelius Agrippa, an occultist who lived in the 15th and 16th centuries, who believed that it represented the five Neo-Platonic elements - namely associating each of the five points to fire, water, air, earth, and idea (spirit) respectively.

Looking at the origins of "pentacle" in other languages, we notice they have terms that sound similar. **'Pentaculum,'** from the prefix 'penta-,' meaning five, and the suffix '-culum,' signifies instrumentality in Latin. **'Pentacolo'** means "anything with five points" in Italian. **'Pentacol'** is a 14th century French term that refers to different magickal or apotropaic* charms that are placed on necklaces or similar devices. The prefix "pend-" means "to hang-" and "-col" means "-from neck."

In a nutshell, pentagrams are frequently seen in pentacles, however this is not always the case. Modern Wiccan pentacles are, in fact, pentacles containing a sacred and magickal symbol, the pentagram.

*APOTROPAIC
Having the power to avert bad luck or evil influences.

Distinguishing between the Two

An easy way to distinguish between a Pentagram and a Pentacle is this:

Pentagram - A five-pointed star. The symbol of Wicca and Witchcraft used all over the world. May or may not be enclosed within a circle, although many would debate that the circle therefore creates a Pentacle, as it now represents a plate or tile. Again, it is completely up to you, as these two terms have been inextricably linked and used interchangeably for hundreds of years.

Pentacle - Typically made from stone, wood, ceramic, clay, or another type of material in the form of a 'tile' or 'plate'. A five-pointed star or Pentagram MAY be engraved or embossed onto a Pentacle, but it can portray an array of different magickal symbols or seals, sigils, mandalas, or sacred geometry.

A brief history

After been popularized by French occultist Éliphas Lévi's (1810—1875) 18th-century work, the term "pentacle" entered Western occult slang in the late 1800s. Lévi spelt it "pantacle" by accident, which reflects the fluidity of language and how the term has changed through time and between countries. However, we shouldn't get too caught up on these differences because they are inherent in the development of any language.

English mystic Aleister Crowley, who claimed to be a reincarnation of Éliphas Lévi, would also use the "pantacle" spelling in a number of his writings as a result of Lévi's influence. Gerald Gardener, the originator of contemporary Wicca, was influenced by Crowley. It's worth mentioning, even if the impact isn't huge. During his lifetime, Crowley had a significant impact on Western occultism, particularly in the English-speaking world.

Occult themes, such as the Rider-Waite representation of pentacle cards as pentagram-inscribed discs, would inspire Gardner's work. The Rider-Waite tarot deck was published in 1910, and Gardener is likely to have encountered it. It's also possible that Gardner was unaware that the term "pentacle" can apply to a variety of magical symbols, not just pentagrams, because of his familiarity with the Key of Solomon literature. It's unclear what Gardner had in mind when he chose to define "pentacle" in this way.

As a symbol, the pentagram dates back to at least 3000 BCE. Ancient Babylonians utilized it in sacred rituals, and relics from Mesopotamia, Greece, and Rome all bear witness to its importance. As a symbol of Christ's five wounds, it has been used in early Christianity for more than 500 years. Because the pentagram can be drawn in one continuous line, the five points indicate the beginning and end (or Alpha and Omega). When Jerusalem was the capital of Judah between 300 and 150 BCE, the pentagram was the city's official seal.

Being around for thousands of years, what does it mean? The pentagram is a symbol of justice, kindness, knowledge, insight, and sublime magnificence in Jewish Kabbalistic tradition. It was regarded by the Sumerians to represent Mercury, Venus, Mars, Jupiter and Saturn. They also called it the "Vault of Heaven." According to Pythagoras, each point of the pentagram represents one of the four elements, with the fifth (spirit) at the upper most point. His Pythagorean followers thought it was the perfect math formula, so it became known as the "Golden Ratio."

Today, the pentagram is most commonly employed in witchcraft rituals and as a symbol of protection. Nature's elements and the Spirit's attribution from Pythagoras is still recognized, and it illustrates how they operate together harmoniously.

Right-Side Up? or Upside-Down?

The pentagram is commonly shown with a single point that rises upwards as it is drawn. When the pentagram is turned upside down, with the solitary point facing downward, there is some disagreement on what it signifies. It can be an indication that the wearer has reached the second degree of study in Wiccan tradition. The term "graduated" here refers to a person who has reached a new degree of expertise in their field or craft. Others see an inverted pentagram as a devilish or evil symbol.

The pentagram, like playing cards, began to appear inverted in the tarot's use of the symbol. Is the pentagram upside down a Christian demonic symbol? Is the right-side up a sign of spirituality and goodness? Depends on who you ask, that is.

The pentagram's link with evil may be traced back to the beginning of the Inquisitions of the Catholic Church's endeavor to exterminate heresy from the people. It was Pope Lucius III, in 1184, who launched the first Inquisition against heresy, which he defined as any view or thought that conflicts with accepted religious teaching, particularly Christian. After this, there was one other Medieval Inquisition that took place before the most famous one of all, the Spanish Inquisition.

In 1855, the pentagram was firmly associated with evil. Alphonse Louis Constant, who wrote under the pen name Eliphas Levi, was a long-time Roman Catholic priest and occult author. He wrote 'Dogme et Rituel de la Haute Magie,' which Arthur Edward Waite, who helped create the Rider-Waite Tarot Deck, translated into English as Transcendental Magic.

A pentagram with two points upwards is a sign of evil that attracts nefarious energies, according to Alphonse in his book. Pentagrams have long been associated with evil energies, but this was the first time they had been shown to be so.

The pentagram also received (and continues to get) media attention. In the 1970s and 1980s, there was an increase in both serial murders and occultism. Many publications and news reports attributed murders to satanic cults, citing the pentagram as their emblem. This symbol of Satanism or black witchcraft has been employed in movies, TV programs, and novels since then. Its place in history has changed, like the downward facing cross, which is actually Peter the Apostle's sign. They are perceived as rejecting the beneficial power that their right-side-up counterparts bring.

I hope this has assisted you in developing a new or better understanding of the pentagram and pentacle. The ability to comprehend the history and context of such taboo matters is a valuable tool, as it allows us to dispel misconceptions that do not need to exist and appreciate how useful something like the pentagram has been to people for generations.

As a symbol of protection and pride for the craft, wear your Pentagram proudly (either hidden in secret or shown to the world - it's up to you), and know that you are part of a beautiful family of individuals from around the globe who share in the same magickal journey that you are on right now. Grow, learn, build, and trust in the magick that is within you.

Using the Pentagram in your Magick

The pentagram is quite a useful symbol when it comes to your spellwork and rituals. Not only used as a powerful symbol of protection, the pentagram can be utilized for evoking and banishing depending on your needs for elemental powers. Evoking only brings the energy into your magickal circle, whereas 'invoking' typically pertains to calling the energy INTO oneself.

Sometimes referred to as keys or portals, the evoking pentagrams open up a 'portal' to allow the elemental energy to come through. Alternatively when banishing, this will close the portal and allow the energies to return to their rightful place and stop the flow into your circle. The image below shows the correct way to draw each of the pentagrams, each displaying the starting point and direction in which they are drawn depending on the element you wish to evoke.

Evoking & Banishing Pentagrams

EVOKING	BANISHING	EVOKING	BANISHING

Spirit (Active)		Spirit (Passive)	

EVOKING	BANISHING	EVOKING	BANISHING

Fire		Air	

EVOKING	BANISHING	EVOKING	BANISHING

Water		Earth	

Intention

Also known as
Hocus Pocus Focus
_{hee hee}

Intention & Magick

An intention is determining what you want to get out of your spell, or what you want your magick to accomplish, and saying it as clearly and precisely as you can. One reason to set a concise intention is to make sure that your desire is very, very clear. You have to tell the universe, your intuition, deities, a higher power, or whatever you are working with to make magick, exactly what you want.

In connection to magick, it is not unusual to hear individuals debate intention. People may say, "Magick is about intention," "What you do doesn't matter; what matters is what you intend to happen," or variations on these phrases. While it is true that your objectives matter, what you say and do about those intentions matters more. "They had good intentions" is basically the epitome of every disastrous conversation, deed, and relationship. "I did not want to offend" does not eliminate or prevent the offence, does it? We don't want to be going and offending spirits do we?

Yes, the words you use while constructing a spell are absolutely important. No one should be passive and "leave it in the hands of the deities" when it comes to troubleshooting spells and figuring out why they aren't working. Magick does not work that way. You must be specific in your requests, so get your adulting underwear on, and do the thing. Everything else is prayer, which is good and in certain cases can border on magick, but it's not magick by itself.

This is especially true when interacting with spirits and invisible forces: do not presume that your objectives are logical and clear to the entity or deity to whom you are submitting a request. This is why people frequently recommend writing down your incantation or spell along with the desired outcome. Writing is not 100% magickal itself; but journaling helps organize your ideas and focuses your wording on what you genuinely desire. Before casting any significant spell, it is recommended to record your thoughts in a notebook and give careful consideration to how the request shall be worded. This is particularly true for requests made to a particular entity, spirit, or deity. Communication is crucial and words matter!

Communication is important and the wording matters, however, there needs to be action taken as well. The action of making a connection with your deity, spirit, higher power or however you may classify it is equally important. Once this connection is made, then the real communication happens, where you can initiate a 'handshake' of sorts with your chosen entity, and let them know what your intention is. The action needed here would be an offering, performing your ritual in their honor, and respecting what basically amounts to protocol, diplomacy and etiquette for the spiritual realm.

Some people keep making the same mistakes until they realize that what you say and do does matter, because they only believed that "magick is all about intention," and nothing more. Clarify, simplify, and be detailed, and do not presume that both parties will comprehend your true intention. The rules are very lenient, as long as you play by them.

How to Set your Intention

Identifying your Goal or Desire

The first step in setting an intention is to figure out what you want. It can be something big or small, like buying a new car, or it can be something more general, like living in the moment. Most people stop there when they set an intention, but sometimes we need to dig a little deeper to figure out how we feel about what we want. Once you know how you feel about your goal, you can put it into words and write the intention exactly as you want it to happen. A sacred creation process begins when you start to feel what you want. The universe, your spirit guide or deity listens and responds when our feelings are deeply connected to our thoughts and intentions. Be sure to vocalize and write down your intention when you have it. This will not only feel cathartic, but it will also hold you accountable. Intentions are more powerful when they are declared or shared outside of your own head.

Be Clear, Be Specific

No matter what your intentions are, you need to be very clear about what you want to accomplish and think about what will happen as a result. Specificity and detailed intentions are what the universe thrives to hear, but try not to get overly complicated in the process. It is important to note that when you are manifesting or setting your intentions, it is a great practice to believe that what you are requesting has already come to fruition. This raises your vibration to experience the joy and happiness that fulfilling your intention would bring. Also, being grateful every day and not taking everything for granted is a huge vibrational booster.

Make sure your Intentions are Positive

Your intention can be anything you want. An intention is just a way to give your energy a place to go when it gets pulled in multiple directions during the day. Just ensure that the intention behind your manifestations is pure and originating from a place of good.

It's important to use positive "I will" statements instead of "I won't" when wording your intention. Research has shown that negative emotions or words can be stronger and over-power positive ones. A popular intention is, "I will be debt free." Now, there is nothing wrong with wanting to be debt free, however, the universe or your deity is only going to hone in on one word - debt. This is a negative word, and the powers that be will take this as a sign to send more of it your way. A better way to phrase this intention would be, "I will be financially stable and free." Can you see how this intention is phrased in a positive way, with no mistaking any word as negative or doubtful?

How to Set your Intention

Keep your Intentions Simple

There is no need to make the task difficult or to write lengthy intentions. This creates confusion if there are more than one specific request tied into your manifesting goal. If you have multiple desires that are closely related, instead of putting them all together, separate each of them into their own intention statement. Keep your intentions short, sweet and to-the-point.

Get rid of any doubt or limiting beliefs

Having limiting beliefs means that you have strong convictions that you think are 100% true, but they actually hold you back. Doubt can act in a similar way by voiding any thoughts or feelings of happiness when you are thinking about your intentions. Believe me when I say that it is hard to filter out the negative thoughts of doubt in todays world, but we have to realize that if we truly want something in our lives, we have to know that we are 100% worth it.

Everything has a vibrational frequency, and it's important to start looking at our world in this way. Positive thoughts and feelings are the best way to raise your vibrations and give your intentions a fighting chance to become reality. Negative emotions, thoughts and feelings lower our vibrational state. Your intentions are about manifesting something that has a vibrational charge, that's all the universe hears.

For example, if your intention is, "I will be happy and grateful to manifest a new car," but your thoughts behind it are wavering because your budget will not allow for it, the universe is only going to hear the part where 'your budget will not allow it.' Because of that ONE negative and doubtful thought, that message is going to be blasted loud and clear to the universe, regardless of how good or positive your intention may be, resulting in more budget-straining circumstances headed your way.

At the end of the day, not believing in your intention is a great way to daydream and accomplish nothing. Not believing that your intention can come true is the greatest barrier you will face. Changing your mindset to match your desires with your belief will undoubtedly propel you forward as you watch your intentions pave the way to a more fulfilling life, time after time.

Is there a Dark Side?

As with all magick, we start by creating an intention to change something, manifest something or protect something, among other things. These intentions, no matter how diverse or different, all come from one source; a desire. We would be helpless without desire. We wouldn't hear the calling from our heart and soul or make choices and decisions. Not only that, but without desire, we would have no appeal to our relationships, no motivation to reach our full potential on this planet, and no reason to keep living.

Desire isn't a problem as long as it doesn't turn into lust. When we want something, we experience desire. Lust, on the other hand, is what we experience when we get too clingy or obsessed over something we want. It is critical to make this distinction.

Desire is required. It is a necessary element of life. Desire is our life force, sexual and spiritual energy. In contrast, lust is a sour form of desire. Lust is the negative side of desire, and we must guard against it. Addiction, jealousy, crimes of passion, hostility, and various forms of pain are all the outcome of lust.

Falling into the depths of lust or greed is the darker side of magick. So be cautious. Evaluate and question your motives. Are your intentions selfless or selfish? In the circle of magick or energy, if you are attempting to manipulate another individuals free will, you are opening the cosmic door to also having others manipulate you. Same goes for harming another. Do you also want someone to harm you in response to initiating it first?

Another significant negative aspect of magick is that it may be used to try to control, manipulate, or otherwise meddle with the lives of other people. Please refrain from trying this. It is not worth the trouble it brings. Whatever manipulative intents you have will come back to bite you multiple times. Even if your intentions are seemingly harmless like casting a spell for someone to love you, the universe will ensure that justice is served if you attempt to interfere with another's free will. What is the takeaway? Concentrate solely on yourself. Maintain control of the ball in your own court. Don't try to meddle in the life of others. Simple.

However, that being said, I offer this as a cautionary statement only. Yes, there absolutely can be a dark side to magick. What you decide to do with your magick and your practice is completely up to you. You have been forewarned.

Intention & Magick

Intention & Magick

Tools of the Craft

Tools of the Craft

When individuals first discover Wicca or another type of Paganism, they often run out to acquire every magickal instrument they can find. After all, the books we read and learn from instruct us to buy this, that, and the kitchen sink, so you should head over to your local Witchy Boutique and stock up immediately. This is not the case. Be mindful that these magickal instruments have a purpose and a function, but they are not absolutely necessary to perform your magick. They are simply a means to focus your energies more directly.

For those who are new to the craft, the quantity of "things" that appears to be necessary might be intimidating, but it doesn't have to be. To begin, it should be stated unequivocally that nothing other than your intellect, heart, and soul is necessary for connecting with the divine. Second, you have choices in terms of your personal practice—not every instrument is required, and you don't even have to break the bank to have a beautiful altar with all of the objects you want to include. Magickal implements are utilized in Wiccan ceremonies to both honor the deities and fulfil your magickal intentions. These tools, in general, direct psychic energy to achieve a certain purpose.

Let's have a look at some of the magickal and ceremonial tools used in various Wiccan and Pagan traditions. Keep in mind that not all traditions employ all of these items, and they aren't always used in the same way. Since the majority of witches nowadays are solitary practitioners with differing views and ideals to the practice of Witchcraft, using or having these tools is completely your choice to make. There is really no written rule that says you have to have these tools or even use them.

Most witches prefer to have some sort of tool on hand to help in some way during spellwork and rituals, and this can be whatever to choose, whatever you feel most comfortable with, and something that you feel most connected with. If you decide that you would like to obtain or create your own implements, it is important to know how to consecrate your tools before using them for your spellwork or magickal workings.

There are some additional spaces for you to record any other tools that you wish to use or come across in your magickal journey, and I have also provided instructions for consecrating your tools so you can prepare them for your spellwork and rituals.

Tools of the Craft

Athame

An athame (ath-uh-may) is a ceremonial sword used in contemporary Witchcraft. It is a (typically) black-handled, double-sided blade in Wicca. The athame is a knife used only for symbolic purposes. The blade is typically straight and dull. For deities, it represents the male aspect and can be used in rituals to cast and cut a circle and direct energy, just like a wand. It can also signify The God or male energy, and it can be utilized as a symbol for the Great Rite.

Bell

People in rural areas knew centuries ago that loud noises scared evil spirits away, and indeed the bell is just a traditional example of a good noisemaker. The ringing of a bell produces vibrations that are a source of enormous power. A bell's variants include the sistrum, the ceremonial rattle, and the "singing bowl." All of these can contribute to the harmony of a magickal circle. The bell is rung to open or close a ritual, or to invoke the Goddess in various traditions of Wicca.

Besom

The besom (bez-um), or broom, is used to sweep a ritual space clean prior to ceremony. A gentle sweep cleanses the space physically and gets rid of any bad energies that may have built up. Because the broom is a purifier, it is associated with the element Water. It's pretty rare to come across witches with broom collections, and if you don't want to buy one, it's fairly simple to construct your own besom. A birch twig bundle, an ash or oak staff, and a willow wand binding are all part of the ancient magickal formula.

Boline

A boline (bow-leen) is a useful tool that may be used for any task that requires a sharp blade for cutting herbs, cords, ribbons, thread, etc., or carving symbols into candles and objects. Traditionally, the handle of the boline is white and is also known as the "white-handled knife." Bolines typically have a single sharpened blade that is sometimes curved like a crescent moon thus also symbolizing the Lunar Goddess. The boline is used in the physical plane as opposed to the Athame which is used in the spiritual or astral plane when used in magickal practices.

Tools of the Craft

Candles

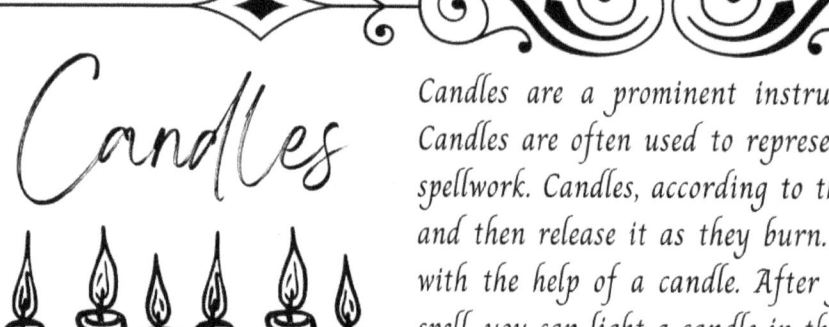

Candles are a prominent instrument in Wiccan and Pagan ceremonies. Candles are often used to represent any deities and the element of fire in spellwork. Candles, according to the belief, may share your personal energy and then release it as they burn. A spell can be "energized" or "activated" with the help of a candle. After putting together the components of your spell, you can light a candle in the among the ingredients to give your spell power and send it into the world. Candles are sometimes left to burn or until they go out on their own. It is sometimes re-lit numerous times over a multi-day ritual or spell.

Cauldron

Like the chalice, the cauldron can be found in many Wiccan traditions that focus on the goddess. Like a womb, it's where life starts. On your altar, the cauldron represents the element of water. The cauldron is linked with Cerridwen, a prophecy-wielding goddess in Celtic mythology. She is the guardian of the Underworld's cauldron of knowledge and inspiration.

Chalice

The chalice, or cup, can be found in many goddess-oriented Wiccan traditions. The chalice, like the cauldron, is feminine and womblike, serving as the vessel in which life starts. It is often a sign of the element of water on the altar. Some covens use the chalice and the athame together to show the female side of the Divine within a symbolic re-enactment of the Great Rite.

Crystals

You can choose from hundreds of stones, but which ones you use will depend on what you want to do. You can't really go wrong if you choose crystals and gemstones based on their correspondences or qualities. Birthstones can also be used in magical rituals. Each month has a different birthstone, and each one has its own magickal qualities. Before using a new crystal or gemstone for the first time, it's important to cleanse it.

Tools of the Craft

Incense

Although many current approaches to incense magick maintain that incense symbolizes all of the elements (the smoke drifts through the Air, is lit by the use of Fire, materials are grown from the Earth, and combustible incense is created using Water), it is commonly utilized in Neopagan and Wiccan rituals to represent the element of Air. It is said to produce a magickal atmosphere suitable for invoking deities and spirits, and burning the incense is thought to unleash the huge quantity of energy held inside natural incense, which may then be utilized for magickal purposes.

Mortar and Pestle

The mortar and pestle set is a useful item that many witches use for crushing and combining herbs and dry substances during a magickal spell. The set is made up of two parts: the mortar, which is normally a bowl but can sometimes be flat, and the pestle, which is held in the hand. The wider end of the pestle is usually made to be more rough or course to help crush or grind any ingredients that you may be working with.

Pentacle

The pentacle is used in nearly every Wiccan tradition (as well as many other Pagan traditions). A pentacle is typically a flat piece of wood, wax, clay or even paper that has carvings of magickal symbols inscribed onto it. The pentagram, on the other hand, is the most widely observed sign, which is why the two names are frequently confused.

The pentacle is employed as a protective talisman in ceremonial magick. In most Wiccan traditions, it is linked to the Earth element and can be used to store items that need to be consecrated at a later time. Feel free to create your own or purchase one, the choice is yours. There are many online resources (such as Etsy) where you can find your own Pentacle in the style that suits you and your practice.

Tools of the Craft

Wand

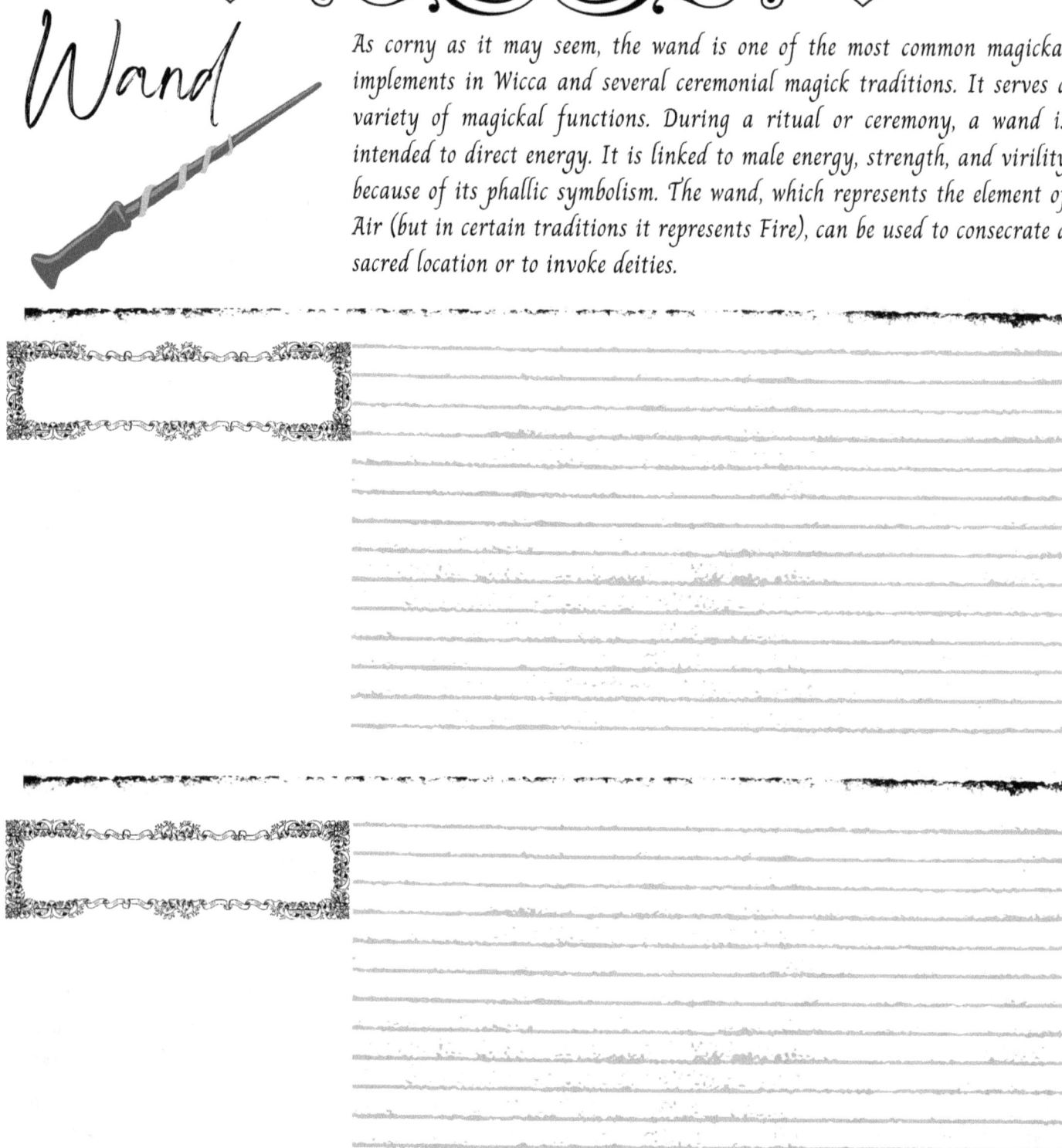

As corny as it may seem, the wand is one of the most common magickal implements in Wicca and several ceremonial magick traditions. It serves a variety of magickal functions. During a ritual or ceremony, a wand is intended to direct energy. It is linked to male energy, strength, and virility because of its phallic symbolism. The wand, which represents the element of Air (but in certain traditions it represents Fire), can be used to consecrate a sacred location or to invoke deities.

Tools of the Craft

The Altar

What is an Altar?

Pagan/Wiccan altars are sacred spaces that include spiritual artefacts that are used for meditation, spells, ritual and divination, as well as for prayers, visualizations and connection with deities. It is a significant component of neo-paganism and wiccan practices.

Wicca, paganism, and witchcraft can be scary thought for some people who have never practiced or even believed in them before. Having been around for over a century, Wicca is a religion/spirituality with a rich history and a wide range of practices. As a result, it's no wonder that when someone is just beginning their magickal adventure, it may be quite overwhelming.

For any witch, an altar is one of the simplest and most essential tools in their toolbox. It is entirely up to the individual to decide how complex or simple their altar should be. You can design your altar in whatever way that works for you and your house or place of worship, and your own personal practice.

Witch altars are sacred and distinctive places that represent your spirituality. It's a place to establish intentions, celebrate, and practice. You may use altars to communicate energy and intention to whichever deity, entity, or energy you're working with at the moment. Your altar can be as simple or fancy as you want. Some witches dedicate a whole room to their altar, while others keep it simple. The altar-maker, you, makes that decision.

Altars are not just used by Wiccans and Pagans. Altars are found in churches, temples, and other religious buildings. It is an altar that represents one's practice. That's why they're a witches best friend. Altars are physical places where the "real" and the "spiritual" meet. We may reach the gods, ancestors and other spirits, as well as our own higher selves.

How to set up your Altar

When it comes to your own personal altar, it can be large and extravagant, or it can be simple, small and even portable depending on what you intend to accomplish. Any kind of altar is a good place to start if you want to learn and grow in your magickal journey.

I will show you some different altar layouts, from large and complex, to more simple and easy. The first thing that you will need to determine is what kind of surface you would like your altar to be placed, which location would best suit your needs, and which direction you would like your altar to face.

Remember the Directions

When setting up your altar, remember the four directions; North, East, South and West.

NORTH - EARTH   EAST - AIR   SOUTH - FIRE   WEST - WATER

Facing the altar north is a common choice for witches. Depending on your own unique preference, you can face your altar in any other direction you like, or a non-descript direction if that isn't of great interest to you. Most witches will default to facing their altars north as this is the direction that most rituals start out with. Keep in mind that altars are personal, so it's always about what works best for you and what doesn't.

Altar surfaces can take several forms, including various pieces of furniture. Furniture like bookcases, desks, cabinets and even a nightstand may be used to make altars. Whether you want it to be large or tiny and in any part of your home, you can make it happen. There are also "travel altars" that may be packed into a bag or container and taken into the wild to be used by witches. Make the space your own by relying on your intuition and the vibes that surround you. It's best to go with what seems most natural to you and your practice.

Choosing what talismans, candles, and other items to place on your altar is the fun part once you've settled on the fundamentals like the surface you're utilizing and the location. Many witches' altars include natural items, in keeping with Wicca's Earth-centered ethos. Anything from nature that calls to you, such as herbs, plants, soil, sand or shells, can be included.

Crystals are a common choice for altars (as well as throughout the home and in one's practice). Charging crystals with the sun and the moon allows them to attract and store a variety of energies that may be used to materialize and heal oneself, others, and help in your magickal workings. There are no restrictions on the crystals, gemstones or spiritual artifacts you can use on your altar. You choose the layout and items to create your own sacred area.

Once your altar is built, you must purify the area. It's crucial to cleanse your altar since bringing in things like gemstones from elsewhere might bring unwanted energy into your sacred space. By smudging your tools and altar with sage, you ensure that they are clear of external energies and ready for your practice.

The following altar layouts are the most common and/or the most popular amongst witches. Some altar layouts are specific to the magickal work that is to be done, and you will see these, as well as basic altar setups. Feel free to create your own altar orientation and use the notes section to draw out your very own personal altar or sacred space.

Altar Layouts

Altar Layout 1 - General Use

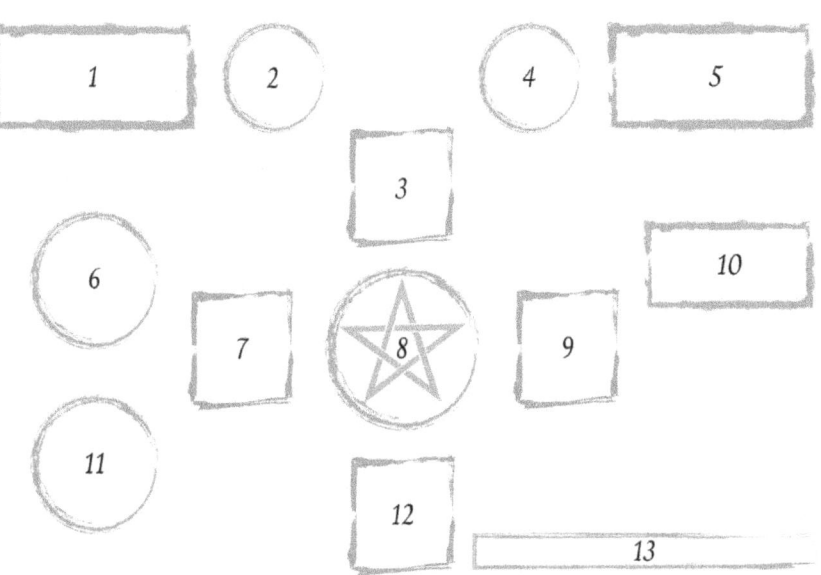

1. Goddess Statue
2. Illuminator Candles
3. Bowl of Salt (Earth)
4. Illuminator Candles
5. God Statue
6. Chalice
7. Bowl of Water
8. Pentacle
9. Feather (Air)
10. Incense and holder
11. Cauldron
12. Candle (Fire)
13. Wand or Athame

Altar Layout 2 - General Use

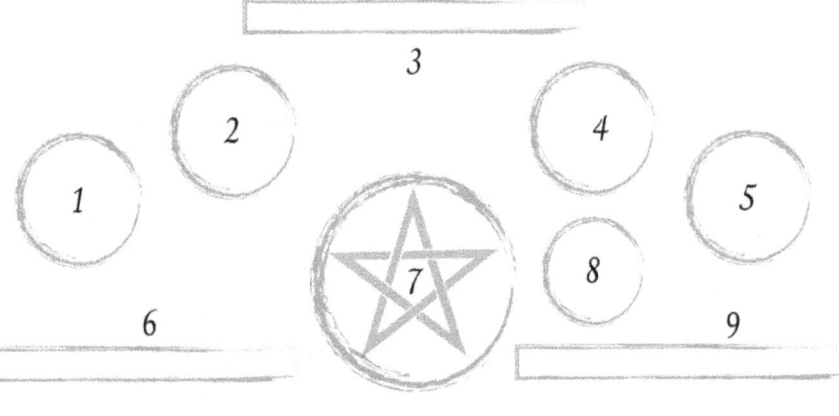

1. Ritual Candle
2. Offering plate
3. Athame
4. Chalice
5. Bell
6. Incense (Air)
7. Pentacle
8. Bowl of Salt (Earth)
9. Wand

PLEASE NOTE: These layouts work great for North facing altars. If you decide to face your altar in a different direction, please be mindful of the items that correspond to the directions and adjust accordingly.

Altar Layouts

Altar Layout 3 – General Use

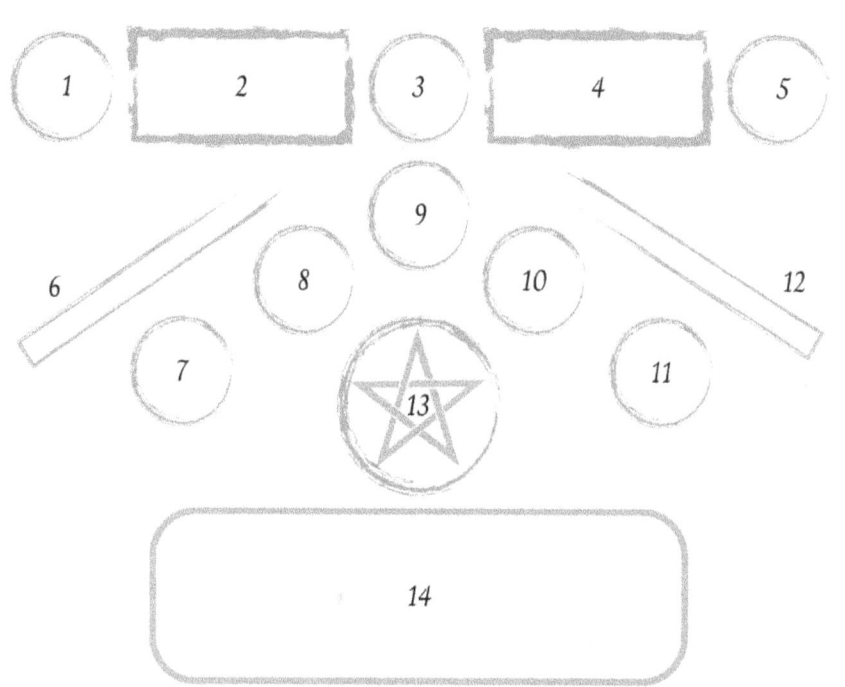

1. Green Goddess Candle
2. Goddess Statue
3. Ritual Candle
4. God Statue
5. Red God Candle
6. Wand
7. Bowl of Water
8. Bowl of Salt (Earth)
9. Chalice
10. Incense / Censer (Air)
11. Candle holder (Fire)
12. Athame
13. Pentacle
14. Workspace

Altar Layout 4 – General Use

1. Goddess Candle
2. Garland of Flowers
3. Ritual Candle
4. God Candle
5. Ale or Cider/Chalice
6. Pentacle
7. Cakes or Cookies
8. Book of Shadows
9. Cauldron
10. Bowl of herbs
11. Athame or Wand

Altar Layouts

Altar Layout 5 - General Use

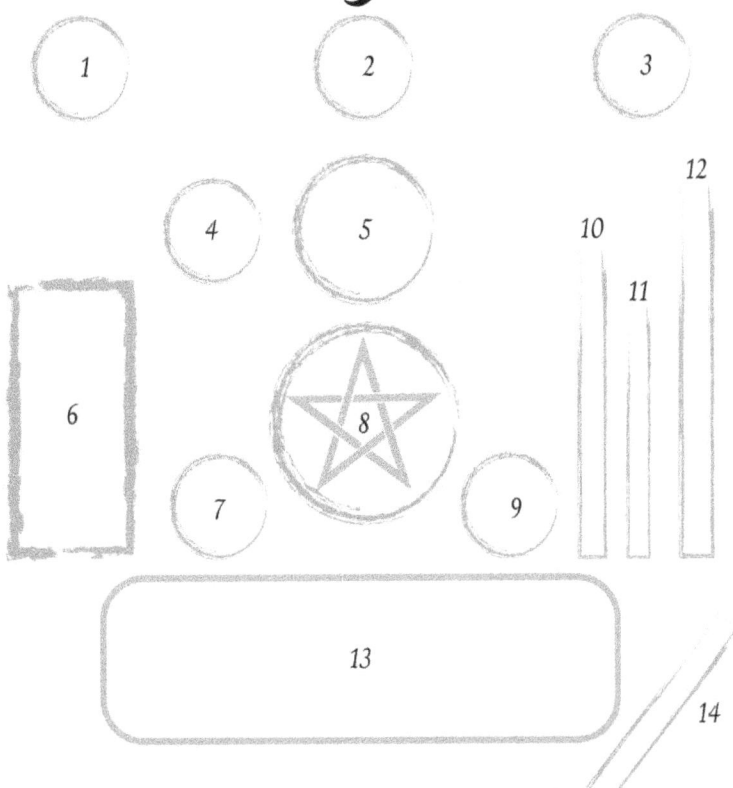

1. Goddess Candle
2. Spirit/Ritual Candle
3. God Candle
4. Chalice
5. Cauldron
6. Book of Shadows
7. Bowl of Water
8. Pentacle
9. Bowl of Salt (Earth)
10. Wand
11. Lighter or Matches (Fire)
12. Incense Sticks (Air)
13. Workspace
14. Athame

Altar 6 - Travel-size/Portable

Using a small container or bag of your choice, you can make a small travel-size altar with only a few essentials.

1. Altar Cloth
2. Small amount of water
3. Small amount of salt (Earth)
4. One small candle (Fire)
5. Small incense such as a cone (Air)

Feel free to add anything else that you may want to use. Try different layouts to find the best one.

Altar Layout 7 - Deity Magick

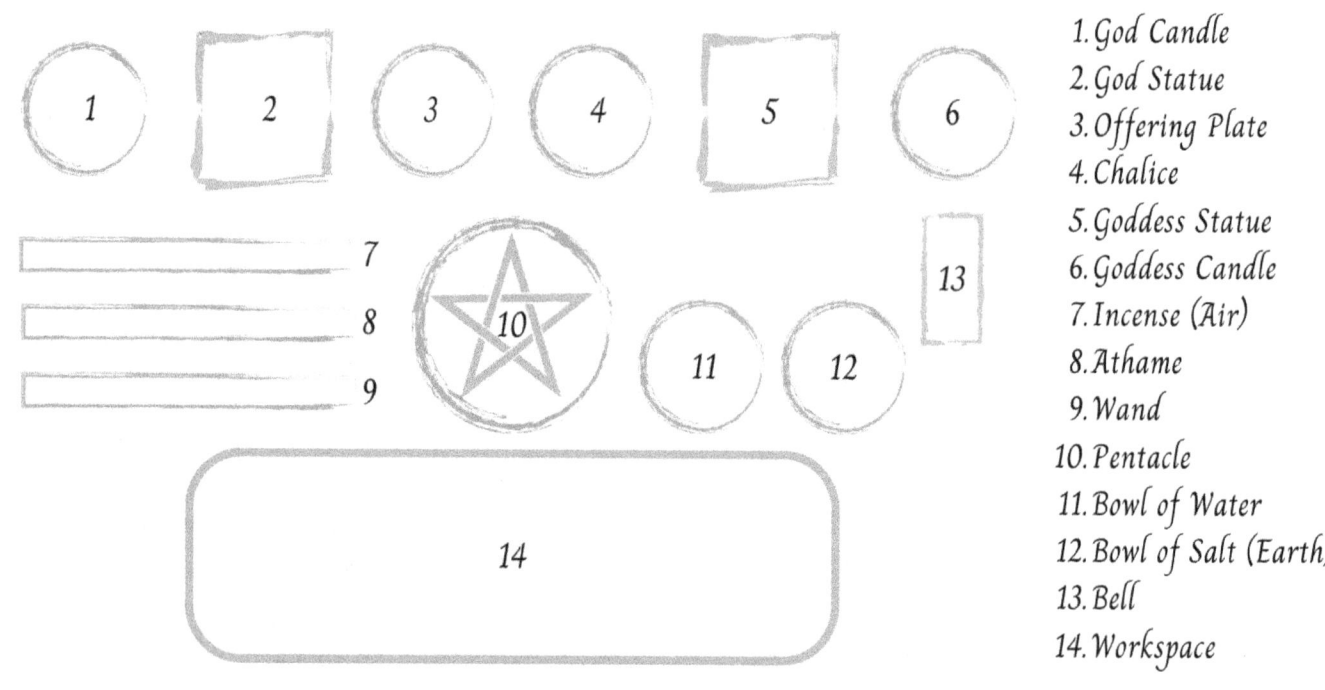

1. God Candle
2. God Statue
3. Offering Plate
4. Chalice
5. Goddess Statue
6. Goddess Candle
7. Incense (Air)
8. Athame
9. Wand
10. Pentacle
11. Bowl of Water
12. Bowl of Salt (Earth)
13. Bell
14. Workspace

Using a Deity Altar

For those who worship a certain deity, why not create a god or goddess altar? This altar honors your belief system's Divine element, whether you worship a single deity or a pantheon.

Include such things as:
Find a statue of your path's deity.
Candles: Use god or goddess candles in colors connected with your deity.
Natural signs: Do you worship an ocean god? Add a seawater bowl. Is your deity linked to a particular tree? Leaves, branches, or seeds are a great addition.
Have you built or created a craft item for your god or goddess? A Brighid's cross, for example, may be added to honor Brighid. Have you crafted a set of prayer beads honoring Cernunnos? Incorporate these into your altar.
Offerings: If your deity accepts offerings, set a bowl, cup, or offering plate on the altar.

Altar Layouts

Altar Layout 8 - Elemental Magick

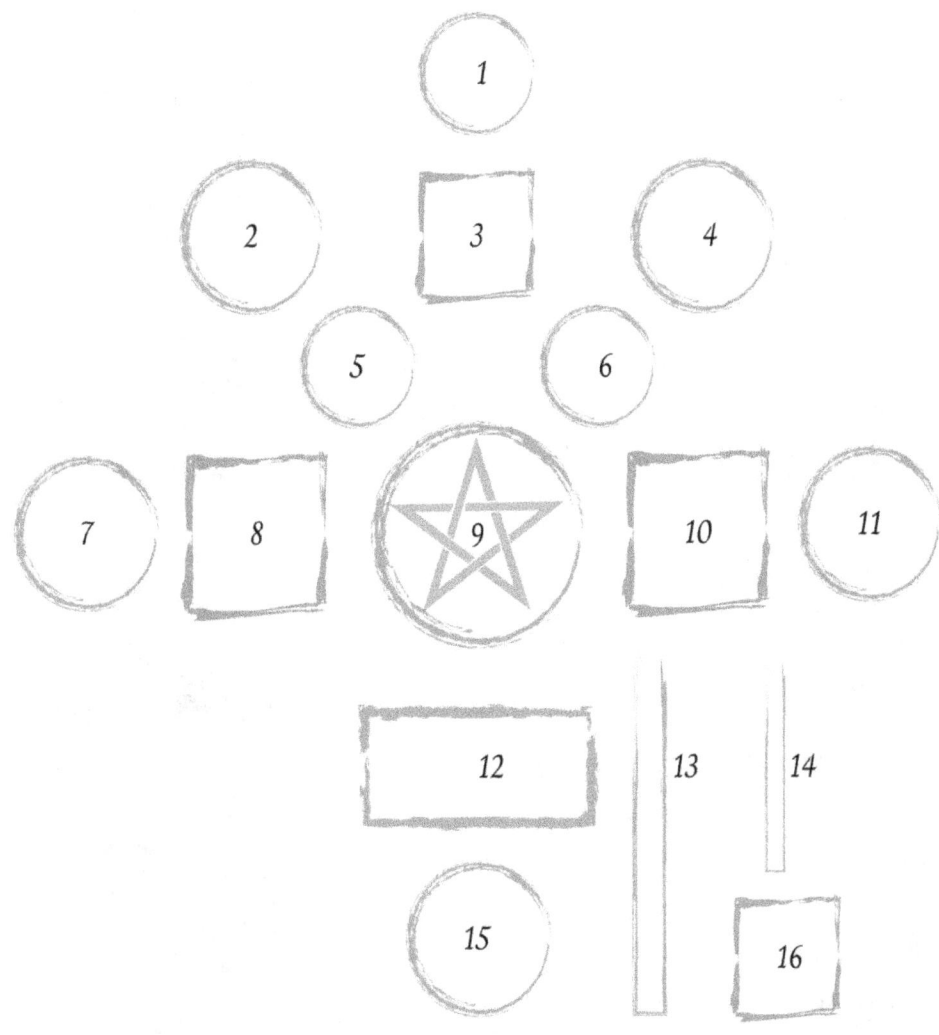

1. Elemental Candle - Green
2. Goddess Candle
3. Bowl of Salt (Earth)
4. God Candle
5. Crackers or Cakes
6. Wine or Cider - Chalice
7. Elemental Candle - Blue
8. Bowl of Water
9. Pentacle
10. Incense (Air)
11. Elemental Candle - Yellow
12. Bowl of Charcoal (Fire)
13. Wand
14. Athame
15. Elemental Candle - Red
16. Matches or Lighter

For many witches, connecting with the powers of the four elements is one of the most important things they do. Earth, air, fire, and water are all elements that move through and inspire us. They assist us in making sense of and describing a complicated reality because they are concepts. Even the most basic altars will generally include some depiction of the Elements.... Some witches have ritual tools dedicated to each of the Elements, which they use in specific rituals.

Altar Smudging & Cleansing Ritual

What you will need:
- Candles - Sage Bundle - Fireproof Bowl or Container - Matches or Lighter

PERFORMING THE RITUAL

1. Set your purpose by lighting a candle (or several) on your altar. Be still and allow the universe to surround you with love and openness and invite it to be your guide in your practice.
2. You can light your sage with a candle, match or a lighter. In the event that ash falls, hold your fireproof container under it to catch it. It will begin to glow red.
3. Speak a cleaning incantation aloud if you're comfortable doing so. Here are a couple examples:

> "With this sage, I cleanse this area and my tools of any bad energy so that they can be used for the greatest good,"
> or "Earth, Air, Fire, Water, cleanse, dismiss, and dispel."

4. The most important thing is to focus on and imagine clearing your environment of bad energy so that positive energy may flow in.
5. Your altar and utensils can be cleansed of bad energy by gently blowing sage smoke over them.
6. Smothering or extinguishing the sage with salt is an alternative to allowing it to burn out naturally in the fireproof container on your altar after you've cleansed your entire area and all of your tools.

After cleansing your altar space, recite a blessing and consecrate it.

> "I honour [insert deity, ancestor, spirit] by dedicating this altar. May this place be a spiritual nurturing space. Blessed be."

You can also meditate and visualize the positive workings you'll accomplish there, if you choose. Congratulations, you have now cleansed your altar, and are ready to perform your magick.

Altar Blessing

Your altar is a sacred space where you can feel comfortable and exercise creative action and intuition.

1. Arrange your tools and items on the altar as you please and light a white candle.
2. Taking three deep breaths, close your eyes and visualize the bright light from the candle flame surrounding you and your altar space.
3. Taking your wand (or Athame or ritual knife) into your dominant hand, point it towards the sky and say:

> By the Moon, the Stars and the Sun,
> By the God, the Goddess, and the Ancient Ones,
> Blessed be this altar, and all here-on,
> Good for all and harming none.

4. Using your wand or athame, start by gently touching the pentacle and taking a deep breath in and out, while visualizing all negative energies exiting the area, leaving only pure good energy in its place. Continue to do this with each item on your altar.
5. Return your wand or athame and say, "May my altar be blessed."
6. Sit (or stand) with you altar for some time, and meditate on all the good that it will bring you: peace, serenity, awareness, intuition.
7. When ready, extinguish the candle and say "Thank you."

Create your own Altar Layouts

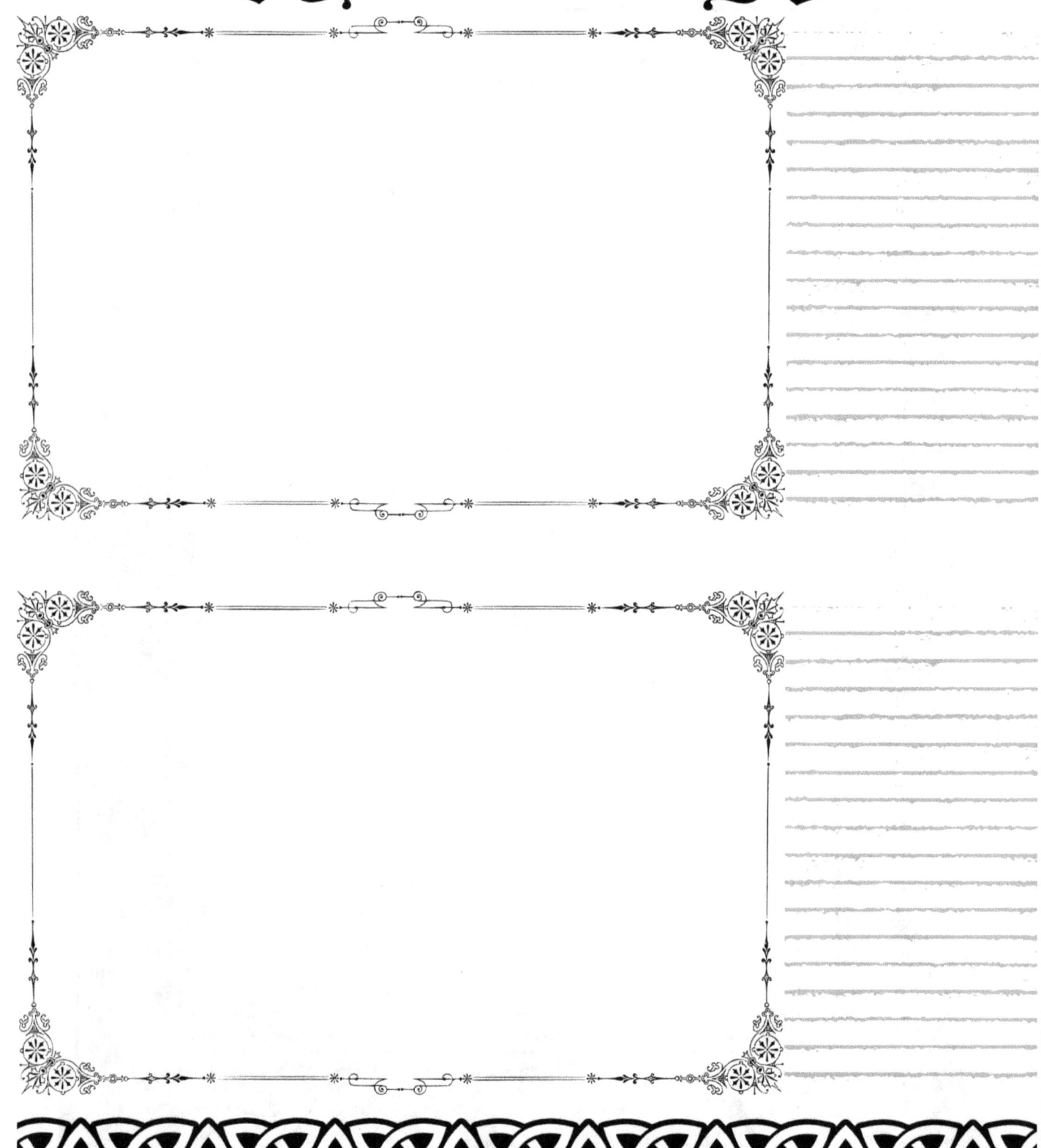

Create your own Altar Layouts

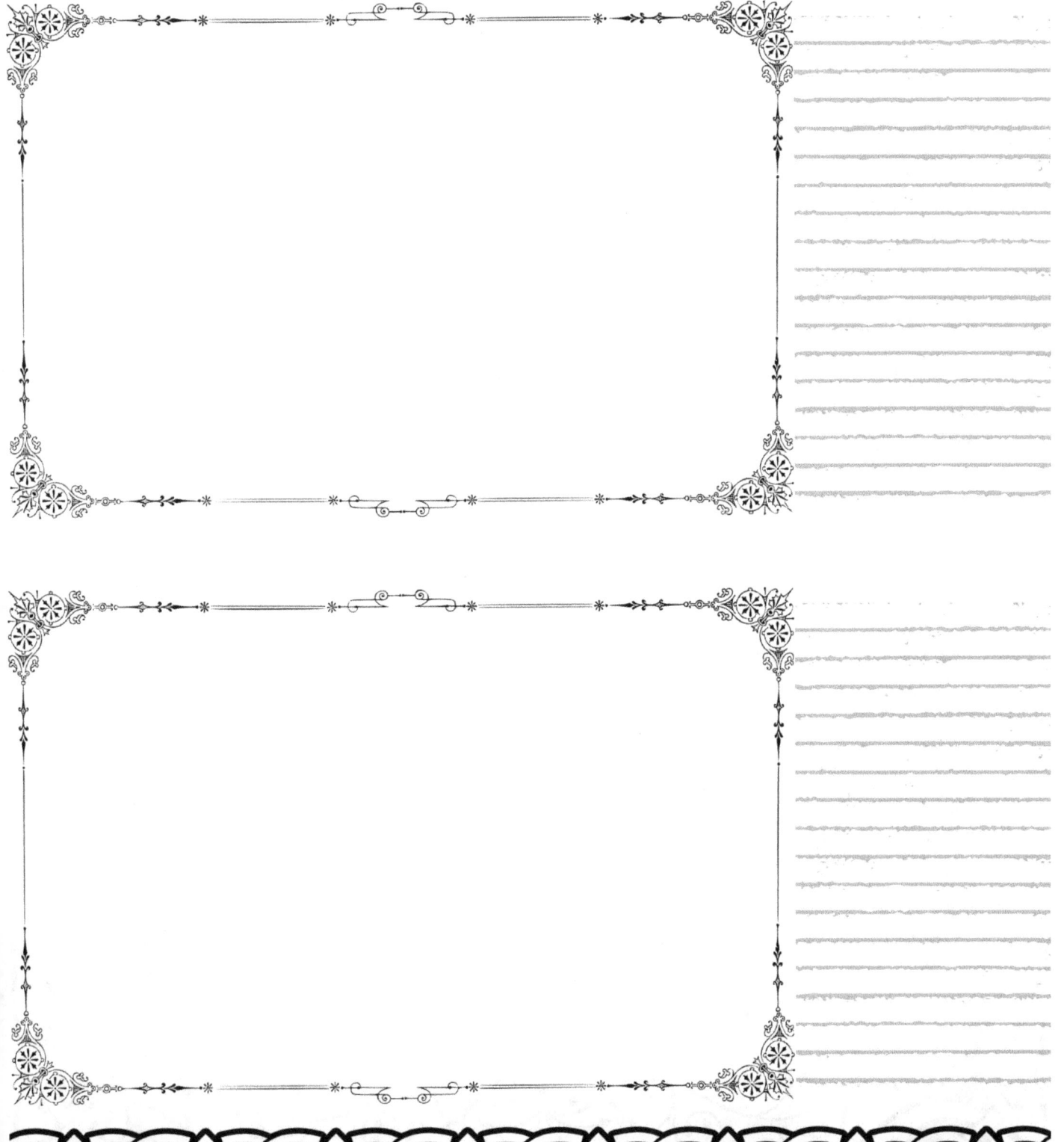

The Altar

Casting a Circle

Casting a Circle

Circle casting is a fundamental tool in the witches toolbox. The witches circle has been an iconic symbol of the witch and the occult for decades, but you do not have to be psychic or Helga Hag of the Woods to apply this esoteric practice. Casting a circle can also benefit highly sensitive people, empaths, and those who come into contact with a variety of various energies during the day.

In the simplest terms, circle casting is the process of creating a protective energy blanket over spiritual activity in order to shield it from harmful energy and other influences. The circle is a portable altar, a safe zone, and an extension of the aura that is stretched into the desired shape by drawing energy from the earth and, depending on the time of day, the sun/moon. The circle may be seen in its whole or in conjunction with candles, décor, and symbolic things.

Certain witches and neo-pagans who practice ritual magick construct sacred circles within which rituals are performed. The circle acts as a gateway to the realm of spirits and deities, as a shield against bad forces, and, more simply, as a psychological instrument to help you achieve the desired frame of mind.

Whether you are a newbie or an experienced practitioner, this is the first step you should do before casting a spell or performing a wiccan ceremony. It is not required (that's the beauty of the craft, you can decide what is required), however, it can enhance the strength of your magick if you do.

Additionally, bear in mind that you may change this according on what you have on hand, the amount of time available, or what seems right to you. If you don't have a lot of room at home, you can easily jump straight to the part when you chant as you light each candle, invoking the spirits of the Old Ones. You may include whatever you choose to signify the season or celebration. If it is Samhain, for instance, Halloween decorations and a few black candles provide the ceremony an appropriately ghastly aspect. And during Yule, evergreens, mistletoe, holly, and Christmas lights lend an extra touch.

Circle casting is often conducted prior to the commencement of ritual practice and then dispersed at the conclusion. Similarly, casting a circle around the car while travelling, around you or your loved ones before sleeping, or even around an object that has to be delivered is beneficial.

There is no hard and fast rule regarding the optimal technique to cast a circle, but the more powerful the visualization, the more powerful your shield will be. The difficulty level increases in some forms of conventional witchcraft with more formal ceremonial procedures than in those who instinctively practice eclectic magick, although neither is wrong. Practicing with your own energy and style will assist you in refining any of these ways to make them uniquely yours. With experience and practice, you will discover what works best for you and the most effective method of enhancing your magick.

How to Cast a Circle

There are many different methods you can use to cast a circle, but as mentioned before, there are no rules that have been written in stone that you must follow. The beauty of the craft is that each and every individual creates their own practice based on their own needs and desires for their own personal magick. Below, you will see some common practices for casting a circle, ranging from simple visualization to more complex and 'ceremonial' rituals. Make it your own, have fun with it, and try different methods to find the one that best suits your own personal practice.

Visualization

Ground and center yourself. Consider white light being drawn up from the earth into your root chakra and down into your crown chakra from the sun. Visualize the energy of the sky and the ground merging in your heart chakra and radiating outward. Visualize a circle of white light rotating from the North/Earth in a clockwise direction to each quarter and its related element: East/Air, South/Fire, and West/Water. As you travel around the circle's edge, invoke the magick and protection of each element by visualizing their protective energies being drawn into the circle. Consider how that circle extends in all directions, forming an orb around you and becoming intertwined with your aura. Make an affirmation, for example, "The circle has been formed. So mote it be."

Visualization with Candles

Using the visualization technique above, you can also add a white candle to each elemental direction as you make your way around your circle. You may also use different colored candles to signify and represent each of the four elements. Light each of the candles when you are facing their dedicated direction, as you work your way around the circle. With the four candles placed at the directional points, you will also have a visual reminder of where your circle border lies if that helps you visualize better. Additionally, you can also incorporate symbols or sigils such as the pentagram, triple goddess, triquetra, or any other symbolism that you are attracted to to create a deeper connection.

Using Sigils & Symbols

Using the visualization with candles method above, you can add an extra layer of power by incorporating sigils and symbols. Placing your candle in the middle, simply use a sigil or symbol that you feel personally connected to. There are many different and unique magickal symbols like the Pentagram, Triquetra, Triple Moon Goddess and many more. Use the Wiccan Symbols section to find one that resonates with you and your intentions for the circle.

How To Cast a Circle

In the craft, a circle is a barrier that keeps your spells and rituals safe. By casting a circle, you are assigning energy to shield you from any undesired or harmful outside forces. You may cast a circle formally or informally, that option is entirely up to you.

In traditional witchcraft, you may invoke a deity or goddess, but a secular witch may invoke the elements or construct a barrier with their own energy. A circle is not required, but it may considerably aid in protection and energy. Here, we will take a look at a more ceremonial approach to casting your circle.

Where to start:

Always begin by cleansing your environment. You may use your mind to push something away, incense to burn it away, or a broom or besom to sweep it away. Once you have determined your strategy for clearing your environment, it is time to define your circle. Space and location are important things to ask yourself when creating your sacred circle. Are you in a your bedroom, bathroom, or outdoors? You can make your circle as big or small as you want. You can define your circle in your mind, or you can use candles or crystals to show the directions or elements. Using the four elements, it is possible to form a cross. If you are using the five elements, one may form a pentacle.

To employ the elements when casting a circle, start by facing east. This is where the realm of air resides. When moving in a clockwise direction, you will finish facing north, where you may begin your ritual or magickal workings. As you begin to relax and concentrate on your breathing, stand in your designated circle. Take as much time as you like with this stage, or until you feel peaceful, centered, and present. You are free to change or modify these rules however you want.

Please note that the fifth element of spirit is included. This is optional or adaptable for your practice. When you have cleansed your space, and you are ready to call upon the elements, continue with the following chants.

CIRCLE CASTING TERMINOLOGY

When casting a circle, the direction of your movement is important. When talking about clockwise and counterclockwise movements, the words deosil and widdershins distinguish between the two.

DEOSIL (Dee-O-Sill): Clockwise or sunwise, positive energy, circle casting motion.
WIDDERSHINS (Widd-ER-Shins): Counterclockwise, negative energy, circle closing motion.

Elemental Circle

Start by facing the East, visualising the wind blowing around you. When you sense a connection to air, embrace it and say:

> "Powers of Air and wisdom, I call upon you. Protect me from harm, and aid me in my magickal workings."

Turn south while travelling clockwise or Deosil in your circle. Imagine flames and the sun's warmth. When you sense a connection with fire, embrace it and say:

> "Powers of Fire and courage, I call upon you. Protect me from harm, and aid me in my magickal workings."

Turn westward. Imagine that your body is surrounded by waves, waterfalls, and streams. When you sense a connection with water, embrace it and say:

> "Powers of Water and intuition, I call upon you. Protect me from harm, and aid me in my magickal workings."

Finally, face north and imagine the scent of the ground after a rainstorm. Imagine the darkness, calm, and serenity of a cave, as well as the sense of having your bare feet firmly placed on the earth. When you sense a connection to the earth, embrace it and say:

> "Powers of Earth and prosperity, I call upon you. Protect me from harm, and aid me in my magickal workings."

Elemental Circle

As you are still facing North, bring awareness to your feet on the floor or ground. Imagine roots of light extending deep down into the earths core, and take a moment to meditate with any feelings you may have.

Bring this beautiful white flowing energy back from the center of the earth, up through your feet and into your body. Imagine that this brilliant white light is extending out from your body to create your circle and say,

> "Earth, Air, Fire and Water, come together
> under the guidance and protection of Spirit.
> As I will it, a circle of protection has been forged.
> As above, So below, and within."

Your circle of protection is now ready for your rituals, spellwork, meditations, or whatever you desire.

CIRCLE TIPS

If you need to leave your circle before you are finished with your magickal work, you can do so without repeating the entire process. You can simply use your wand, athame, or a crystal to 'cut open' a door for exit and re-entry. Holding your wand, athame, or crystal, make a cutting motion at the barrier of your circle and say, "I use this (tool used) to open a door." When you return to your circle, you can close the door again by reversing the process.

CIRCLE of SALT

Salt is very popular in the craft as it provides very powerful protection. When you are casting your circle, it's important to note that some witches also trace the border of their circles with salt, in addition to the vocal invocations, this gives an extra layer of defence. Some practitioners may argue this, but you can also simply cast a circle by tracing a large circle of salt around the area where you desire to practice, then activate it with intention for protection.

Closing The Circle

Also known as opening a circle, this is a technique to release the energy you've created and to express gratitude to the elements for their support. Moving counter-clockwise this time, the act of opening a circle begins by looking north and saying,

"Earth, thank you for your energy and protection. I bid thee farewell."

Next, turn to the west to release the element of water: Say:

"Water, thank you for your energy and protection. I bid thee farewell."

Then, you will turn to the south to release the element of fire. Say:

"Fire, thank you for your energy and protection. I bid thee farewell."

After that, you will turn to the east to release the element of air. Say:

"Air, thank you for your energy and protection. I bid thee farewell."

You will then return to the north to release spirit and the circle by saying,

"Spirit, I bid you farewell. I release the energy back into the earth and open this circle."

Ceremonial Circle Casting

Using a ritual broom, sweep the area to cleanse it. Next, use four candles to mark your elemental and cardinal points. If you choose to use coloured candles, the north is represented by green, the east by yellow, the south by red, and the west by blue. Start from the north and travel clockwise to illuminate each candle. Now, using salt (or other markers, such as flowers or pine branches), create a circle with the cardinal point markers contained inside the boundary of your circle. Light some incense. While raising your athame or wand, touch its point to a cup or bowl of water, recite:

I cleanse and bless this water so that it may be worthy for use inside the sacred circle. In the power and light of the Mother Goddess and Father God [or the names of your chosen deities], I dedicate this water.

Imagine your knife or wand expelling any negative energy from the water.

Then, while touching the tip of your knife or wand to a dish of salt, say:

I consecrate this salt so that it may be worthy for use inside the sacred circle. I bless this salt, in the power and light of the Mother Goddess and Father God.

Now, stand at the edge of the circle facing north. Knife or wand should be held at waist level.

As you carefully move deosil around the edge of your circle, empower it with your words and energy. Visualize the energy as creating a whole sphere, half above and half below the earth, and say:

Here the circle has been formed.
Nothing besides love may enter.
Nothing besides love will emanate from within.
Charge this with your might, Ancient Ones!

Ceremonial Circle Casting

Once you have returned to the north, place your athame or wand on the altar.
Spread the salt in a clockwise (deosil) manner around the circle, starting and ending in the north.

Next, carry the incense clockwise (deosil) around the circle.

Then, sprinkle water around the circle in a clockwise direction (deosil).

Finally, carry your lit candle clockwise (deosil) around the circle.

The circle is now sealed, however there is still more to be done.

Facing North, hold your wand slightly above your head with arm extended out and say:

> Great spirits of the North,
> Ancient Ones of Earth,
> I call upon your power, join my circle.
> Imbue this with your energy, Old Ones!

Envision a green mist rising and twisting from the candle's flame, transforming into something natural. Lower your wand and face east after the spirit presents itself. Raising your wand again, say:

> Great spirits of the East,
> Ancient Ones of Air,
> I call upon your power, join my circle.
> Imbue this with your energy, Old Ones!

Envision a yellow mist rising and twisting from the candle's flame, transforming into a whirlwind. Lower your wand and face south after the spirit presents itself. Raising your wand, say:

> Great spirits of the South,
> Ancient Ones of Fire,
> I call upon your power, join my circle.
> Imbue this with your energy, Old Ones!

Ceremonial Circle Casting

Envision a red mist rising and twisting from the candle's flame, transforming into flames. Lower your wand and face west after the spirit presents itself. Raise your wand again and say:

> Great spirits of the West,
> Ancient Ones of Water,
> I call upon your power, join my circle.
> Imbue this with your energy, Old Ones!

Envision a blue mist rising and twisting from the candle's flame, transforming into a wave of water.

The circle is alive with your energy and it breathes around you. The spirits of the elements are protecting you and your sacred space. Feel their energy, hold still for a moment and visualize the circle glowing and gaining strength.

Now, the circle is complete. You may invoke the Goddess and God, or any other deities of your choosing, and perform your magick as you desire.

Popular phrases for Casting a Circle:

- I call upon the Guardian of (direction) and the element of (element), to watch over and protect this circle.
- Hail to the Guardian of the watchtowers of the (direction), spirits of (element), hear me, protect me, and join my sacred circle.

Popular phrases for Closing a Circle:

- The circle has opened, but will never be broken. Forever in my heart will reside the energy and love of [deity name].
- Merry meet and merry part, until merry meet again.
- Blessed be, element of (element), I thank you for your protection and energy. I bid you farewell.

Casting a Circle

Casting a Circle

Consecrating your Tools

Con·se·crate

/känsəkrāt/

verb

present participle: consecrating

1. make or declare (something, typically a church) sacred; dedicate formally to a religious or divine purpose.

Why Consecrate?

Before using magickal instruments, many modern Pagan traditions consecrate them. This does two things. First, it cleanses the object before it is utilized to engage with the Divine. Second, it clears the tool of any bad energy. This is especially useful if you don't know the history of an item or who had it before it got to you.

In many forms of magick, you don't have to consecrate a tool before you use it. Some practitioners don't bother with this step because they think it's not necessary. Their personal energy is channeled into their instruments without the ceremonial act, in their opinion, and going through the rituals of consecrating would interrupt their natural energy flow. The distinction between conscious and unconscious energy direction is an intriguing concept for many witches to grasp. If a witch thinks that his or her instruments or ritual items need to be consecrated, then they do. Some witches may apply it in some rituals but not in others. As in all parts of the craft, everything is decided by each individual.

Consecrating

You can consecrate your tools in a lot of different ways. I have included a ritual for you on the following pages. If you don't feel that an elaborate ritual is needed, that is absolutely okay. Not every practitioner likes to do full rituals for everything, and as mentioned before, this is your craft, and you can practice however you feel most comfortable. Below are some quick methods of consecrating. Not all witches will adopt these methods in the same way, so feel free to explore the options that suit your needs.

Quick Consecration Methods

Moonlight

Although this may not be the 'fastest' option, it can be quite quick if the moon is at the right position in the night sky when you need to consecrate a tool or item to use in your magickal practice.

Depending on which phase the moon is in, you can simply leave your tool or water out overnight to soak up all the lunar energy to help cleanse, purify, and consecrate your items.

Smoke

Herb sticks and bundles are probably the fastest way to cleanse and purify a tool or item for consecration. If you have some Sage or Palo Santo, all you need to do is simply light the one of your choice, and pass the item through the smoke to help purify, cleanse, and consecrate your item or tool.

Herbs are often tied together as cleansing bundles. You can make your own bundles if you have other dried plants that you feel a connection to.

Crystals

If you have an affinity for crystals, and you have your own collection, then using these gemstones can also be a quick and easy way to consecrate. Simply place your tool or item in the middle, and make a circle around it with the crystals of your choice. Crystal grids work great for this purpose. You can do some quick research to see what the magickal properties of each crystal are, but it is also important to have your own personal connection to the crystals in order to effectively consecrate your tools.

Declaration

Another simple way of consecrating your tools is simply stating or declaring that they are now consecrated for your intended purpose. This is a far faster and easier way if you have time constraints, plus you don't have to go through a complex ritual just to make your tools sacred.

Self Consecration

Many witches also prefer to consecrate themselves to show their dedication to the craft, and to become intrinsically connected to their own power and magick. This can be done by meditating, taking a cleansing ritual bath, or simply declaring your own person as consecrated and dedicated to the craft.

Consecrating Ritual

This is a simple ritual for blessing your magickal items, clothes, jewellery, or even the altar itself. Your instrument or tool will be made sacred by offering it to the energies and power of the four elements. This will ensure that it becomes consecrated from all directions.

Remember that, as with many other aspects of ritual, there is rarely a right or wrong way to accomplish things. This rite is only an example of how things might be done; many traditions have their own distinct technique of consecration.

WHAT YOU WILL NEED:
- White Candle
- Cup of Water (Just a cup with water in it, not actually 1 metric cup of water)
- Small bowl of Salt
- Incense of your own choosing

Each of these items corresponds to one of the four cardinal directions in your ritual, and you will find that these items will be used a lot throughout your practice as you learn and grow.

NORTH = EARTH (SALT)
EAST = AIR (INCENSE)
SOUTH = FIRE (CANDLE)
WEST = WATER (WATER)

If your style or tradition requires you to cast a circle, then you can go ahead and do that now. If not, it's okay. We will cover this later on. Go ahead and light the candle and incense, and clear your mind.

Holding the item or tool in your hands, face toward the North, and pass it over the bowl of salt while saying:

Consecrating Ritual

Guardians of the North,
Forces of the Earth,
I bless this [name of item]
and imbue it with your power.
I make this tool sacred and cleansed this [day/night].

Turn to face the East, and while gently passing your tool through the smoke of the incense, say:

Guardians of the East,
Forces of Air,
I bless this [name of item]
and imbue it with your power.
I make this tool sacred and cleansed this [day/night].

Next, face the South and slowly pass your item or tool through or slightly above the flame of the candle.
Be extremely cautious not to ignite the object or instrument.
When you are ready, say:

Consecrating Ritual

Guardians of the South,

Forces of Fire,

I bless this [name of item]

and imbue it with your power.

I make this tool sacred and cleansed this [day/night].

Finally, face West and pass the object or instrument over the cup of water while saying:

Guardians of the West,

Forces of Water,

I bless this [name of item]

and imbue it with your power.

I make this tool sacred and cleansed this [day/night].

After you have completed all four directions, face your altar and hold your tool or object toward the sky while reciting:

Consecrating Ritual

*I bless this [name of tool or item] in the
name of the Ancients & Old Ones,
the Sun, the Moon and the Stars.
By the forces of
Earth, Air, Fire and Water.
I dispel the energies of any previous owners,
it is now cleansed and renewed.
I consecrate my [name of tool or item],
for thine own spellwork and ritual, and it is mine.*

You've not only blessed the instrument, but also taken possession of it. Many Pagan traditions, including certain varieties of Wicca, believe that putting the object to use right away helps to bond the consecration and increase the energy of the tool. You can use a consecrated wand, athame, or chalice in a ritual to consecrate another instrument. Begin to wear any jewelry or clothing that has been consecrated immediately.

Remember to record and keep track of your ritual. If you have any notes or changes that were made, please use the following pages to jot down your thoughts, ideas and feelings.

TOOL OR ITEM	DATE & METHOD

CONSECRATING RECORD

TOOL OR ITEM	DATE & METHOD

Consecrating

Cleansing

In many magickal traditions, it is important to purify or cleanse an area before performing any type of ritual. There are several methods to accomplish this, and how you do it will rely in part on your tradition's laws or principles. If you are a lone or solitary individual, or if your practice is eclectic, you may select the method that works best for you.

Typically, when a space is cleansed, it is done so in a clockwise, or deosil, orientation; however, this may vary from tradition to tradition, or your personal preference. Keep in mind that your intention and focus will help with cleansing efforts. Here's how to begin detoxifying and cleansing your sacred environment.

Smoke Cleansing

You can use sage, sweetgrass, or other botanicals for smoke cleansing. You may also choose to use incense, wood, bark and other herbs that have protective or cleansing properties. The objective of smoke cleansing is to clear an area of bad energy using smoke.

When you light your herb bundle, allow it to burn for a short period before putting it out. This will leave you with a bundle of burning herbs that will produce smoke. Some witches actually plant and grow sage to make their own smoke cleansing bundles. It is a great way to connect and infuse your intentions of protection with the sage itself for when it comes time to utilize it.

A good way to distribute the smoke into all areas of your sacred space is to use a feather. This can be any feather that you find out in nature, or you can purchase a peacock, crow, raven or any other feather that you feel will suit your purpose and intentions.

SMOKE CLEANSING TIPS

Work in a clockwise pattern around your home (often beginning at the front door) while gently waving the smoke into the air. Spend a little more time cleansing the corners of the room because that's where energy tends to build up and become stagnant. Additionally, open the closet doors and cleanse the interior. Don't forget about places like the basement, garage, and laundry room.

The Ethics of Burning Sage

In recent years, social media has favored more witchy content, and individuals express their need to cleanse their homes or spaces of negative energies. The trendy activity of cleansing one's surroundings is known as smudging, saging or smoke cleansing which typically refers to the use of white sage. If you follow social media circles pertaining to smoke cleansing, you probably heard and may be wondering: Is smudging cultural appropriation?

White sage is found in the Mojave and Sonoran deserts of northern Mexico and the southwestern United States. White sage is by far the most popular, and it is also considered sacred by various Indigenous groups, including the Lakota, Cheyenne, and Navajo. This popular plant is used for healing by the Chumash people of California to detoxify and purify the central nervous system.

It is fair to question if smudging is cultural appropriation. Burning sage may prove problematic by conveying cultural insensitivity and being environmentally unsustainable. If you are not inherently from an indigenous background or ancestry, the following information will be beneficial.

Smudging is distinctly Indigenous. It is a sacred ceremonial purification rite or prayer practiced by many North American Indigenous nations. These ceremonies also do not specifically call for the use of white sage. Many Native groups, depending on location, utilize different medicines other than smudges and/or white sage. Smudging has a long and rich history that predates the white witchy Instagram posts you see on your feed. Smudging was actually prohibited — at least for Indigenous peoples — and was often violently supressed before it became 'fashionable.'

When non-Native people 'smudge' their surroundings, they are infringing on the cultural significance and authenticity of the ritual and prayer, and therefore, it is cultural appropriation. If you choose to incorporate 'smudging' into your practice, it should not be taken lightly.

Dr. Adrienne Keene from Brown University and a citizen of the Cherokee Nation states, "That smudge stick represents the deep pain, sacrifice, resistance, and refusal of Native peoples. It represents a continuing legacy of marginalizing and punishing Native spirituality. So, when our religious practices are mocked through these products, or folks are commodifying and making money off our ceremonies, it's not about who has the 'right' to buy or sell. It's about power."

Because of its recent popularity, white sage is in high demand. Overharvesting, as Keene also says, jeopardizes Indigenous peoples' capacity to access and use the wild herb in ways their ancestors have practiced for thousands of years, but stores continue to sell white sage despite Native communities' disapproval and objections. Ruth Hopkins, a Dakota/Lakota Sioux writer says, "It's exploitative and amounts to silencing Native voices and erasing our cultural heritage."

The Ethics of Burning Sage

The appropriation of white sage is worsened by improper harvesting of the plant. "When we pick sage, we use it sustainably, and we always leave the root and say a prayer of thanks for our harvest. This is as much a part of smudging (or saging) as burning the plant is," Hopkins says. In other words, preserving the plant's root is critical since this is how the plant regrows. If someone harvests white sage improperly, they prevent further plants from developing and harming the species.

Smoke Cleansing Vs. Smudging

White sage has gained popularity among practitioners of witchcraft and health practices influenced by witchcraft. Sage is not traditionally associated with European witchcraft, from which many current witchcraft practices are derived from.

If you have previously utilized herbs to cleanse your environment and enjoy the practice, you don't need to stop in order to be culturally sensitive. Smoke purification and cleansing is an alternative to smudging for non-Indigenous individuals, whereas smudging is a distinct cultural and spiritual practice. This cleansing method may appear similar to smudging, but it is simply the process of burning herbs, wood, bark, incense, or other safe-to-burn items that have cleansing properties — including cloves, lavender, thyme and pine, which are not environmentally endangered like white sage.

As a side note, if you are looking for alternatives to white sage, you may also see or hear that Palo Santo is becoming quite popular as a reasonable substitute. Palo Santo, which translates to "Holy Wood," is a Central and South American tree bark utilized by Amazonian tribes. Because of its rising popularity as an alternative, this tree may very well become endangered similar to white sage. Although the tree is far from extinction, its recent overharvesting may very well put it on that path.

It is essential to respect Indigenous customs and the ecology throughout any cleansing ritual. This may involve educating yourself and others about white sage, appropriation, and smoke cleansing; gathering your own sage or other herbs in a sustainable manner; contacting businesses to encourage them to stop selling white sage who are not providing credit to Native cultures; or practice your cleansing with different herbs and plants. Being intentional about how you integrate this practice into your craft, being informed and mindful, and respecting its origins and significance is extremely beneficial to everyone.

It may be personally satisfying to discover if and what your ancestors burned for their cleansing practices, and unless you are a descendent of Indigenous North American people, they probably weren't burning white sage.

INFORMATION CITED
TO READ THE FULL ARTICLE, PLEASE VISIT:
Is Burning Sage Cultural Appropriation? What You Should Know
(bustle.com)

Cleansing

Different Types of Sage

Sage is revered by the First Nations and the Métis people. Sage is widely used by both First Nations and Native Americans for a variety of reasons. Similar to sweetgrass, it is used in several regions of North America. Sage should be respected in your practice to honor the traditions of its origin and history.

White Sage

As mentioned earlier, white sage is the most popular and is quickly becoming an endangered plant species. Unless you are from Indigenous descent, it is recommended to use an alternative. These smudges are used for meditation, protection, purifying the body, warding off bad spirits, and preventing illnesses. If you choose to use white sage in your practice, please respect its history. Research, study and understand its origins, and if possible, learn from an Indigenous elder or teacher.

Blue Sage

Blue Sage has a gentle, sweet perfume that cleanses your home's energy and induces quiet and relaxation. Blue Sage's soothing smell makes it ideal for meditation or relaxation. It's a good option if you find the white sages scent too overwhelming.

Black Sage

Black Sage's powerful scent is said to transport your energy and mind into different realms. This plant promotes reflection and healing. Black Sage, also called Dream Weed, Magickal sage, and Mugwort, promotes tranquil sleep and dreams. It's used by Shamans to safeguard them during astral journeys.

Lavender Sage

Traditional healers call Lavender Sage 'the mother plant' for its medicinal powers. Despite their physical likeness and abundance of purple blossoms, Lavender Sage is not related to Lavender. Lavender Sage clears bad energy, harmonizes the psyche, promotes intuition, and encourages love. Lavender Sage's relaxing, sedating qualities make it ideal for nighttime.

Desert Sage

Desert Sage's warm, herbaceous, peppery scent purifies, strengthens, and cleanses. Desert Sage's fragrance is considered to treat headaches, calm anxiety, and induce happy thoughts, while the smoke cleanses, heals, and blesses individuals and the environment.
Desert Magick, Sagebrush Smudge, Mountain Sage, Grey Sage are some commonly known alternative names.

Cleansing

Asperging

In certain instances, you may want to utilize asperging to clean an area. Asperging is the process of utilizing liquid or the power of water to cleanse a space. Traditionally, this is done by sprinkling sacred/moon water around the edge of the area. However, you can also asperge with honey, milk, or wine.

In many magickal traditions, water or other liquids are made sacred by putting them in the moonlight (moon water), charging them with the power of the sun, or even putting magickal plants and stones in them. Don't just splash liquid about in a circle if you're asperging your area with it. Instead, put it in a bowl and sprinkle it lightly as you walk around the edge. Not only is this more relaxing than simply spraying water everywhere, but milk, honey, or wine cleanup will be much simpler and not as messy.

ASPERGING TIPS

Instead of just using your fingers to sprinkle the water around your circle or space, many practitioners tend to use a birch branch or any other kind of tree that you may feel connected to. The smaller the branches the better, so you can dip them into your bowl of water to help sprinkle around the perimeter. Another alternative would be to use a besom or a sprig of your favorite protection herb, such as rosemary. These are typically made up of smaller and thinner branches or twigs which would make for a great asperging technique.

Cleansing

Sweeping

The broom is usually associated with cleaning and getting rid of 'dirt.' You can go around the area with a broom or besom and sweep away any bad feelings and negativity as you go. It is advisable to begin and end near a door so that bad energy can quite literally be whisked outside. Consider creating your own besom, or broom, for cleansing rituals. You may even wish to chant a bit while you sweep to assist in expelling any lingering negative energy.

Keep in mind that you shouldn't use the same broom that you're using for magickal purposes to clean your house. Instead, designate a distinct besom or broom for magick and ritual.

SWEEPING TIPS

There is more to sweeping than the physical act of cleansing your home. It is also about clearing space. Mentally and emotionally, you are cleaning the area of any negativity and sweeping it away. If, for example, you are angry with the individual who cut you off in traffic this morning, you should 'sweep away' such thoughts, and remain grateful that you have a vehicle, and you were not in any sort of accident.

When sweeping, it is also recommended that you sweep from East to West if possible, as this is the motion that builds positive protective energies at the same time you are dispelling negative ones.

Cleansing

Salt

For many millennia, salt has been a popular choice for cleansing and purifying. Use a small bowl of sea salt and sprinkle across the space that you wish to purify and cleanse. Some folks also enjoy using salt crystal lamps. These are a great alternative to sweeping up the salt after you are finished with your ritual or spellwork. As with any other purification item, you should consecrate your salt before sprinkling it; otherwise, you'll just be making a mess and not cleansing anything on the metaphysical level at all.

The reason salt must be consecrated prior to usage in this manner is because it has a natural inclination to absorb energies, especially negative ones. In fact, salt is one of nature's most potent absorbers of bad energy, which is why it is so effective in cleansing, purifying, and exorcism ceremonies. Unconsecrated salt acquires bad energy simply by sitting on a shelf.

SALT TIPS

Salt is among the most revered minerals on the planet. Salt is symbolic of prosperity and protection. Salt is connected with financial abundance since it was historically used as currency and to pay salaries, especially when combined with green vegetables and other items associated with success and money. Use salt to purify both physical and nonphysical energy. One of the most common applications for salt is to create protective magickal barriers, or a 'circle of salt.'

Cleansing

Black Salt

In certain forms of folk magick, black salt is utilised as a protective agent. It may be mixed and strewn about your property to protect it from invaders and troublemakers. It is historically believed to ward off evil and may be sprinkled in the footsteps of a bothersome individual to drive them away.

In a sense, black salt can be used to cleanse you and your space by absorbing negative energies, repelling toxic people, driving away bad moods and protecting your home and space.

Recipe

- Course Salt (or Sea Salt or Kosher Salt)

ANY ONE INGREDIENT BELOW OF YOUR CHOOSING:

- Ash or residue from your cauldron
- Powdered black food coloring (Liquid will make it clumpy)
- Black Pepper
- Activated Charcoal Powder
- Ash from your left over incense cones or sticks

Combine all of your chosen ingredients together and mix well. Place your Black Salt in a sealable container. Before the first use, charge and activate your Black Salt under the Dark or New Moon to imbue it with lunar energy and strengthen the protective qualities. Add any additional ingredients that you choose. This can be essential oils, small crystals or different herbs.

Magickal Uses

- Guard your home by sprinkling it around the outside perimeter.
- Charge and cleanse protection crystals by placing them in a bag of Black Salt.
- Add Black Salt to any protection charms or amulets for an added boost.
- A small container with Black Salt and cinnamon oil will protect your heart from ill-intended lovers.
- All forms of protection.

Cleansing

Fire

In a number of civilizations, fire is utilized to purify and cleanse a location. You may accomplish this by burning a candle and slowly moving around the perimeter of your circle or space, or by dusting cooled ashes around the perimeter. If you are using ashes inside, be forewarned that this can be quite messy, so think about the space you are working with, and go with the best option.

By moving about the space with a little fire in a bowl or dish, you can eliminate any negativity that may have accumulated. If you wish to chant or speak to the fire element while you do this, that is completely up to you. As you conduct ritual or spellwork, you can also light candles and arrange them in the four cardinal directions (north, south, east, and west), creating the four marker points for the barrier or outer points of your sacred circle.

FIRE TIPS

Never leave a burning candle unattended.

Always remember to use fire-safe or fire-proof containers to hold your fire, and always check that you are in a big enough space to mitigate the harm to yourself or others.

Fire cleansing, also known as a burning ceremony, evolved from a religious rite, and can also be utilized as a means of letting go of the past, negativity, old resentments, hurt, grudges, or suffering in order to concentrate on what is more important, by simply clearing your mind, writing down what no longer serves you, and ritually burning the paper to release it from your life.

Cleansing

Ritual Cleansing Bath

As much as cleansing your ritual space is important, keep in mind that it is also important that we cleanse ourselves in preparation for rituals and spellwork. Many witches prefer to cleanse their ritual space and themselves, but again, if this is not your style, you don't have to adopt this method.

Cleansing baths are ancient rituals used by devotees of all the old gods, and they remain a healing and effective method of expelling unwanted energy from your life today. They are a crucial component of preparing for sabbats because they purify the mind, body, and spirit, but they are also valuable contributions to other forms of magick.

If a witch feels the heavy presence of a hex or negativity on themselves, which would hinder their own spellwork, a cleansing bath commonly referred to as an 'uncrossing,' unbinds hexes and curses from the witch, either by itself or in conjunction with other measures.

By infusing the water and surrounding the bath (including the environment) with items and aromas that you resonate with, meditation goals are enhanced and the experience becomes rather potent. If you have a full-size bathtub, you may add aromatics to the water and bathe your entire body in it. If neither is available, build the "bath" in a large basin or big cauldron and purify yourself with scoops of infused water.

RITUAL BATH TIPS

When bathing, if you are intending to attract favor and good energy to you, start with your feet and wash your way up.

If you are intending to remove negativity or bad energies, start at the top of your head and wash your way down.

Cleansing

4 Additional Methods

CANDLE MEDITATION: Purge your energies of negativity by burning incense and meditating while gazing at a lit candle positioned at eye level. Focus on your intention of cleansing your energy while doing so. Place one drop of Peppermint essential oil to the heated wax (while the flame is out).

SINGING: Using your voice is highly soothing and purifying; while laying your palm on your heart and focusing on your intention to cleanse bad energy, softly sing the sound "Aah" (diffuse your favorite oils as you sing).

FULL MOON JOURNALING: Create a letter detailing your intention to release whatever negativity you're experiencing, then burn it beneath the moonlight. You may also spritz yourself with your favorite cleansing essential oil while doing so. (Make sure the oil is skin safe)

NATURE CLEANSE: Being held by nature is one of the most effective methods I know to eliminate bad energy; you are physically being replenished by the energy of nature. Sit on the grass for an hour with your essential oils and you will feel amazingly cleansed and refreshed.

Cleansing

Essential Oils for Cleansing Negative Energy

Lemongrass
Cypress
Frankincense
Lemon
Lemon Eucalyptus
Rosemary
Peppermint
Sweet Orange
Eucalyptus

Essential Oils for Protecting Against Negative Energy

Cedarwood
Sandalwood
Patchouli
Vetiver
Ylang Ylang
Black Spruce
Myrrh
Rose

Cleansing

Cleansing

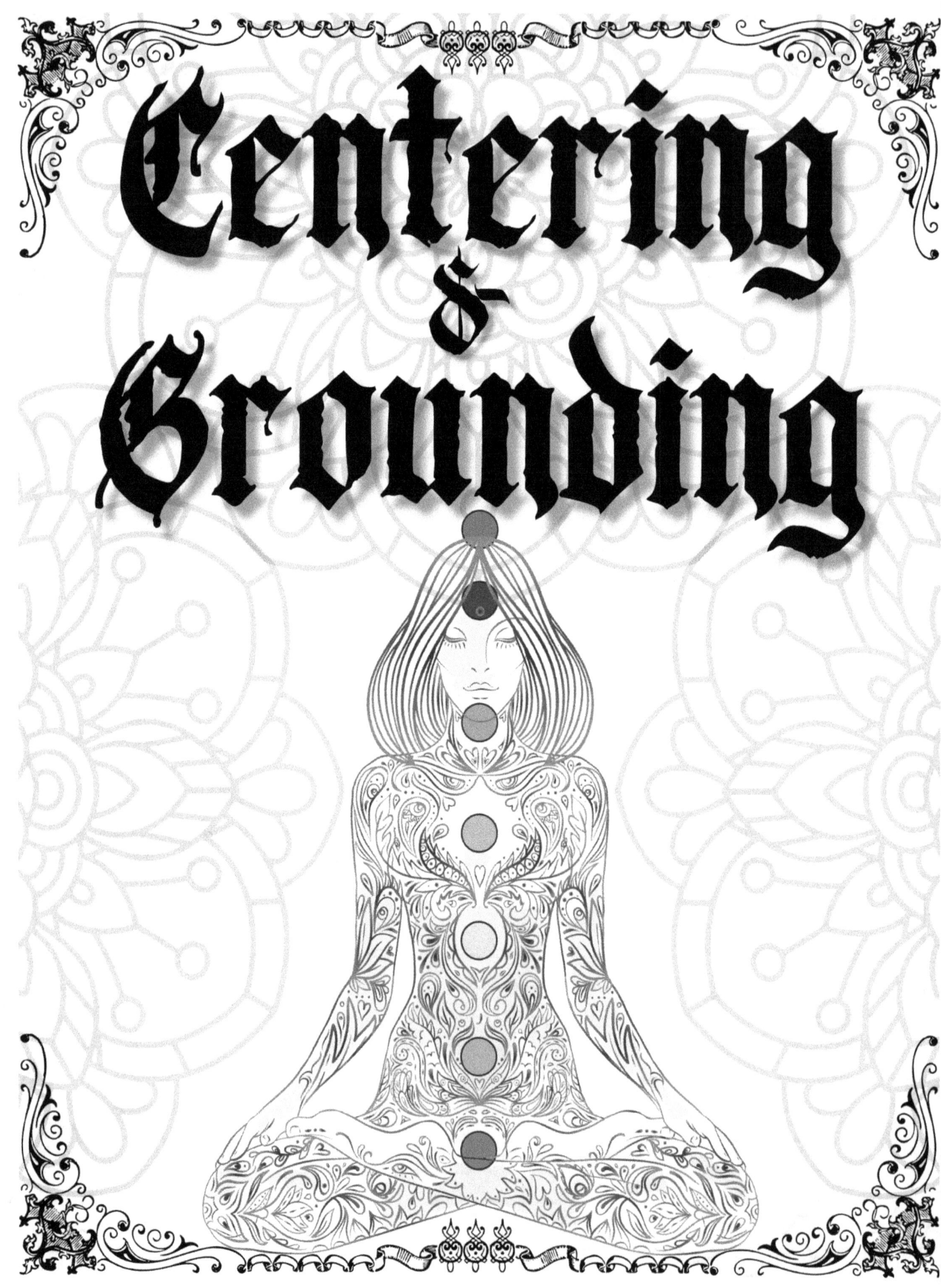

CENTERING & GROUNDING

Someone from the pagan community may discuss centering and grounding rituals at some point in time. Many traditions insist that you learn to accomplish these things before you start doing magick. Centering is the fundamental building block of energy work and, by extension, magick. Grounding is a technique for releasing excess energy that has accumulated during a ritual or spellwork.

Centering Techniques

Centering is the initial starting point in energy work, thus if your magickal practices rely on energy manipulation, you must learn to center. If you've practiced any meditating before, you might find it easier to focus because it employs many of the same principles.

Take note that each magickal tradition defines centering differently. Though this may be a simple exercise to help, centering could have a different meaning in other traditions. This is absolutely fine, because we are all different in our magickal paths, and if you choose, feel free to research the other options for centering.

First, choose a quiet location where you can work uninterrupted. If you are at home, remove all distractions such as your phone and tv, and lock the door to ensure privacy. You should aim to do this while seated, mainly because some individuals fall asleep if they become too comfortable lying down. Once sitting, inhale deeply and exhale slowly. Repeat this several times until you are breathing evenly and consistently. This will assist you in relaxing. Some people find it simpler to control their breathing by counting or chanting a basic tone, such as "Om," as they breathe in and out. This will become much easier with consistent practice.

When your breathing is even and regulated, it's time to start visualizing energy. It may seem strange or odd at first, but start by rubbing your hands together as if you were trying to keep them warm in the cold. Then, slowly start to separate them by an inch or two. A charge, warmth, or a tingling feeling between your hands should be there. That is your bodies force of energy and power. Don't be discouraged if you can't feel anything right away, it may take a couple of tries. Just keep practicing and you will feel that 'spark' soon enough. You'll eventually realize that the area between your hands feels different. If you gently put them back together, it's almost as if there's some resistance pulsing there.

CENTERING & GROUNDING

You can start working with energy once you've mastered this and can tell what it feels like. This allows you to concentrate on the region of resistance. Close your eyes and experience it. Consider how that tingling spot expands and contracts like a balloon. Some claim that you may extend this energy field by spreading your hands apart as if you were pulling on taffy.

Visualize the energy extending until it completely surrounds your body. According to certain stories, after some practice, you'll be able to hurl it between each hand, as if you were flinging a ball back and forth. Bring it into your body and bring it within, forming an energy ball within yourself. It's vital to remember that this energy (known as an aura in certain cultures) is always present around us. You are not producing something new, but rather utilizing what is already present.

This process will be repeated whenever you center. Begin by focusing on your breathing. Then concentrate on your energy. You should eventually be able to entirely control it. The core of your energy may be located wherever seems most natural for you—for most individuals, it's best to maintain their energy concentrated around the solar plexus, while some find the heart chakra to be the greatest spot to focus on it.

It will become natural and easy after a while of doing this. You'll be able to concentrate and center yourself anywhere, at any moment, whether you're on a packed bus, trapped in a dull meeting, or even when you are making dinner (which you should probably keep your eyes open for this). By learning to center, you will lay the groundwork for energy work in a variety of magickal traditions, and ultimately, your own magickal practice.

If you prefer to say some spoken words to help you center, you can use this simple chant:

Focus on this purpose of mine,
Mind, body and spirit combine,
Intricate energy in harmony center,
Strength and clarity shall be my mentor.

CENTERING & GROUNDING

Grounding Techniques

Have you ever performed a ritual and then felt restless and weak afterwards? Have you ever done a spell only to wake up in the middle of the night with an unusually heightened feeling of clarity and awareness?

If we don't properly center ourselves before a ritual, we might wind up a little off-kilter. In other words, you've enhanced your energy level using magickal means, and now you have to burn part of it away. This is when a grounding exercise becomes useful. It's a technique of releasing some of the surplus energy you've accumulated. Once this is accomplished, you'll again be able to exercise self-control and feel normal.

Grounding is a simple process. Remember how you can manipulate energy when you first learned to center yourself? Instead of drawing that energy in, you will push it out, into something else, to ground yourself. Focus on your energies by closing your eyes. Control it so that it's workable, and then press it into the ground, a bowl of water, a tree, or another absorbing item using your hands.

Some individuals like to expend their energy by flinging it into the air, however, one should caution—if you're among other magickally inclined people, one of them may unwittingly absorb what you're expelling, putting them in the same situation as you.

Another approach is to channel the excess energy into your legs, feet, and into the ground. Feel your excess energy draining away, like if someone had pulled the plug out of your foot. Some folks find that hopping a little helps to shake out the rest of the surplus energy.

If you need to feel something more concrete, consider one of the following options:

- Carry a stone or crystal with you. Allow the stone to absorb the extra when you're feeling an abundance of energy creeping up on you.
- Make a container of "mad soil." Keep a container of this soil outside your front door. When you need to let go of surplus energy, put your hands in the earth and expel the extra energy.
- Make a catchphrase to signal grounding—it may be as easy as "Aaaaaand it's gone!" When you need to release some energy, use this sentence or something that works for you. Have fun and be creative with it.

CENTERING & GROUNDING

To help you ground more effectively, you can also use the following chant to help you focus better:

I am bound to the ground,
My roots go deep all around,
One with Earth, Fire, Water and Air,
I am now focussed and acutely aware.

You don't always have to go through a huge experience to ground; if you're reasonably well grounded, you may use a variety of fast and simple approaches. Here are a few other easy methods to help with grounding:

- Consume some food that is natural or organic. Carrots, potatoes, apples, pears, or bananas are other good sources of carbs, which are great for grounding.
- Make use of a crystal. Natural grounding stones include smoky quartz, blue or black kyanite, and black tourmaline. Remember to wash (cleanse) and charge your crystals before wearing or carrying them.
- Try different herbs. Use incense to imbue yourself. Sage is good, as is a combination of sage and sandalwood. Patchouli has also shown to be effective.
- Bathe. Include some salts in the water, and if desired, add herbs such as sage or lavender to help cleanse and soothe you.
- Stand or lie down on the bare Earth. Find a wonderful piece of grass or soil and lie down. Feel a connection to the world. Also known as 'Earthing.'
- Practice drumming. Any form of drum or percussion instrument is an excellent technique to ground yourself. It doesn't have to be large or complex; any tiny drum-like item would suffice. Alternately, listen to steady percussion music that characterizes the pulse of Mother Earths heartbeat.
- Perform meditation, such as yoga or tai chi, to help you ground.

CENTERING & GROUNDING

CENTERING & GROUNDING

Clearing & Charging

Clearing & Charging

Magick is all about energy—your own energy, universal energy, the energy of the gods and goddesses, elementals, guardians, and other nonphysical creatures with whom you may interact, and the energy of the intention for which you are practicing magick. Because of this, the energy of the physical tools you use is a big part of how well your magick works and how well any ceremonies or rituals you do as part of your wiccan practice work. Before utilizing new ritual instruments or spell ingredients in ritual or spellwork, it's critical to clear them of any undesired leftover energy and charge them with intended, good energy.

Clearing

Energy that you don't want can come from many places, including brand-new ritual items. Almost every product, from a candle to a cauldron, needs the work of more than one person to make, ship, and sell. If you buy something second-hand, the object has even more powerful energy from its prior owner(s). Have you ever felt your mood shift drastically when visiting a thrift store, after picking up or touching an item? That is the leftover, residual energy from someone else.

There is no need to be concerned about leftover, undesirable, or "outside" energy in your ritual equipment and magickal objects. Everything is merely energy debris that may be removed like dust from furniture. However, the clearing process is essential if you need a "static-free" link to the non-physical realm through these items.

So, how can you get rid of negative or unwanted energy? There are several approaches, and some are more suited to specific objects than others. Sea salt, for example, is a tried-and-true method to clean crystals and candles with heavier energies. It works by absorption; simply bury the object in a bowl of salt for several hours overnight, then remove and rinse (be sure to discard the salt). You may also soak or spray your items with a mixture of sea salt and water. However, not all items keep well in a salt bath, depending on their specific chemistry, so it is wise to do some research to find out what items can handle being soaked in water.

Sunlight is an additional natural method of clearing. Place your ritual objects in the sunlight for at least one hour to dispel any negative energy. This will leave them cleansed, cleared and ready for you to charge them with your own energy, giving you the best results. Moonlight works the same way, and it is better for things that could be damaged by the sun's light and heat. This is especially true for crystals and plants that you may wish to utilize in spellwork.

Clearing & Charging

Smudging using sage, rosemary, lavender, and/or other purifying herbs is a centuries-old technique done by shamanic peoples all over the world. It removes negative energy from items, physical environments, and even people. Sound is another great technique to disperse and break up stagnant energy; try ringing a bell or some chimes over your more delicate ritual instruments and ingredients to clear them for magickal usage.

Charging

The next stage in ritual tool and spellwork preparation is to charge them with the energy of your specific intention for their usage. For example, you may charge a citrine crystal with cheerful, confident energy so that you can call on it whenever you need, simply by holding the stone in your palm. When charging a candle for a specific spell, you'll concentrate on the link between the candle and the intention you're attempting to manifest.

Both sunshine and moonlight act as charging agents, allowing you to clear and charge simultaneously. Just make sure that if you're charging for a specific objective, you put your intention into the item when you lay it down under your chosen celestial body. Another straightforward technique is to place your item on a pentacle slab (which has already been cleared and charged). Place the pentacle in the sunlight or moonlight for an added "boost." Because amethyst and quartz crystals are wonderful chargers in their own right, you may add herbs, smaller stones, ritual jewelry, or any other items that will sit on top of these dazzling beauties.

The key to the process is the energy of your own intended purpose, regardless of the technique you choose. When charging your ritual equipment and magickal supplies, visualize the desired outcome. A quick and easy method of transferring your power to your desired item is to simply hold the object in your hands, or place the item on a flat surface and put your fingers on it. Speaking words of intention can help you focus, so think of some phrases that describe your desire here. The following is an example of what you can say for a specific spell, but feel free to change these words to your own style and make it your own.

> "This [name of object] is charged,
> by the power of the universe.
> May it help manifest [magickal intention]
> within my life.
> So mote it be."

Clearing & Charging

Is there a difference between Consecrating & Charging?

Consecrating and Charging are similar, but there is a distinct difference between the two.

When you are consecrating an item or ritual tool, you are dedicating that object to the sole purpose of working with your magick, therefore dedicating and making that item sacred to you and your practice.

When you are charging an item or ritual tool, you are imbuing that object with your own personal power, energy, and intention for the spellwork or ritual that you are currently working.

Typically, once an item is consecrated, you can use it for any and all rituals and spellwork going forward, the only thing that you would need to do is clear and/or cleanse and charge prior to each use.

Clearing & Charging

Clearing & Charging

Banishing

Banishing

Banishing is used in various Pagan traditions to get rid of negative or unwelcome energy, as well as persons who may be causing issues in our life. While some traditions frown upon banishment as manipulative magic since it interferes with another's free will, if your tradition has no restrictions against such things, there's no reason you can't cast a banishing spell.

Banishing is utilized in all types of magick. It's similar to a common spice in food that you don't often notice it's there, but when it's gone, something appears strange and off, or an entire meal is ruined.

A successful banishment can be accomplished through a variety of means. Which one you select will depend on how familiar you are with the various approaches and what you want to achieve.

Banishing refers to one or more rituals used in ceremonial magick to eliminate non-physical entities such as ghosts or bad energies. Although banishing rituals are frequently utilized as parts of larger ceremonies, they can also be done on their own. Banishing is one of various magickal practices, closely connected to ritual cleansing and a common precursor for consecration and invocation.

What is Banishing?

Banishing something involves putting it in the past and removing it from the present and anticipated future. It is a desirable or necessary loss. Most changes, especially planned ones, entail some type of loss or banishment. This might include both major and minor things.

When you dust your home, you are technically banishing since you are removing the dust. New dust will settle with time, but the old dust has been removed from the present. That is a form of banishment. Banishing an abuser, especially one who is stalking or obsessive, is a large banishment that requires a lot more work, but when done properly, it can help avoid a reappearance of the problem in your life and in the future.

Banishing may be used on energetic locations, items, people, situations, spirits, habits, shadow work, and other things. If anything can change and disappear from your life, it can be banished.

Difference between Banishing & Cleansing

Both cleansing and banishing remove negative energy, yet they are not the same thing. So, what is the distinction? Please bear in mind that there are many various interpretations, so feel free to use your own discretion in how you practice cleansing and banishing.

Because the core concept of cleansing is "clean," most cleansing spells include baths, washing, or some form of physical cleaning. It is a gentle method for eliminating energy. It's similar like washing away the metaphysical dirt that accumulates with time or sanitizing your hands after coming into contact with others. Cleansing, to some, is a more positive polarity, right-sided, yin act. This is because it is simple to carry out and should be done on a frequent basis.

Banishing, on the other hand, is a far more aggressive and powerful method of eliminating energy or entities. It may be likened to removing dead leaves or weeds; things that have taken root and grown and must be removed. Like a person you believed was a friend, you've established some roots or attachments, but now you see they're impeding your progress and growth, therefore you have to remove them from your life in order to push forward. To some, banishing is a negative polarity, left-sided, yang act. This is due to the negative connotations associated with banishment, such as sadness and hurt feelings, rage, and the fortitude and courage required to remove someone/something out of your life.

These are key considerations when determining what type of magick to perform. If you're exhausted after a long day or your energy flow feels low or stuck, you probably need to cleanse. If you are feeling angry, scared, depressed, or if you feel that your energy has changed or shifted, a banishing may be more appropriate.

Banishing

If uncertain, it is advisable to reflect on what constitutes banishment. Consider what the term "banishing" means to you and research its implications.

Below you can discover some typical questions to consider while deciding whether or not to banish. Feel free to write down your thoughts and ideas on the next page.

- What does banishment mean to you in terms of the people you know?
- What does banishment signify in terms of the items you possess, encounter, or come into touch with?
- What does it involve to banish energy from objects or locations?
- What does banishment symbolize in terms of your own energies, whether they are a part of you or something you picked up over the day?
- What does banishment symbolize in connection to your life circumstances, such as relationships and careers?
- What does the act of banishing have to do with spirits who occupy the same locations as you?
- What does expulsion mean in terms of sickness or injury?
- What does banishment imply about your actions, such as routines, instinctive responses, or how you see or treat yourself?
- What does banishment imply in terms of shadow work, healing, and confronting trauma and hidden elements of yourself?

Banishing

Banishing

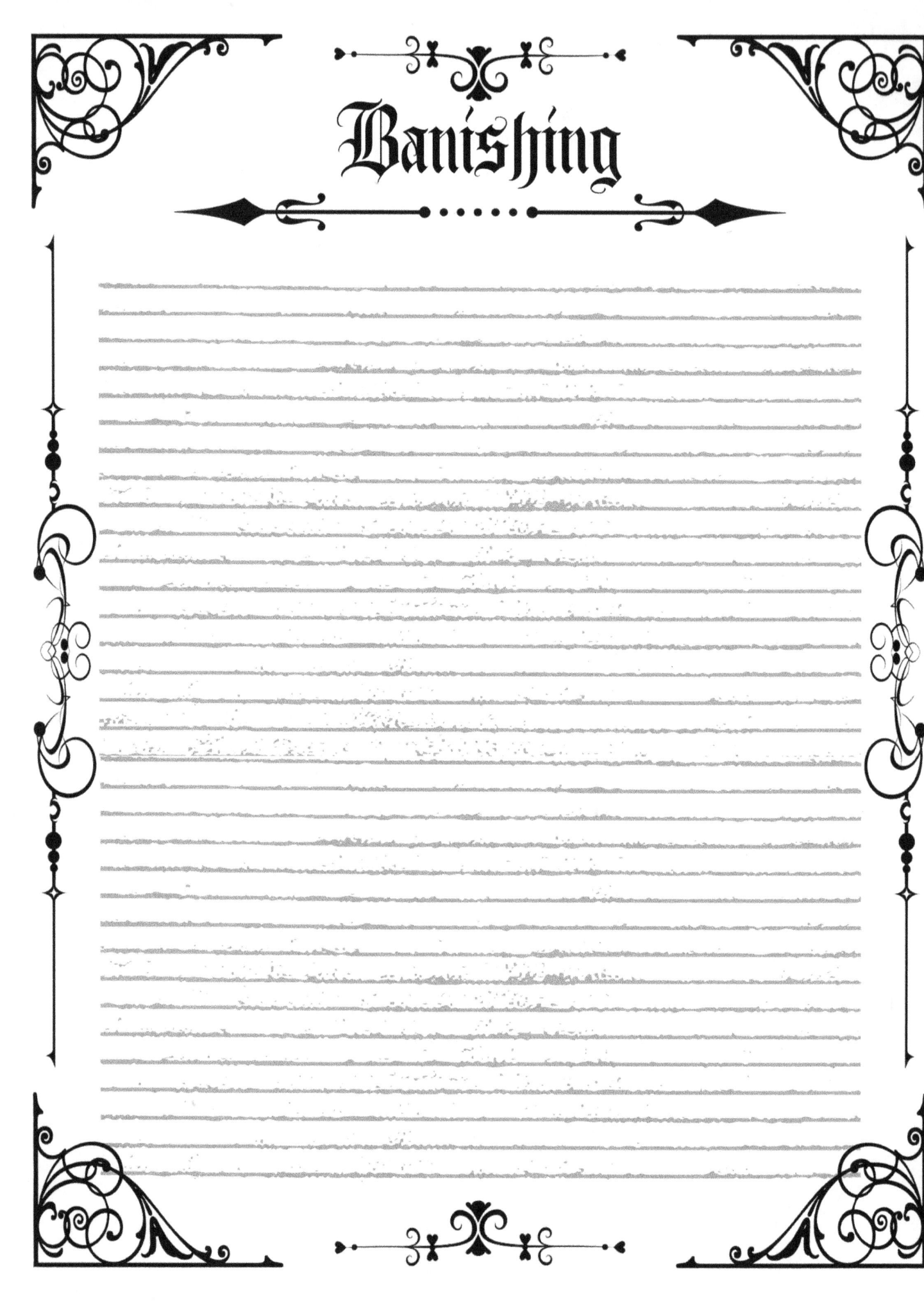

Banishing

THE PROCESS OF GRIEF

Banishment is a type of loss. Even good or necessary losses can cause pain at times. Certainly, not everything you get rid of will bring you sadness (I won't be grieving dust). When you do find yourself suffering, you must give yourself time to grieve and live in your loss. Even if you are pleased for the changes that sparked the grieving, it is absolutely acceptable to miss what was or what may have been, had things gone differently.

TO BANISH, OR NOT?

If you want to cast a banishment spell, you must be determined. If you have any doubts, especially major ones, the spellwork may fail, wasting your time and energy. When you think banishing is a good idea but aren't convinced, do this exercise:

Using the chart on the following page, write out the benefits, neutral changes, and drawbacks of 'banishing X,' where X is the subject of your intended banishing (the blank line). Use a pencil so you can easily edit your list if you would like to make changes later. Think about what would change if the issue was gone. Sort as much as you can into columns.

Sorting out the possible consequences can help you decide whether or not to cast the banishing magick. Banishing spells are most effective when you have carefully considered your options and are totally determined to removing the issue from your life. If you have misgivings, the spell is likely to fail. Conviction and confidence are really important. If you wait, you can usually conduct the banishment later if you change your mind and determine it is still necessary.

A second option is to focus the spell for a brief banishment or a lessened effect. Thus, you may approach your spell in a manner similar to snoozing a Facebook friend you cannot manage at the moment or using the "play this less often" option in a music streaming service. Getting some distance and time away from the issue may help you return rejuvenated, or it may reaffirm that the subject must be removed permanently.

Banishing

BANISHING _____

BENEFITS	NEUTRAL CHANGES	DRAWBACKS

BANISHING _____

BENEFITS	NEUTRAL CHANGES	DRAWBACKS

Banishing

BANISHING _____

BENEFITS	NEUTRAL CHANGES	DRAWBACKS

BANISHING _____

BENEFITS	NEUTRAL CHANGES	DRAWBACKS

Banishing

HOW TO BANISH

Saying that there is unlimited methods to perform a banishing is an understatement. Every culture, and every adept witch, has a few dozen distinct methods for banishment. The specifics of your banishment will be determined by the scenario as well as your personal path and practice. The same is true if you include banishing aspects in a bigger spell. Look to others for inspiration, but follow your heart and instincts, and tailor spells to you and your personal situation.

Smoke purification, salt, chants, prayers, sigils or wards, stones or crystals, bells, spell jars, baths, hand gestures, gardening, burning paper, direct energy manipulation, cooking, candles, cleaning, meditation, poppets, and so on are common techniques of working banishing spells.

Remember that the durability or effectiveness of banishing is partially determined by what you are intending to banish. Be mindful that some banishments are permanent and unchangeable. Some banishing's will help mundane attempts to get rid of troublesome items that are difficult to remove. Some banishments may need constant replenishment and recharging in order to continue resisting ongoing threats. Some banishments will serve to minimize the number or severity of events, especially if they are widespread and inescapable (like household pests or online trolls). Some banishing's simply will not work because what you seek is not achievable (banishment can remove toxic individuals from your life, but it cannot make what they did disappear - you must still work through it to process the trauma).

The one thing that all successful banishing's have in common is a clear intent. Be confident about what you are banishing, and be precise about why you are doing so.

When we have people in our lives that bring us difficulties, a banishing spell can be helpful. You can attempt a variety of approaches; just make sure that none of them break any of your own particular moral or ethical rules.

DISCLAIMER: The following methods are provided with the idea of assisting beginners get a better understanding of banishing, and may need to be changed to match your specific needs. Please keep in mind that if your specific belief system forbids you from casting certain kinds of spells, you should probably not cast them—however, it's vital to note that not all magickal traditions follow the same set of standards when it comes to spellwork.

Banishing Methods

Giving Orders

If you want to get rid of an unwanted spirit, one of the best things you can do is just tell it to leave. Say something like, "This is not the place for you, and it's time for you to leave." If it makes you feel better, you could offer a blessing or well wishes and say, "It's time for you to move on, and we wish you the best in your new place." Typically, this will be sufficient to resolve any difficulties you may be experiencing.

Elemental Banishing

People often use the elements, like fire or water, to get rid of something. By destroying things, fire can be used to cleanse and make things better. Water is used in many religions for different things, like getting rid of bad energies. To use in rituals, you can make your own consecrated water (moon water).

Salt is also an effective approach to eliminate things. In some magickal traditions, it stands for the earth, and for hundreds of years, it has been used to get rid of bad energy. Some forms of folk magick use black salt, which is a mix of sea salt and something else, like charcoal, which is used as a protective barrier. Utilize fire to destroy a symbol of what you want to get rid of, or bury it in the ground using earth.

The Poppet

A poppet resembles a person, like a doll or puppet. This is beneficial to use when you don't just want the person to leave you alone; you want them out of your life completely. Light two black candles, one on either side of your working space. Black is for getting rid of things.

Make a poppet from whatever you want (cloth, clay, wax, etc.). As you put the poppet together, make sure to tell it how much you hate it and how much better your life would be if it would just leave. Be sure to use a magickal connection, like a picture, so the poppet knows who it stands for.

If you want to get rid of the person quickly, you can use the candles to "light a fire under their butt" (important safety tip here, make sure you only SINGE the bottom of the poppet rather than actually lighting it on fire). Take it to the edge of your town and bury it there. If it's made of clay, you can smash it instead of burying it. Let the candles burn out until there are none left.

Banishing Methods

Ritual & Spellwork

In some situations, you may need to do more than just throw some salt on someone or something and tell them to leave. For example, if someone is bothering you, it might be time to do a full-fledged ritual to get rid of them. A banishing ritual to get rid of something (or someone) usually contains a variety of the following:

- The individual you wish to eliminate from your life.
- A thorough and detailed description of your intended result. "Make Karen a better person," for example, is too vague and passive. Instead, try "Karen will stop bothering me at work."
- A magickal link to the person you want to get rid of, also called a "taglock," which could be a picture of the individual, or more extremely, a strand of their hair. Be careful as this may go against some traditions.

A lot of magick is based on symbols, so use this to your benefit when you want to get rid of something. By magickally binding someone, you can stop them from acting badly or even send their bad behavior back at them. Some easy ways to do this are:

- A basic binding (which can be as simple as wrapping black ribbon around their picture) which essentially metaphysically binds the hands of the individual.
- If you are struggling with someone spreading false or slanderous stories about you, you can use a tongue-binding spell.
- Using a box that has mirrors on the inside, will reflect the negativity back to the person or individual that is harassing or bothering you.

You can make your own spell to get rid of something or someone and use it when you need to. You can make your banishing spell or ritual as extreme and over the top as you want. Getting rid of someone who is hurting you or breaking your heart is a big deal, so use as much magickal pizzazz as you think you need. However, be mindful of going against someone's free will if you follow or adopt the threefold rule.

Banishing Methods

To make someone leave you alone

This one helps when you can't get away from someone, like a co-worker or classmate, but you're sick of being bothered by them. They will still be present, but they will be less bothersome.

Write the person's name on paper. Burn the edges of the paper with a black candle, which is associated with banishment. As you do this, tell them that you are burning away any bad feelings they may have toward you, whether it's anger, lust, jealousy, or something else. Burn the paper around the name, as close as you can, until it is the only thing remaining.

Take the last piece of paper to where you usually find them, like work or school, dig a hole, and bury it there. You could also rip the paper into small pieces and blow it away or spread it around.

Cord Burning Ritual

This one is quite simple. All you need is a two candles (quick burn or small pillars are ideal) and a long piece of string. Each of the candles represent you and your enemy. Place both candles a couple inches apart on a fire-safe plate. Wrap the thread around each candle about an inch below the wick. This signifies the connection between you and this individual. You can use some wax or hot glue to keep the string in place.

When you are ready, light both candles. As both candles burn down, it will reach the string and set it aflame. When this happens, visualize the bond between you and this person being cut off. Let the entirety of the string be destroyed. Allow both candles to extinguish on their own, and when both flames go out, your banishment is sealed and complete.

Four Thieves Banishing Spell

Some Hoodoo and folk magick uses something called "Four Thieves Vinegar." Before beginning, you must prepare a batch. On the next page is a recipe you can follow. You can use this spell to keep someone from bothering you.

Write down your targets name on paper. Some traditions say to use parchment or brown paper. Using the vinegar brew, soak the paper. Fold the paper as tiny as possible and bury it in the ground outdoors. One option is to bury it in a flower pot, especially beneath a plant such as a cactus, so that no one will ever discover or disturb it.

Four Thieves Vinegar

WHAT YOU NEED
- Apple Cider Vinegar or Red Wine Vinegar
- Four garlic cloves
- Jar with a lid

First thing you need to do is find the best vinegar you can get your hands on. Apple Cider Vinegar is a great choice, and Red Wine Vinegar is a very popular option as well.

In the jar, place your selected choice of vinegar.

Add the four garlic cloves, which are peeled and minced, to the vinegar.

In the traditional story of the Four Thieves, each of them contributed a single ingredient. Following this tradition, choose any four of the following ingredients, and add them to the jar with the vinegar and garlic, and place the lid on.

Black pepper, chili pepper, coriander, lavender, mint, rosemary, rue, sage, thyme, wormwood.

Allow your mixture of Four Thieves Vinegar to sit for four days. Some people prefer to place it in direct sunlight to charge it magickally, and others prefer to hide it away in a dark cabinet. Use the method you prefer. REMEMBER: On each of the four days, shake the brew to keep things mixed up.

After the fourth day, your Four Thieves Vinegar is ready to use in your spellwork and magick.

USE FOR: Banishing, ending a relationship, protection, healing.

Banishing Methods

Banishing Methods

Banishing

BANISHING SITUATIONS

There are certainly an unlimited number of reasons to banish. Banishing may be used in almost any type of magick. It certainly is a useful tool in a witches arsenal. If you wish to get rid of anything or bring about change (and, let's face it, most magick is about bringing about change of some kind), then banishing is likely to play a role.

Following is a list of situations where you may discover banishment in typical types of workings, as well as situations when it can be beneficial to expressly bring out banishing as a magickal instrument of choice. It is also recommended that you do your own research to find other beneficial ways to conduct a banishing ritual that work best for your needs, your intentions and your practice.

Baneful Magick

When baneful magic is used responsibly, it is generally often in response to the terrible actions of others. It is typically useful to include an aspect of banishing the undesirable behaviors or the toxic individual. When used responsibly, baneful magick is a form of 'return to sender' spell. You are simply speeding up the process of karma, and sending someone else's negative energy and ill-intention back to them, which will bite them in the ass sooner than later. On the flipside, baneful magick can be quite harmful and destructive, so be cautious of how you practice this method.

Boundaries & Self Respect

Setting boundaries is a form of self-respect in which you recognize that some items, actions, and individuals are either unacceptable to you or actively damaging to you. What those boundaries are will vary greatly for each individual and situation. Understanding your own limits is critical to your general health and well-being.

Banishing comes into play by building your boundaries to keep those toxic things out of your environment, and especially to throw them out when limits are eventually breached.

Banishing

Chemical Dependence

If you are willing to put in the effort to eliminate drug dependency, banishment is a useful magickal tool to assist you. What you banish will be determined by your circumstances, what you're using, and why you're using it, so try to focus on banishing the things that are the most difficult for you to let go of. This may imply eliminating urges, access to the substance, or individuals or events that cause you to use again. Alternatively, you may need to banish more temporary aspects such as mental loops, anxiety spirals, self-doubt, self-destructive ideas or actions, traumas, or other difficulties that may fall under shadow work.

Cleansing

As previously mentioned, there are different views around banishing and cleansing as different practices. Because cleansing is a specific, energy-focused method of "making something go away," it can be considered a subcategory of banishing. Cleansing usually focuses on removing invasive or unwelcome energies, but occasionally the purpose is to make the object or environment an energetic clean slate in preparation for future work.

Consecrating

To guarantee that the object or space being consecrated is prepped and ready for its new purpose, the first step is usually to banish any old and lingering energy.

Creating a Peaceful Environment

Banishing behaviors or situations could be a better focus rather than individual people. If your mostly-OK neighbor produces too much noise at inconvenient times, you may cultivate harmony by banishing the noise from those inappropriate times. You deserve a pleasant lifestyle just as much as everyone else, so give it a go. Another related circumstance is hearing regular yelling arguments, which is never good. If you banish it, it benefits you and them.

Banishing

Creating a Successful Event or Gathering

If you're casting spells to assist in ensuring a successful event or gathering, it might be useful to banish and ward off anything you don't want to happen. Oppositional or snobbish conduct, racism, bigotry, stereotyping, transphobia, antisemitism, discrimination, prejudice, bullying, thievery, charlatans and scam artists, white supremacists, abusers, rapists, and pedophiles are all things to consider banishing to ensure equality amongst guests and a successful event.

Social Media

When you want to rid your social media of trolls and other toxic people, banishing may be quite useful.

Residual Memories or Echoes

Often, what appear to be spirits or ghosts are echoes of previous occurrences or leftover energy memories. If there is no genuine consciousness or awareness, you can end the experiences by banishing the energies or echoes that cause them.

Self Energy Maintenance

We pick up and internalize outside energies when we engage with the environment, no matter how meticulous we are at shielding and warding. Banishing is an excellent practice for maintaining your energy body, free of harmful forces that are not your own.

Garden Magick

Banishing can be used in spellwork to keep unwanted pests, invasive plants, or the neighbor's dog from digging up your yard, at bay. It may also be used to assist with spells to prevent difficulties caused by heat, cold, over or under watering, and so on.

Banishing

Unwanted Spirits & Ghosts

Most spirits, ghosts, and other nonphysical creatures who coexist with humans on Earth are better left alone or handled with respect. They do their thing, we do ours, and the world continues to spin. If you find yourself living with a troublesome ghost or spirit and discussions aren't working, banishment can be useful for reducing disruptive behaviors or occurrences, or completely eradicating the apparition. Please be cautious, as banishment in this scenario might be interpreted as a hostile move, similar to throwing out a roommate who lived there first. The entity may react negatively to such attempts, and if you are unsuccessful, it may worsen the matter.

Healing

One method for boosting healing magick is to banish disease, symptoms, or harm. No, it will not heal everything, but it can aid with symptom management and improve the effectiveness of medical treatment.

Insomnia

Banishing sleeplessness, restlessness, nightmares, and so forth can be a beneficial component in larger spells to improve sleep quality and consistency.

Looking for a New Home

If you have deal-breakers with a potential new residence, it is appropriate to banish and ward against such things. This will save you time looking at areas that you would find unpleasant or uncomfortable. Banishing's can also be useful if you want bad neighbors to leave you alone, but remember to ward as well to keep additional horrible neighbors from moving in after they depart.

Banishing

Manifesting

Some manifestations need a simultaneous loss. For example, if you seek financial prosperity, you might think about it in terms of eliminating poverty. To magickally approach the problem from several aspects, the banishment and manifestation may often be intentionally integrated into the same spell at the same time.

Pet Behaviors

Banishing may be an important component of spells that assist dogs in ceasing undesirable behaviours like barking, urinating on the floor, waking you up at night, or something else completely. Remember to conduct basic duties such as walking your dog (if your dog remains inside for ten hours straight, it will urinate on the floor), cleaning the litter box, training, etc. It is also important to understand and read messages that your pet or familiar may be sending your way to determine if they are only acting out of protection for you, which in the end, may not require an actual banishing.

Protection & Warding

Banishing and warding often go hand in hand, since warding against something suggests that you do not want for it to remain. To put it another way, if you cast a ward and it still appears, you want it to vanish or be banished. Additionally, banishing persons or things that do damage may be extremely beneficial as a component in other sorts of defensive magick. Wards and protective spells must be recharged and updated on a regular basis in order to stay effective.

Removing Toxic or Abusive People

Some toxic individuals aren't abusers. Many people are toxic because of unresolved personal concerns. Sometimes toxic individuals are OK with others. Abusers are just as effective at cultivating allies as victims, so don't ignore someone who claims to have been mistreated by someone friendly to you. Abusing or toxic individuals are never entertaining or worthwhile. Banishing can help eliminate such people from your life forever.

Banishing

Ritual or Circle Casting

Almost all rituals, notably circle casting, involve banishment. Preparing the space by eliminating harmful energy that might interfere with the task is generally the first step. Banishing in the completion of the ritual removes any residual energy and returns the environment to normal.

Seasonal Shifts

Spring cleaning is a type of banishing in which you get rid of the old to create room for the new. Most seasons or festivals include some kind of cleansing or transformation to signify the passage from the past to the future.

Shadow Work

The idea of using banishment to help with shadow work is simple, but it takes a lot of hard work and dedication to do it. You can't just make your problems go away without doing anything about them. That doesn't work.

Banishing magick may help you deal with negative aspects of your shadow, such as prior traumas, poor self-esteem, self-destructive tendencies, and so on, if you choose to confront them. You have the ability to eliminate any undesirable behaviour on your own. You can get rid of being hard on yourself if you want to. Take things carefully, one step at a time, and know that the magick will aid in bringing it to the surface so you can deal with it, fix it, and release it. The magick will not eliminate it instantly.

UNLOCK THE MYSTERY - JOIN OUR FACEBOOK COMMUNITY TO RECEIVE A FREE SECRET CHAPTER OF SHADOW WORK

Simplifying & Decluttering

When things get too hard or too complicated, it can be very helpful to take a step back and make things easier. Minor or temporary banishments can help clear up your emotional, mental, spiritual, and physical space by getting rid of smaller things that aren't as important. This allows you to concentrate on what is most essential to you.

Banishing

Waning & New Moon

When the moon is getting smaller or waning, its energy is all about letting go. This is a great time to focus on getting rid of things. During the moon cycle, the New Moon is the most powerful time to utilize banishing energy.

Can Banishing Be Done
TOO OFTEN OR TOO MUCH?

It can be very freeing to get rid of things, especially when they are actively hurting us or keeping us from being happy. But it is possible to banish too much and too often, especially if it is an aspect of toxic positivity.

Both excessive and insufficient banishing has its place. If you do it too much, it can make you feel alone. Too little, if you don't set enough boundaries, you'll be overrun by things that aren't good for you and are not even necessary.

Getting rid of too much can also be a way to avoid something. There are lots of uncomfortable, hard, or painful things in life, and not all of them are bad. In truth, some of the most essential aspects of life are also painful, difficult, and unpleasant. It is thus essential to carefully consider what you wish to banish and why. If you do this in an honest way, you will be in a much better position to move forward with your decision to banish or make peace with the way things are.

Banishing

Banishing

Shielding & Warding

Shielding

A shield is a barrier of energy that functions similarly to a window screen. It filters the energy that passes through it and protects the practitioner from the bad or negative energy of others. It also prevents psychic powers from being used against you. Empaths can use shields to keep the emotions of others isolated from their own.

Creating a Shield

Begin by properly thinking through your shield's purpose. Why are you in need of a shield? What do you want it to accomplish precisely? Will it block all energy or only the sort that is harmful? Is it a temporary or permanent situation? Will it be purely defensive, or will it strike in response to bad energy?

Begin pulling energy and spinning it around you after you have a clear intention. Imagine the energy as anything you choose. Common sights include soap bubbles, waterfalls, balls of lights, flames, greenery, gemstones, feathered wings or hair, tank iron, and armour. Choose a thought-provoking image that isn't too crowded or hefty. Circulate your energy. Release when you believe the shield is sufficiently powerful. It will continue to serve the purpose intended when it was established. If the shield deteriorates over time. Repeat to enhance the energy level.

Shield Effects

A shield may have several effects, either individually or in combination. A shield can keep the energy on either side, or it might operate as a filter, allowing only particular types of energy in. It has the capability to transform energy into another form, thus eliminating the need for a filter. Empaths can use shields to keep some of the additional emotional energy out so they don't experience overwhelming emotion. Shields also create boundaries that individuals will typically not breach. They frequently may not comprehend why they have stopped. A shield's edge acts as a psychological alert. The shield will give its owner a mental alert when someone else has crossed the threshold into their space. Shields have the effects you desire when you make them. Energy, like any psychic skill, follows thought. Whatever you consider when crafting the shield affects its construction. You are not limited to the shield effects listed here; you may create anything you can imagine.

Shielding

Maintaining your Shield

Stress can sometimes make it difficult to maintain a shield. Under normal circumstances, a shield can maintain its power for quite some time. Large amounts of negativity, attacks, disease, and a lack of sleep, on the other hand, all deplete a shield.

The most prevalent problem with shielding is daily stress. While a shield frequently keeps mental energy from adding to the stress, the shield eventually weakens. The greatest treatments include more rest, scheduled alone time, self-care, meditation, and avoiding stress. Meditation on a daily or monthly basis restores a depleted shield and promotes relaxation.

Empathic overload is like stress, but more extreme. Crowds, schools, and cities are emotionally charged. Empaths who are sensitive to this, construct strong shields to isolate their emotions from those around. If an empath hasn't built a strong enough shield, the first few days in an emotionally charged setting might be exhausting. Meditation and self-examination shield empaths from emotionally overwhelming settings. Meditation calms tension and emotions. It helps distinguish between empathetic and personal feelings. By properly defining yourself (emotionally), you add a layer to the "self" and "other" shield. This makes external feelings harmlessly bounce away.

It's a good idea to envision the surface of your energy shield as mirrored when you're creating it. This not only shields you from harmful influences and energies, but it also has the ability to reflect them back to their source. Another way to think about it is like your car's tinted windows—just enough to let in sunshine and positive things while keeping out all the bad.

If you are frequently impacted by the emotions of others—if certain individuals drain and deplete you just by being in their presence—then you should practice shielding strategies.

Other types of visualizations to create your Shield

- Surrounded by trees
- Inside a strong eggshell
- Inside a diamond
- Surrounded by white light
- Surrounded by Angel wings
- Surrounded by Golden Light
- Inside your favorite planet
- Visualizing a force field
- Inside a tube of lipstick
- Surrounded by hedges
- Mirrors around you to reflect negativity away

Shielding

Shielding & Wards

WARD/ing: to guard; protect

Much like shielding, warding is a form of magick in which you create an energetic barrier around yourself, your house, an object, and so on. Usually created to last long term, you can decide if they will be permanent or temporary. They have the power to expel or turn away anything you desire. Warding is a valuable talent to have since it can keep you and others safe, and with practice, you can execute it at any moment using almost any item, object or material you have on hand.

Warding is a practical method of magickal protection that uses physical items as energy anchor points, whereas shielding is most often only an energetic barrier. It is a preventative step that uses your magick to tap into sacred and ancient powers in order to transform everyday items into strong wards.

When should you Ward?

Most individuals routinely ward their house, oneself, or their area of practice whenever they desire an energy barrier of protection around them. Some folks even ward their space before casting a spell. It should be done on a regular basis in any place you want to protect, but where and how often is totally up to you. Shielding and warding can be done at the same time, and overlapped if you wish. You can never have too much protection.

Cleanse before warding since it is an energy barrier that keeps things out while also keeping things in. You wouldn't want an unwanted 'something' trapped inside your ward would you? Just remember to cleanse yourself and your space before warding either one. Refer to the cleansing section to see different ways you can purify your space before attempting to activate any wards.

Warding

Preparing for Wards

When you intend to ward a space, there are several steps that must be done in order to effectively protect the area. You will put your new knowledge to the test as preparing will incorporate cleansing (and banishing if required), centering, grounding and charging. Before you start, you can also select your item or object that you wish to use as your ward so you can cleanse it at the same time.

Part of preparing is deciding what kind of object or material you would like to use for your ward. This can be simple or complex depending on your preference, but it should be something that you feel deeply connected with in order to charge the item effectively. Below is a list of different materials and items that are popular to use as wards:

MATERIALS: Wood, glass, stone, granite, metal, paper, plastic, or any other material that you wish.

ITEMS: Necklace, rings, crystals, jewelry, wind chimes, witches bottles, or any item that you feel a connection with. This can be a spoon if you really wanted.

When you are making a selection for your ward material or item, there are a few things to consider. Is your intention to ward yourself? Then utilizing a small personal item would work better than a larger one. Do you want to ward and protect your home? Using a material that is weather proof might be something to consider. Are you going to be carving or drawing any protective symbols onto your ward? Maybe something like wood, granite, paper or plastic will work better. There are also natural wards that can be used as well. For instance, if you have wind chimes around your home, you have wards that are already in place. They simply need to be charged with your intention of what you would like to keep out.

There are also many different herbs that offer protective qualities, and some say that planting rosemary near the entrance or gate to your yard or property is a ward all in itself. You can be creative when selecting your wards, and yes, you can absolutely have more than one ward activated at a time.

Warding

Starting the Process

Now that you have selected your material or item, it is time to start the process of cleansing your home or space, banishing any entities or negative forces, centering and grounding, and finally, charging your ward with your intentions. Go ahead and review the previous chapters if you need to, and return here once you feel that you have sufficiently cleansed your space, yourself and you feel centered and grounded.

REMINDER: Do not forget to be thorough when you are cleansing. You will want to be sure that you are covering ALL corners of your home or space including the ceilings and floors. If you are only focusing on the walls, windows and doorways, the spirits will likely see that as a weak protection and invite themselves in to wreak havoc for you.

START CLEANSING YOUR HOME OR SPACE NOW.

Using Protective Symbols

Once you have finished cleansing your space and the material for your ward, you can decide whether or not you would like to incorporate any protective symbols. Referring to the Wiccan Symbols section, you can select any symbol that you feel connected to for this task. You can paint, carve or draw your desired symbol directly onto your material.

If you would like to get creative and have a symbol that is very powerful, you also have the option of creating your very own sigil. A sigil is a single glyph that represents an intention. They are a tremendously helpful magickal form. They are encoded with your unique intention and can only be decrypted by you, allowing you to keep your intention hidden while the universe works to align and fulfil your wish. This grants them amazing power.

If you would like to create your very own sigil, please refer to the sigils section, otherwise, continue with your material or item of choice. If you do not wish to use any protective symbols, which is completely okay, you can now go ahead and refer to the Charging section to imbue your intention or desire into your selected ward to activate it. Once it has been charged, you can place your ward in a spot that protects well, such as your front door, gate or other prominent location.

Shielding

Shielding

Sigils

Sigils

A sigil is a symbol that you make in order to change your reality in line with your intentions. All sigils are encoded with a specific objective in mind, such as attracting a loving partner, setting firm boundaries, becoming more financially wealthy, or healing your inner child — the options are endless.

While sigils were formerly used to represent and conjure spirits, they are now employed on a more intimate level to symbolically represent and actualize our own wishes. The formal process of constructing sigils (or intention-charged symbols) to affect your world is known as sigil magick. Sigil practitioners use self-reflection, creativity, willpower, and ritual to actualize their objectives. Sigil magick is founded on the idea that we co-create our world. As a result, we have the ability to make the changes we want, as long as they are consistent with our ultimate destiny and the will of life.

Sigils are quickly becoming very popular in the magickal world of the craft, and witches are using them to cast spells, manifest their intentions, and protect their home and ritual spaces all the same. If you are hesitant about using sigils, here are the top 11 reasons why people like to utilize their power:

- You feel strong and more empowered.
- You feel more accountable for your life, decisions, and actions.
- You become more aware of the interconnection of reality.
- Opportunities to showcase your creative side.
- You become more determined and thoughtful.
- You are more inspired.
- The distinction between lust and desire is now more apparent.
- You acknowledge that you are a conscious co-creator of your existence.
- You feel more profoundly linked to Life/Divine.
- You gain hope when you realize that most situations can be changed if you want them to.
- You can change your life drastically and for the better based on your intentions.

Sigils

How do Sigils work?

Sigils are small seeds that are placed into the unconscious mind. Many things enter our brains, yet not all of them are placed there on purpose or take root. The energy and intention behind sigils give them their strength, and this is what allows them to grow and blossom into manifestation. The sigils symbolic character also aids in bypassing the reasoning (skeptical) mind and entering the unconscious, where possibilities are limitless.

Because the deep minds language is symbolic, sigils essentially 'speak' to your unconscious. Pretty cool huh?

Deciding on your type of Sigil?

There are three different types of sigils that you can create: Destructible, temporary, or permanent. The type of sigil you choose will determine how you create and charge it. Here are the definitions of each type:

DESTRUCTIBLE: Becomes active when they are destroyed. The act of destroying generates the burst of energy that gives the symbol its power. This is often accomplished by writing your symbol on a piece of paper and then burning it with fire; however, you can also carve the sigil onto food and then ingest it.

TEMPORARY: Sigils that will fade away over time. These sigils might be sketched with a marker on your skin or carved into a candle that would inevitably melt.

PERMANENT: Built to last and to be active for an extended length of time. Permanent sigils are powered up on a regular basis to keep the energy active. These sigils might be turned into pottery as an art work, or they could be written on a piece of paper and placed behind a picture or beneath a piece of furniture. Great for warding.

Check your Motivations

Always ask yourself, is it necessary to create a sigil? Be wary of becoming sigil-crazy and creating complicated symbols in order to attract a new computer (when you can simply have it fixed) or improved connections with friends (when you can stop being an a-hole to your current friends).

Sigils are not a substitute for action. Yes, sigils may help you materialize almost anything - but you must also put in the effort. Don't be a slacker. Inner changes will be brought about through sigils, but you must first be accountable for bringing about outside changes.

I propose utilizing oracle and tarot cards if you need a more objective approach to examine your motivations and intentions. There are different kinds of cards, including religious, new age, and secular ones. Tarot and oracle cards are fantastic tools for self-reflection and looking at things from many perspectives.

Creating your Sigil

There is no common method for designing a sigil. To find a method that works with your tradition and practice, try different techniques. It will work as long as you design a single unique symbol from your intention that feels powerful to you. I will show you two popular methods of creating your sigils, but feel free to explore and try different things. You can really let your creativity shine during this process because there is no right or wrong way.

Creating a Sigil using an Intention Phrase or Sentence

STEP 1: Choose which type of Sigil you would like to create. Is it going to be a destructible, temporary or permanent sigil?

STEP 2: Write down your intention in the form of a sentence. Avoid being too complex or vague. Be specific. Here are two examples of being too complex and vague:
- "I want to have more confidence around my boss when we are at the 2pm meeting this afternoon," and "More confidence."

Can you see how these two examples are too complex and too vague? Instead, to be more specific, you would try something like, "More confidence around my boss." Simple, specific and to the point.

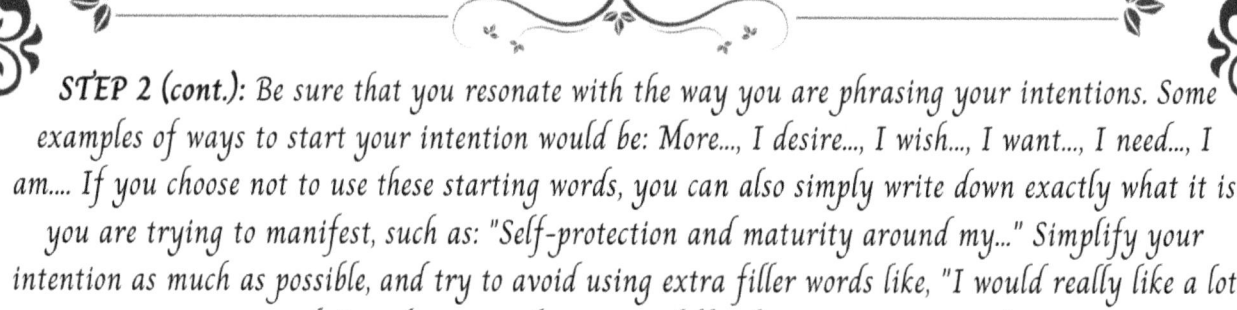

Sigils

STEP 2 (cont.): *Be sure that you resonate with the way you are phrasing your intentions. Some examples of ways to start your intention would be: More..., I desire..., I wish..., I want..., I need..., I am.... If you choose not to use these starting words, you can also simply write down exactly what it is you are trying to manifest, such as: "Self-protection and maturity around my..." Simplify your intention as much as possible, and try to avoid using extra filler words like, "I would really like a lot more of..." as this can make it quite difficult to create your sigil.*

EACH INTENTION SHOULD HAVE ITS OWN SIGIL! *If you desire to have a loving family with 3 kids, living in a nice big house down by the ocean, you need to create a sigil for each of those individual desires. Trying to cram all of those into one sigil will conflict and confuse the energies and chances are your magick will fall flat.*

Use your common sense and be realistic. Do not create a sigil for becoming a millionaire if you do not intend to work hard and exert effort in the actual world. Also, if you are not qualified for something like becoming the CEO of a company, don't waste your time. Similarly, it's also impractical to create a sigil for something that is most likely to happen anyways. Always aim for the middle ground or a 50/50 likelihood of occurrence.

And lastly, while stating your intention, strive to be as optimistic as possible. So instead of saying something like, "I will not feel scared or anxious around my peers," try this instead, "I feel calm and empowered around my peers." Magick and the universe have a funny way of locking in on words with negative connotations. So if the vibrations for 'scared' and 'anxious,' are prevalent, then that's what is going to manifest in your reality. **BE CAREFUL HOW YOU WORD YOUR INTENTIONS.**

STEP 2 EXAMPLE:
MORE CONFIDENCE AROUND MY BOSS

STEP 3: *Eliminate all of the vowels and repeating letters.*

STEP 3 EXAMPLE:
MR CNFD BS

Sigils

STEP 4: After you have simplified your sentence and reduced it down to only single letters, you will use those remaining letters to create your sigil. Don't be concerned if you can't make an elegant-looking symbol right away. Continue to experiment until you discover something you like. You don't have to be an artist, and your symbol doesn't even have to resemble a sigil — just make something that speaks to you. If you enjoy the final design, you've done great!

Rearrange the letters in whatever manner you like. For example, you may flip certain letters upside down, magnify others, shrink the rest, or merge two letters together. You can also add different elements like hearts, stars, swirls, dots, squiggly lines, different colors, other symbols that compliment your desire, and whatever else you want. If a letter(s) is not working with your vision, you can also leave them out. Have fun, enjoy the process and just let your heart guide you.

Take a minute to congratulate yourself after you're finished. You've completed your first sigil! In the next step, we will charge and activate it.

STEP 4 EXAMPLE: MR CNFD BS

Sigils

STEP 5: Now it is time to charge your sigil. Numerous methods exist for imbuing your sigil with power. If you are creating a destructible sigil, the act of burning will charge it. Some witches like to take a few seconds to place their hands on the sigil and imagine a warm light streaming from their palms and onto the paper. You may also charge a sigil by dancing, chanting, or clapping, so select the manner that best suits the sort of sigil you're making.

Make sure you're in a secure, peaceful place with no distractions when you burn the symbol. After the symbol has been entirely burnt, it is now charged, and the ashes can be discarded. Alternatively, you can also refer to the 'Charging' section of this book to charge your sigil in other ways. Remember to record your sigil ceremony so you can reflect back later to see what has manifested in your life.

STEP 6: The majority of the work has now been completed. Don't try to control it, you can't influence what happens next. But the most important point to remember is to forget and let go. Don't obsess with your sigil. Don't get caught up in it. Don't become attached to it. Allow the universal will to do its job. If you constantly think about it, the greater chance your conscious mind will get involved. This is comparable to planting a seed and then digging it up every day to see if it is growing. Leave it alone!

Close your ritual place and go on with your daily life.

TYPE OF SIGIL: D | T | P (*Destructible, Temporary, Permanent*)

INTENTION PHRASE:

REMOVE VOWELS & REPEATING LETTERS:

SIGIL CREATION & DESIGN:

Sigils

TYPE OF SIGIL: D | T | P (Destructible, Temporary, Permanent)

INTENTION PHRASE:

REMOVE VOWELS & REPEATING LETTERS:

SIGIL CREATION & DESIGN:

TYPE OF SIGIL: D | T | P (Destructible, Temporary, Permanent)

INTENTION PHRASE:

REMOVE VOWELS & REPEATING LETTERS:

SIGIL CREATION & DESIGN:

Sigils

TYPE OF SIGIL: D | T | P (*Destructible, Temporary, Permanent*)

INTENTION PHRASE:

REMOVE VOWELS & REPEATING LETTERS:

SIGIL CREATION & DESIGN:

TYPE OF SIGIL: D | T | P (*Destructible, Temporary, Permanent*)

INTENTION PHRASE:

REMOVE VOWELS & REPEATING LETTERS:

SIGIL CREATION & DESIGN:

Sigils

TYPE OF SIGIL: D | T | P (*Destructible, Temporary, Permanent*)
INTENTION PHRASE:

REMOVE VOWELS & REPEATING LETTERS:
SIGIL CREATION & DESIGN:

TYPE OF SIGIL: D | T | P (*Destructible, Temporary, Permanent*)
INTENTION PHRASE:

REMOVE VOWELS & REPEATING LETTERS:
SIGIL CREATION & DESIGN:

Sigils

Creating a Sigil using a Magick Square

Let's begin with the history of the Lo Shu grid, the most well-known magick square. The Chinese emperor Yu found a 3x3 grid on the back of a tortoise shell and believed it to be a perfect magick square. The Lo Shu grid was frequently used in astrology, divination, talismans, and Taoist magick as a symbol of harmony.

When the sum of the numbers horizontally, vertically, and diagonally in a magick square is the same, the square is considered magickal. In the sample Lo Shu Grid below, each direction adds up to 15.

Lo Shu Grid

4	9	2
3	5	7
8	1	6

During the Middle Ages, magick squares became quite popular and began to appear in the work and literature of numerous fields such as mathematics, astrology, mysticism, alchemical, and other academics.

Alchemists frequently fashioned sigils to coincide with and reflect the energy and wisdom of a planet. These might then be utilized in ceremonies and rituals to depict or invoke the power of the planet.

You can make your own sigils with magick squares. Begin with your intention or desire in mind. In this case, we'll use — 'My prosperity is inevitable.' Then, narrow it down to a single keyword or small phrase. As an example, we will use prosperity.

Alternatively, you can also use a single word intention instead of trying to think of a phrase. Some examples of single word intentions can be:

- PROTECTION
- MONEY
- FERTILITY
- HEALING
- MANIFESTING
- CHANGE
- HEALTH
- ABUNDANCE

Sigils

Now we are going to take our intention word, Prosperity, and figure out which numbers correlate to each letter. To do this, we will work with the chart below, which is also utilized in numerology:

1	2	3	4	5	6	7	8	9
A	B	C	D	E	F	G	H	I
J	K	L	M	N	O	P	Q	R
S	T	U	V	W	X	Y	Z	

PROSPERITY = 7961759927

Now that we have our intention word in the form of a number, we can go ahead and utilize the Lo Shu Grid to create our 'Prosperity' sigil. There are several methods to do this. Some witches like to remove any repeating numbers to create a sigil with one clean line. Others, like myself, prefer to keep all the numbers involved as it creates a unique design, and packs an extra magickal punch. How you choose to create your sigil is entirely up to you. We will go over both examples so you can see the difference.

When drawing or tracing out your design on the grid, there are a couple of things that you should be aware of:

- THE FIRST AND LAST NUMBERS WILL HAVE A SMALL CIRCLE ON THE CHART TO DEPICT THE BEGINNING AND END OF YOUR SIGIL.

- IF USING REPEATING NUMBERS, WHEN YOU GET TO THE NUMBER A SECOND TIME DURING YOUR DRAWING, A SMALL 'BUMP' OR UPSIDE DOWN 'U' WILL BE PLACED.

Lets go ahead and create two different sigils for our intention word of 'PROSPERITY.'

Sigils

PROSPERITY = 7961759927

With repeating numbers

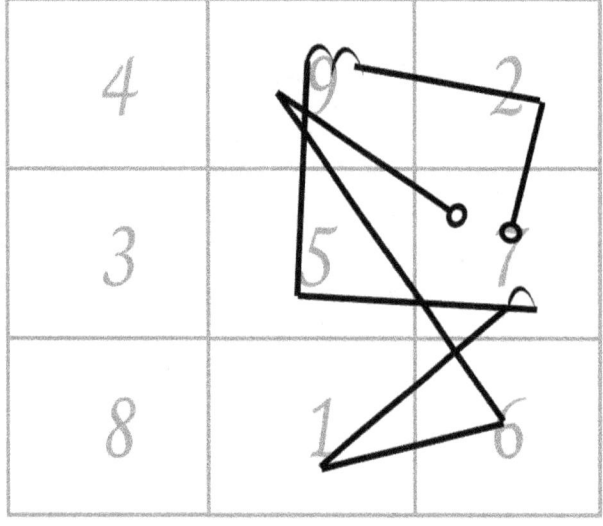

Finished Design

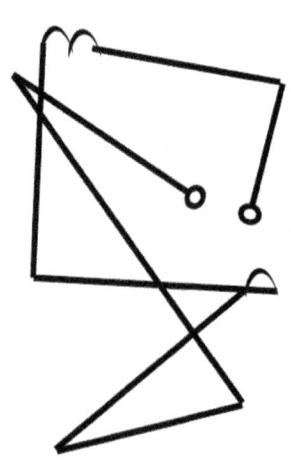

PROSPERITY = 796152

Without repeating numbers

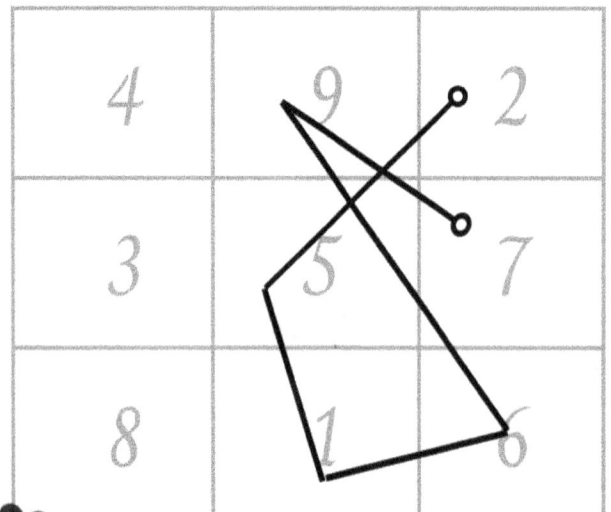

Finished Design

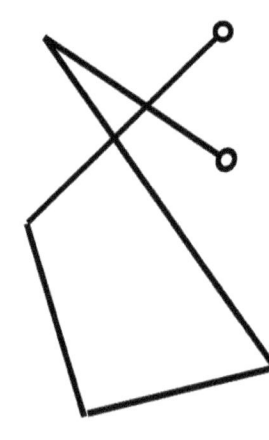

These are the two different designs you can make with or without the repeating numbers. You can also go ahead and add any additional elements like before; hearts, stars, swirls, or any other added extra that you prefer.

Sigils

Now you have created three different types of sigils by learning two different methods. It is time to put your creativity to good use and go out into the world and manifest the crap out of what it is you want to manifest in your life. Remember, have fun, let your heart and intuition guide you, and good luck.

TYPE OF SIGIL: D | T | P (Destructible, Temporary, Permanent)
INTENTION WORD:
NUMBERED INTENTION WORD:
(Optional) REMOVE REPEATING NUMBERS:

1	2	3	4	5	6	7	8	9
A	B	C	D	E	F	G	H	I
J	K	L	M	N	O	P	Q	R
S	T	U	V	W	X	Y	Z	

COMPLETED SIGIL

SIGIL TIP:
If you don't like the way your sigil is oriented, feel free to rotate it to the way you like!

Sigils

TYPE OF SIGIL: D | T | P (*Destructible, Temporary, Permanent*)
INTENTION WORD:
NUMBERED INTENTION WORD:
(*Optional*) REMOVE REPEATING NUMBERS:

1	2	3	4	5	6	7	8	9
A	B	C	D	E	F	G	H	I
J	K	L	M	N	O	P	Q	R
S	T	U	V	W	X	Y	Z	

4	9	2
3	5	7
8	1	6

COMPLETED SIGIL

NOTES:

Sigils

TYPE OF SIGIL: D | T | P (Destructible, Temporary, Permanent)
INTENTION WORD:
NUMBERED INTENTION WORD:
(Optional) REMOVE REPEATING NUMBERS:

1	2	3	4	5	6	7	8	9
A	B	C	D	E	F	G	H	I
J	K	L	M	N	O	P	Q	R
S	T	U	V	W	X	Y	Z	

COMPLETED SIGIL

4	9	2
3	5	7
8	1	6

NOTES:

Sigils

TYPE OF SIGIL: D | T | P (*Destructible, Temporary, Permanent*)
INTENTION WORD:
NUMBERED INTENTION WORD:
(*Optional*) REMOVE REPEATING NUMBERS:

1	2	3	4	5	6	7	8	9
A	B	C	D	E	F	G	H	I
J	K	L	M	N	O	P	Q	R
S	T	U	V	W	X	Y	Z	

COMPLETED SIGIL

4	9	2
3	5	7
8	1	6

NOTES:

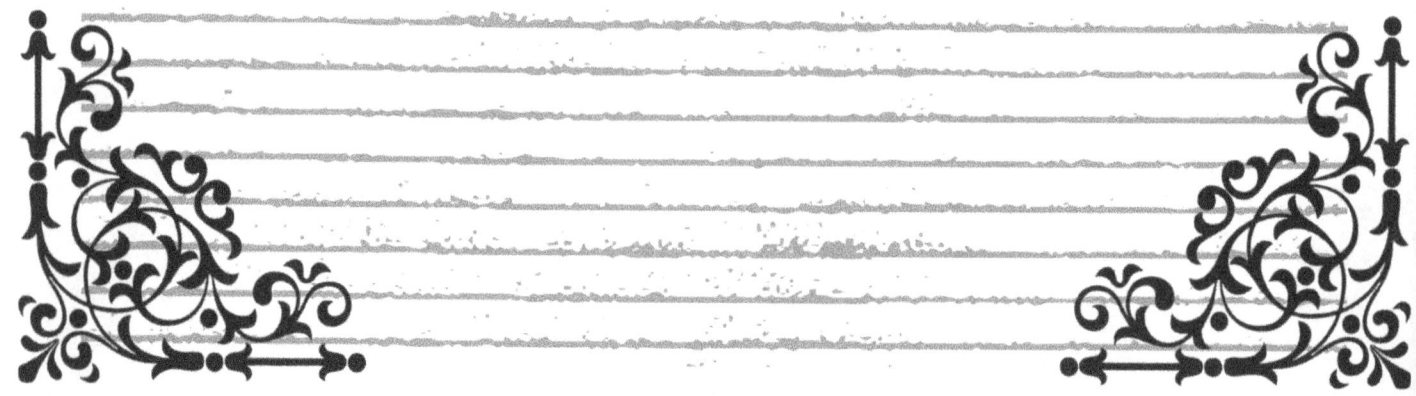

Sigils

TYPE OF SIGIL: D | T | P (*Destructible, Temporary, Permanent*)
INTENTION WORD:
NUMBERED INTENTION WORD:
(*Optional*) REMOVE REPEATING NUMBERS:

1	2	3	4	5	6	7	8	9
A	B	C	D	E	F	G	H	I
J	K	L	M	N	O	P	Q	R
S	T	U	V	W	X	Y	Z	

4	9	2
3	5	7
8	1	6

COMPLETED SIGIL

NOTES:

Sigils

Sigils

Witchcraft Symbols

WITCHCRAFT SYMBOLS

Numerous modern Pagan religions include symbols into their rituals and spells. Some symbols signify elements, while others represent concepts. Many witches use these symbols as talismans or sigils to wear on jewelry or clothing, carved onto candles or to strengthen their spellwork and rituals.

There are several "denominations" of Wicca known as traditions, hence the significance and meaning of the symbols used, will change depending on which tradition you are following. The moon goddess and horned god are considered deities in many traditions. There is a wide variety of various witchcraft emblems within these beliefs.

These are some of the most prevalent symbols used in wicca and other kinds of paganism today.

Pentagram or Pentacle

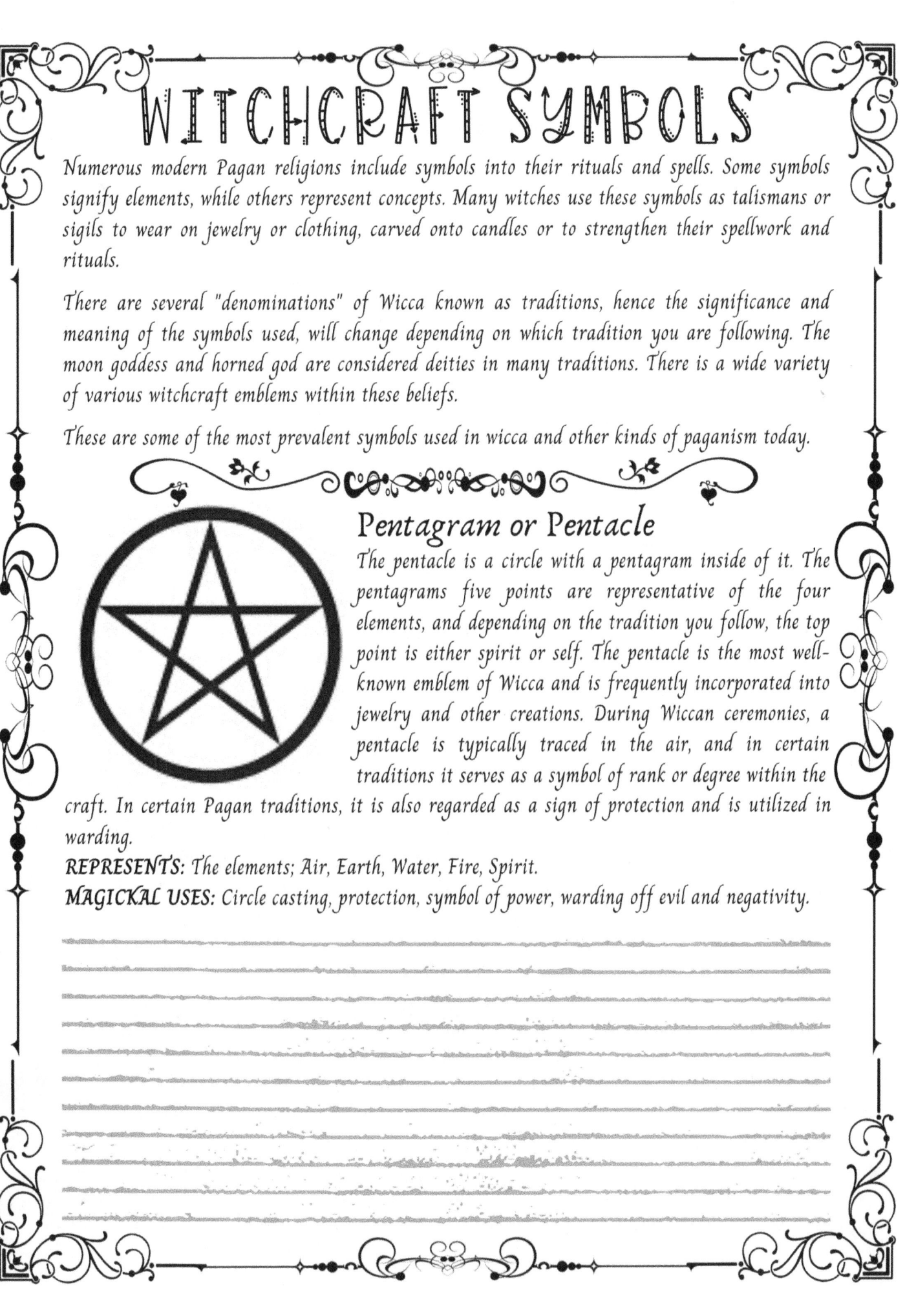

The pentacle is a circle with a pentagram inside of it. The pentagrams five points are representative of the four elements, and depending on the tradition you follow, the top point is either spirit or self. The pentacle is the most well-known emblem of Wicca and is frequently incorporated into jewelry and other creations. During Wiccan ceremonies, a pentacle is typically traced in the air, and in certain traditions it serves as a symbol of rank or degree within the craft. In certain Pagan traditions, it is also regarded as a sign of protection and is utilized in warding.

REPRESENTS: The elements; Air, Earth, Water, Fire, Spirit.
MAGICKAL USES: Circle casting, protection, symbol of power, warding off evil and negativity.

WITCHCRAFT SYMBOLS

Triple Moon Goddess

Unsurprisingly, the sign depicts both the moon, its phases and the stages of womanhood (Maiden, Mother, Crone).

REPRESENTS: Divine feminine, the moon.
MAGICKAL USES: Abundance, fulfillment, growth, knowledge.

The Horned God

In several Wiccan traditions, the horned god is one of two major deities and represents male energy. It is depicted as a horn-topped circle. This symbol is utilized in magick when practitioners wish to convey masculine energy.

REPRESENTS: Masculine or Male energy.
MAGICKAL USES: Fertility, invoking the Horned God.

WITCHCRAFT SYMBOLS

Triquetra or Celtic Knot

Triquetra is the Latin word for triangle. In the Christian faith, this emblem refers to the holy trinity. In Wicca, this type of Celtic knot is used to show the three realms, which are the earth, the sea, and the sky, or the mind, body, and soul.

REPRESENTS: Earth, sea, sky or mind, body, soul.

MAGICKAL USES: Signifies three objects, situations or things that you want to be connected together.

Triple Spiral, Triskele, or Triskelion

In Ireland and western Europe, the triskele is engraved into Neolithic stones. Modern pagans and wiccans sometimes use it to represent the three Celtic kingdoms of earth, sea, and sky.

REPRESENTS: The three kingdoms of earth, sky and sea. Also utilized as a symbol for a place or country.

MAGICKAL USES: To signify a specific place or to earth, sky and sea.

WITCHCRAFT SYMBOLS

Hecate's Wheel

The three stages of femininity (Maiden, Mother, and Crone) are represented by this symbol, same as the Triple Moon Goddess. Much like the decisions that must be made between each stage of a woman's life, Hecate is the Greek goddess of such 'crossroads.' The wheel depicts a labyrinth depicting the strength and understanding of travelling through life.

REPRESENTS: Woman, transformation.
MAGICKAL USES: Invoking change and transformation.

Spiral Goddess

The spiral goddess symbolizes inner feminine strength. There are several sculptures and pendants depicting a goddess with a spiral in her belly. This spiral depicts the creative energy that emanates from the sacral chakra, which connects to the menstrual cycle, desires, sexuality, and relationships.

REPRESENTS: Feminine power, fertility, celebration, life cycles, surrender.
MAGICKAL USES: Fertility, the vital magick of life, goddess energy.

WITCHCRAFT SYMBOLS

Witches Knot or Witches Charm

The Witch's Knot is said to be a protective symbol against evil witchcraft. Its power comes from its endless design with no beginning or end. The four loops are intended to safeguard the bearer from bad intent from all directions.

REPRESENTS: Witches used knotted ropes to "tie up" the weather, form protective rings, and magickally bind objects.

MAGICKAL USES: Protection, fertility, birth, feminine sexuality.

Wheel of the Year or Sun Wheel

The sun wheel is a circle bisected by four lines, like the sun cross. It may be used as a calendar, with each part indicating the period between an equinox or solstice, and the four seasons balanced. Commonly referred to as the "Eight-Spoked Wheel."

REPRESENTS: Fire, four seasons, masculine energy, south, sun.

MAGICKAL USES: Celebrating the seasons, sun invocation.

WITCHCRAFT SYMBOLS

Unicursal Hexagram

The unicursal (drawn in a single line) hexagram is a more common six-sided shape in Wiccan tradition and is a more complex design. It is often thought that the uppermost vertex represents the Divine, while the downward-pointing vertex represents Man or the earthly domain.

REPRESENTS: That magick can help you manifest your true will, cosmic forces of the sun, moon, planets and the balance between them.

MAGICKAL USES: Banishing, invoking elemental influences, union of two halves, freedom, power, love, confidence, achieving your goals.

Solar Cross or Sun Cross

The sun cross is a pre-Bronze Age emblem. This insignia originally symbolized the wheel's power for humankind. Later, the circle signified the sun, and the cross as the interior. Ancient monarchs used it as a sign of power since the sun represented the ultimate authority.

REPRESENTS: Creation, growth, hope.

MAGICKAL USES: Good fortune, happiness, harmony, new beginnings, transformation.

WITCHCRAFT SYMBOLS

The All-Seeing Eye

Regarded as the goddess's supreme protection. It is an eye formed from sunshine rays. This emblem is also known as the eye of providence because it represents the divine protection and intervention provided by justice.

REPRESENTS: God and Goddess, the divine.
MAGICKAL USES: Justice, protection, warding.

Elven Star, Septagram or Faery Star

In Kabbalistic tradition, this star signifies Venus' sphere and the power of love, which is one of the earliest known interpretations of its significance. In Wicca today, the seven points are associated with many different things to enhance the magick we practice.

REPRESENTS: 7 chakras, 7 days of the week, 7 directions, 7 elements, 7 planets, heaven.
MAGICKAL USES: Harmony, protection, faery magick, elemental magick.

The Seven Points
(Planet - Direction - Element)

1. VENUS - ABOVE - STARS
2. SUN - WITHIN - HONOR/SELF
3. MERCURY - EAST - AIR
4. MOON - BELOW - MAGICK
5. MARS - SOUTH - FIRE
6. JUPITER - WEST - WATER
7. SATURN - NORTH - EARTH

WITCHCRAFT SYMBOLS

Earth

The alchemical sign for Earth is a triangle that points down and has a line across it. Used in ritual to connect to the divine feminine, growth, life, motherhood, nature.

REPRESENTS: Dependable, patience, truth, being centered.

MAGICKAL USES: Fertility, grounding, healing, money, stability, strength, success, wisdom.

Air

When a practitioner wishes to emphasize knowledge or communication, he or she will employ air in rituals, as it represents life in general, breath, and of course the east and air.

REPRESENTS: Intelligence, practicality, optimism.

MAGICKAL USES: Divination, intuition, knowledge, memory, psychic work, wisdom.

WITCHCRAFT SYMBOLS

Fire

If change of masculine energy is needed, fire is often employed in rituals. It is a strong energy that starts something new, cleanses, destroys, and starts over.

REPRESENTS: Courage, devotion, endurance, enthusiasm, willpower.

MAGICKAL USES: Cleansing, courage, destruction, divination, energy, healing, power, self knowledge, sexuality, strength, will.

Water

When a Wiccan practitioner desires to emphasize feminine energy, water is utilized in rituals. It can also represent the west or water.

REPRESENTS: Love, compassion, flexibility, forgiveness.

MAGICKAL USES: Fertility, intuition, lunar energy, psychic ability, reflection, self-healing.

WITCHCRAFT SYMBOLS

Triple Horn of Odin

The Odin Triple Horn is another Norse icon. Odin is the father of all Norse deities, and his insignia consists of three drinking horns. The emblem is festive, conjuring the picture of Odin raising his drinking horns in a toast.

REPRESENTS: Ceremony, celebration.
MAGICKAL USES: Community, connection, inspiration, wisdom.

Thors Hammer - Mjölnir

Thor's hammer, which is also called Mjölnir, is a Norse symbol of the god Thor. Often said to be stronger than lightning and thunder, this iconic weapon is said to have the power to level entire mountain ranges. The shape of the hammer changes from region to region, so you likely will see differing images.

REPRESENTS: Unfailing protection.
MAGICKAL USES: Defense, power, protection.

WITCHCRAFT SYMBOLS

Celtic Shield Knot

Celtic knots (Icovellavna) are unending knot designs that spiral in on themselves. When shaped as a shield, it's utilized to guard against bad energy. These are frequently used as tattoos or protective jewelry.

REPRESENTS: The 4 elements.

MAGICKAL USES: Inspiration, protection, shielding.

Seax Wica

Seax Wica is a Wiccan tradition. In the Seax Wica tradition, this symbol represents the eight wiccan sabbats or feasts, as well as the sun and moon.

REPRESENTS: The moon, sun, seasons, the eight sabbats, the Seax Wica tradition.

MAGICKAL USES: Anything pertaining to the Seax Wica tradition.

WITCHCRAFT SYMBOLS

Eye of Horus

Ancient Egyptians used the Eye of Horus for protection, power, and health. The sign represents change, healing, and redemption since it derives from Horus, an ancient Egyptian sky deity whose eye was wounded and later healed. This is also called a wedjat.

REPRESENTS: Egyptian God Horus, change, redemption, healing, air.
MAGICKAL USES: Protection, healing, divination, inner sight.

Eye of Ra

Ancient Egyptians also employed the Eye of Ra as a sign of protection. It is an authoritative sign derived from Ra, the Egyptian sun deity. This symbol is also called an udjat.

REPRESENTS: Egyptian God Ra, fire, the elements, seasons.
MAGICKAL USES: Protection, sun magick.

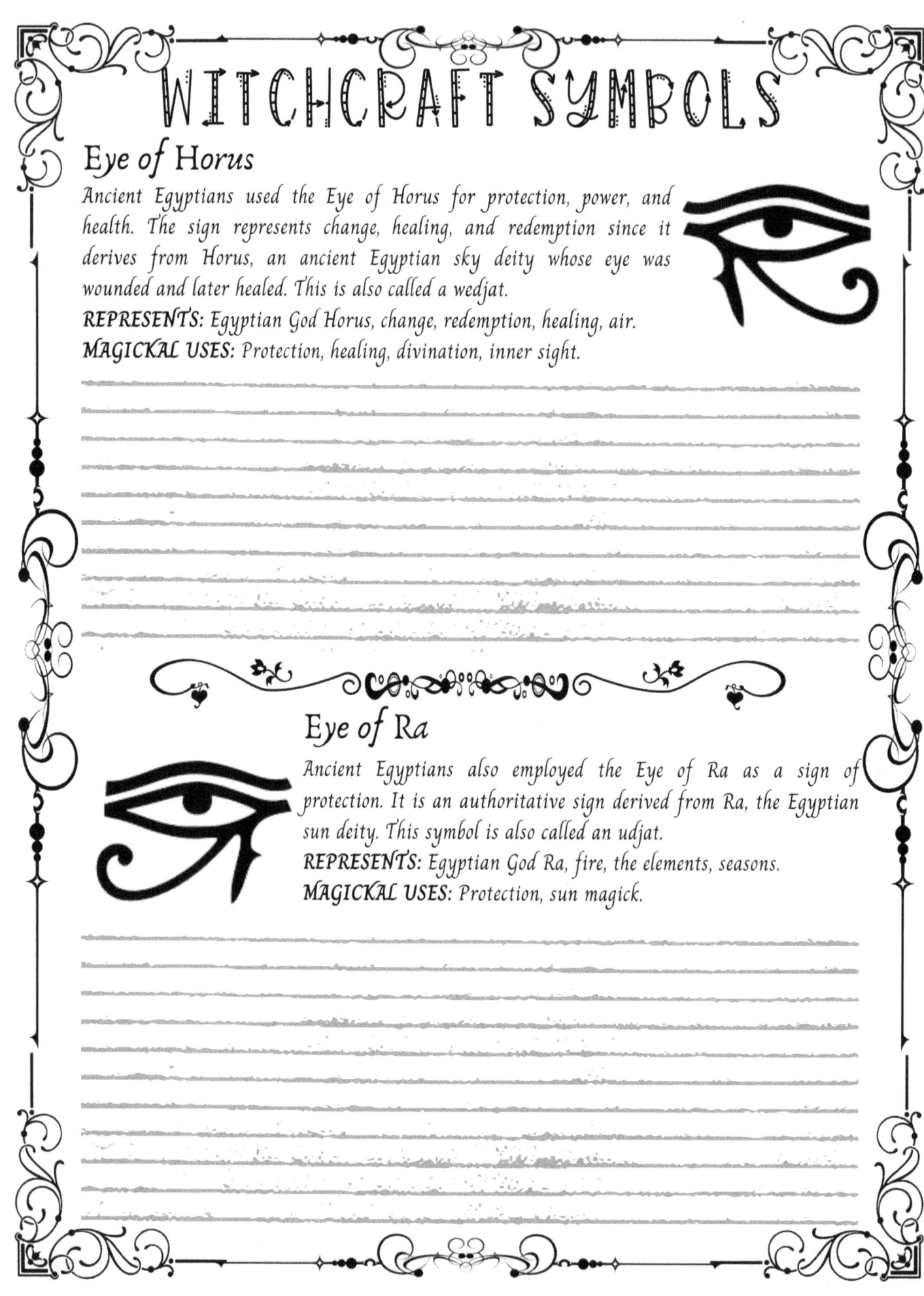

WITCHCRAFT SYMBOLS

Ankh

In wiccan tradition, the Ankh represents life, and comes from Egyptian culture and history. This prominent hieroglyph appears on numerous Egyptian god, goddess, and Pharaoh-related objects. Symbolizes protection and eternal life today.

REPRESENTS: Eternal life, feminine energy, the sun.

MAGICKAL USES: Protection, magick relating to Isis or Osiris, communicating with spirits.

Yin-Yang

This is a Chinese symbol that stands for duality, balance, and ideology. It shows how everything is connected and depends on each other.

REPRESENTS: Balance, duality, good and bad, light and dark.

MAGICKAL USES: Balance, harmony, rebirth, revealing something that has been hidden.

WITCHCRAFT SYMBOLS

WITCHCRAFT SYMBOLS

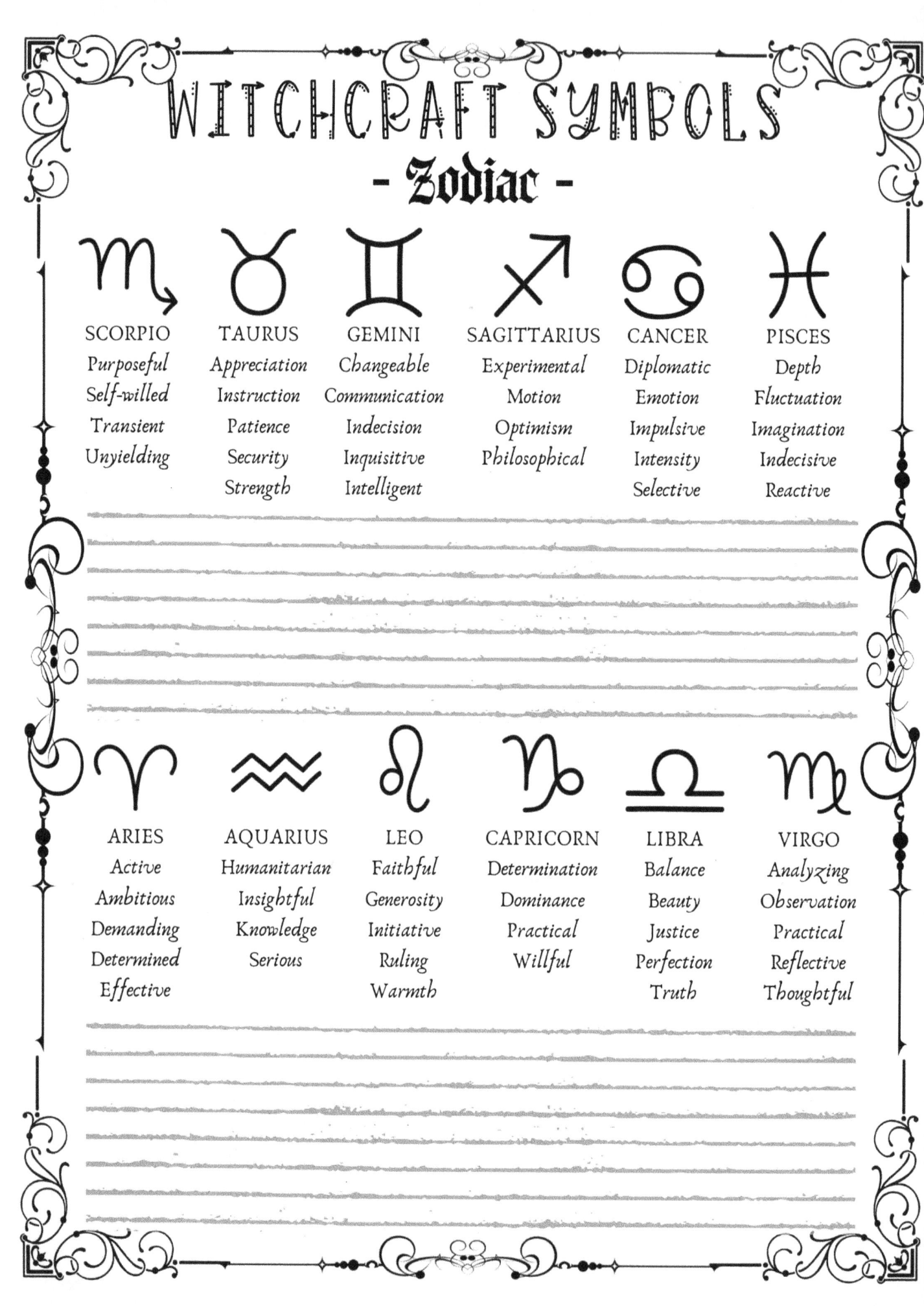

WITCHCRAFT SYMBOLS
- Zodiac -

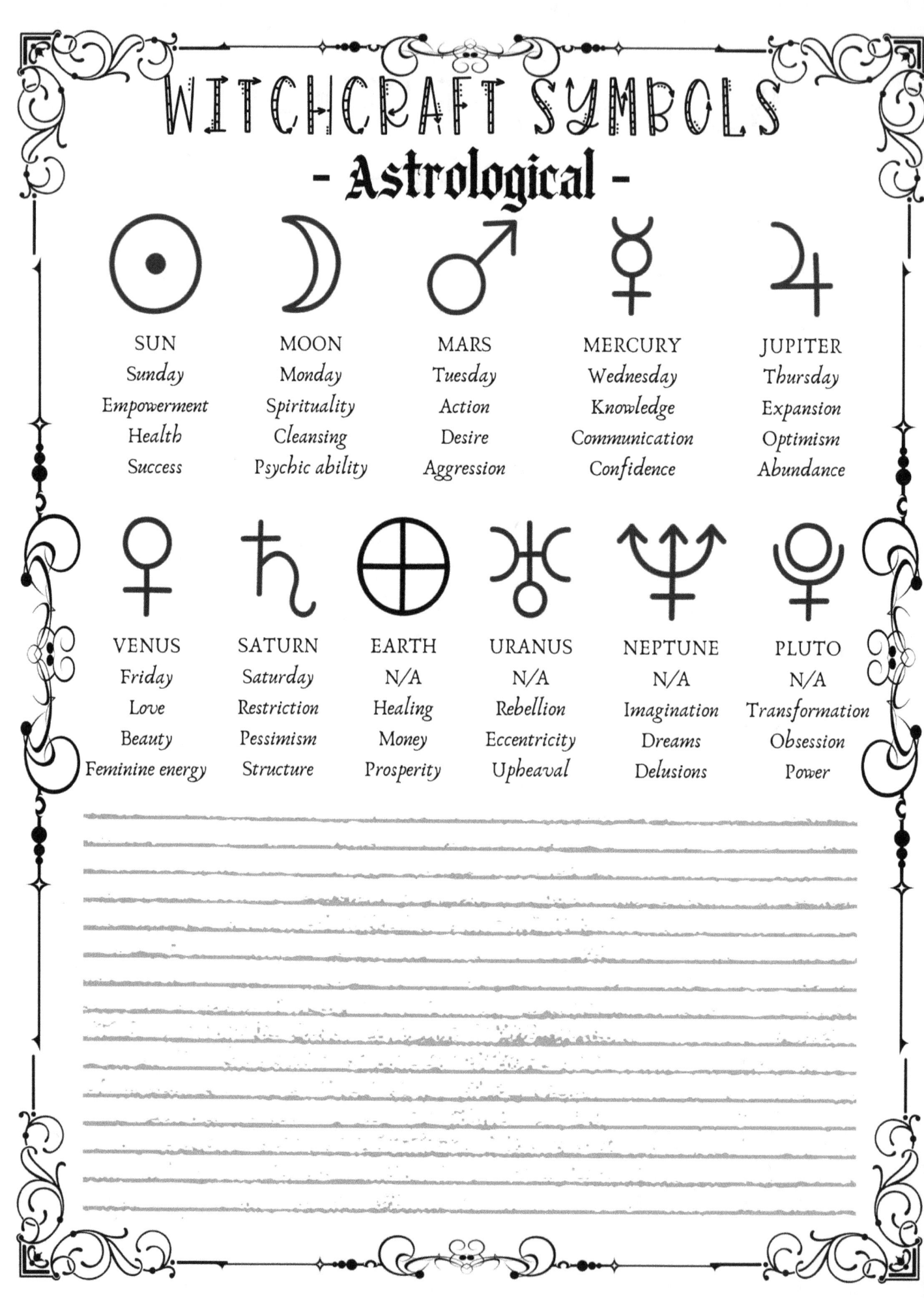

WITCHCRAFT SYMBOLS
- Astrological -

Alphabets & Writing

ALPHABETS & WRITING

Throughout the years, many witches have adopted the use of two main alphabets; The Witches Alphabet and the Elder Futhark Runes. Both of these 'languages' or 'alphabets' have long been used throughout history, and in more recent times, they have been more closely associated with the craft. Modern day witches tend to use these characters as a means to write in their Book of Shadows to conceal or hide what they have written, to keep their power from prying eyes.

Witches Alphabet

Referred to commonly as the 'Honorian Script' or 'Theban Alphabet.' Its origins are unknown, and some believe this was done on purpose by the creator, who intended to remain anonymous. You will see that, unlike the Elder Futhark Runes, the Witches Alphabet has various curves and would not be appropriate for carving into wood.

Wiccans (Witches) are the most common users of the Theban alphabet, however these symbols are not exclusive to their discipline.

The astronomer Johannes Trithemius was the first person who chronicled the alphabet. He included it in his book 'Polygraphia,' which was a publication in 1518. According to Trithemius, the alphabet originated with Theban Honorius and was revealed by Petries de Apono (also known as Pietro D'Abano).

It just so happens that Heinrich Cornelius Agrippa was one of Trithemius' students. In his work, 'Three Books of Occult Philosophy,' Agrippa began referring to this writing as the Theban Alphabet, claiming it came from Honorius of Thebes.

Some assume the source is Petries de Apono, who was connected to Pope Honorius IV, or his granduncle, Pope Honorious III. However, there is no confirmation of this because none of them produced any work including this alphabet, including the book called 'Grimoire du Pape Honorius' penned by Pope Honorious III.

Honorius of Thebes wrote a book called 'The Sworn Book of Honorius' in the 1300s. This book may have been connected to an entirely different concept. Honorius of Thebes, according to legend, was a scribe who compiled this material during a great gathering of highly knowledgeable magickal practitioners. There may be hearsay behind the history because the one and only copy of 'The Sworn Book of Honorius' claims that Agrippa created the Theban Alphabet.

There is also no way of knowing if he's speaking about Thebes in Greece or Thebes in Egypt.

THEBAN ALPHABET

The period when the Theban alphabet was created is likewise a little hazy and unverified. Here are a few possible scenarios:

- 1500-1000 BCE, inspired by an alchemical cypher from Avestan text, which is derived from Aramaic writing.

- Because of its tight correspondences with Latin letters and the lack of matching symbols for J, V, and W (these letters having not yet been formed), it was popular at the start of the Middle Ages. In his work 'Polygraphia,' Johannes Trithemius merged them using a single sign.

- Because it may have been derived from Hebrew, which similarly offers just one letter for I and J and one for U, V, and W, it was probably about the 10th century BCE.

In 1801 Francis Barrett produced the 'Magus,' which had three books in a single volume. His purpose was to update and make available information from ancient and obscure sources. This contributed to the revival of magickal theories and beliefs, such as The Theban alphabet from the works of Johannes Trithemius and Heinrich Cornelius Agrippa. His idea of modernizing historic customs and folklore is most likely where the concept of creating your Grimoire or Book of Shadows came from.

In the late nineteen and early twentieth centuries, magickal societies such as the Hermetic Order of the Golden Dawn started to emerge, along with numerous English occultists. They used the Magus as the centre of their spiritual practice. Gerald Gardner, the founder of Wicca, was influenced by Trithemius, Agrippa, Barrett, and the Hermetic Order of the Golden Dawn, and incorporated their teachings into his Wiccan spiritual practice.

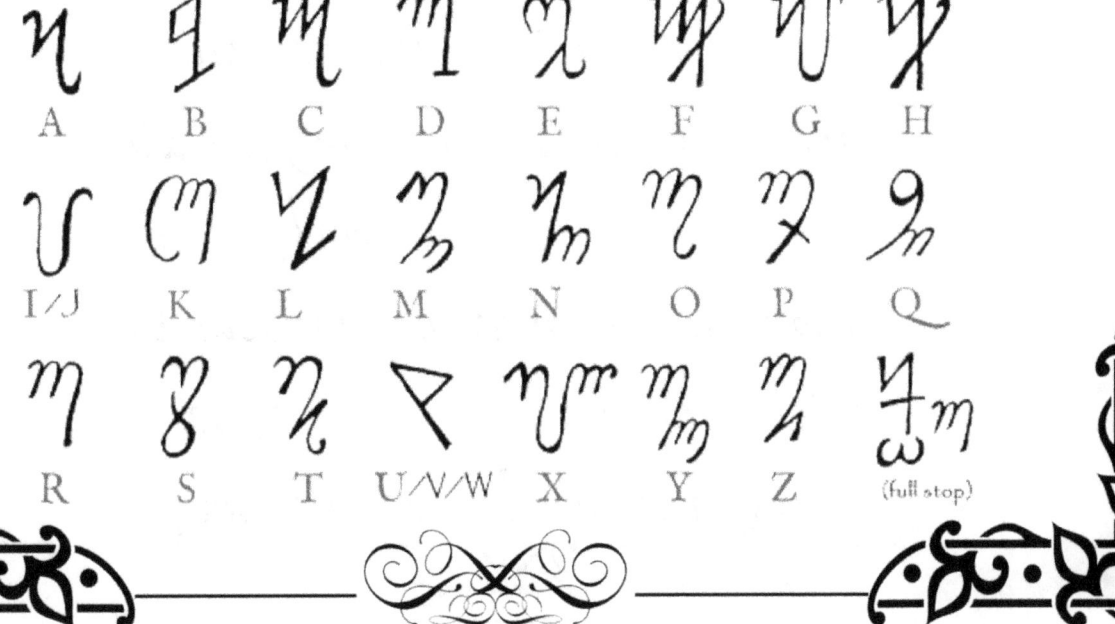

THEBAN ALPHABET

Witches Alphabet Uses

One of the most popular reasons for using the Witches Alphabet during ritual work is to encourage the spiritual practitioner to concentrate fully on the issue at hand because it is not a language in which they are proficient. Some think that employing the Theban Alphabet would strengthen your intentions or spells. Here are some more ways to use the Theban alphabet in your practice:

- Inscribe Talismans or amulets.
- Write in your Book of Shadows or Grimoire (I would not recommend this if you are not fluent in the Theban alphabet).
- Carve intentions onto candles.
- Writing spells or incantations.
- Incorporate into sigil creation.
- Place poems or writings on your altar.
- Use in a spiritual artwork project.
- Draw or write intentions on your body with sacred oils or moon water.
- Engrave into homemade soap.

THEBAN ALPHABET

Try Writing these phrases:

I AM MAGICK

I AM POWERFUL AND VIBRANT

EARTH, AIR, FIRE, WATER, SPIRIT

MY MAGICK COMES FROM WITHIN

BLESSED BE, SO MOTE IT BE

AS ABOVE, SO BELOW

THEBAN ALPHABET

ALPHABETS & WRITING

Elder Futhark Runes

Norse runes are incredibly ancient symbols discovered etched on stones throughout Northern Europe. Runes are a collection of symbols that comprise the written alphabet and many spoken languages of Europe's Germanic peoples. It is thought that Norse runes date back to at least 150 AD.

You may have seen Norse Runes online, in films with Thor and Loki, or on the Goblet of Fire in Harry Potter. If you're a Tolkien lover, you've probably seen them in his work 'The Hobbit.' The Elder Futhark (foo-th-ark) runes are the earliest known Norse runic alphabet, consisting of 24 distinct symbols. Please know that there is A LOT of information to learn about the Elder Futhark runic alphabet, and this is only a quick overview suited for a beginner, while also being informative and simple.

If you are interested in learning more about the Elder Futhark runic alphabet, grab your copy of these other titles for beginners from J.C. Marco on Amazon:

- RUNE DIVINATION & FORTUNE TELLING
A Guide to Elder Futhark Runes - Interpretations & Layouts

- ELDER FUTHARK BINDRUNES
A Beginners Guide to Creating Bindrunes
+ Manifesting & Intention-Setting with Purpose

ELDER FUTHARK RUNES

The term 'rune' comes from an early Anglo-Saxon word that means 'mystery' or 'secret.' It is also notable to mention that the originating word for the Rowan tree, which was highly revered spiritually, is 'runa.' The 24 letters of the Norse runic alphabet are divided into three Aett groups of eight runes each. An Aett also means a family or clan. Below is the 3 Aett's and their corresponding runes:

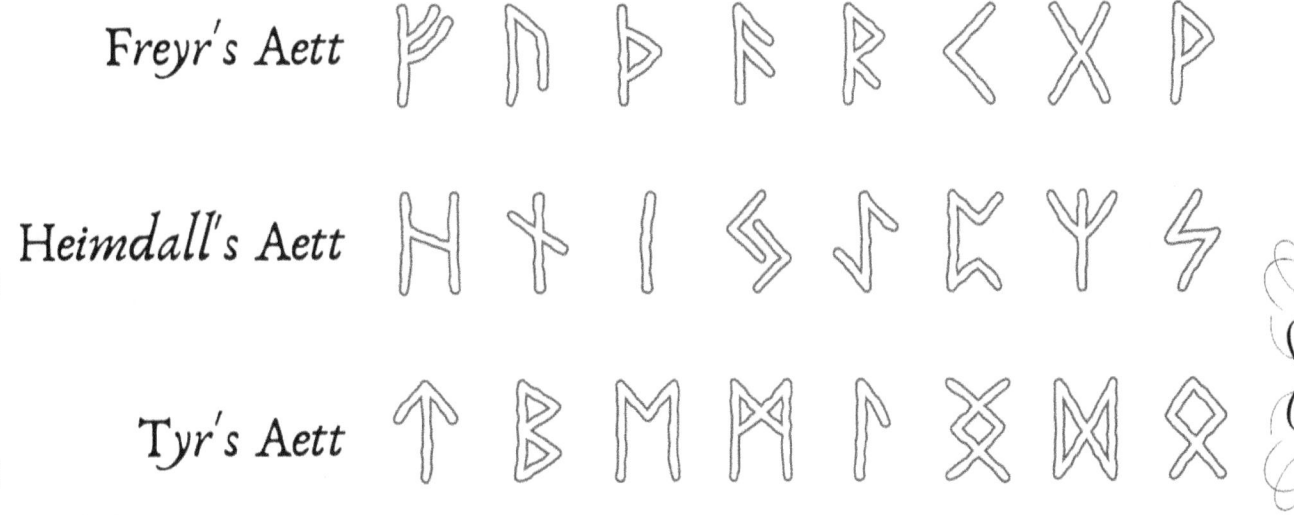

Feyr's Aett symbolizes the material plane and our position within it. This Aett has runes that may be used to predict wealth, communication, abundance, skill, and strength.

Heimdall's Aett reflects our own development and maturity. This Aett contains runes that may be used to predict barriers, abundance, destiny, challenges, and prosperity.

Tyr's Aett recognizes our history and our evolving spirituality. This Aett's runes can represent beginnings, society, instincts, heritage, and inheritance.

As you can see, the runes have a myriad of unique characteristics and applications. Many witches like to write in runes to record important notes in their Book of Shadows. This prevents prying eyes or negative entities from reading your magickal information. Both the Theban Alphabet and the Elder Futhark Runes will take time to learn if you choose to use them in your writings, however, runes are typically easier to learn because of their short straight lines.

ELDER FUTHARK RUNES

RUNE	NAME	LETTER ASSOCIATION	WRITING PRACTICE
ᚠ	FEHU *'Fay-hoo'*	F	
ᚢ	URUZ *'Oo-rooze'*	U	
ᚦ	THURISAZ *'Thur-ee-saws'*	TH <u>TH</u>ING	
ᚨ	ANSUZ *'Awn-sooz'*	A	
ᚱ	RAIDHO *'Rye-though'*	R	
ᚲ	KENAZ *'Cane-awes'*	C, K, Q	
ᚷ	GEBO *'Yee-boo'*	G	
ᚹ	WUNJO *'Woon-yo'*	W, V	

ELDER FUTHARK RUNES

RUNE	NAME	LETTER ASSOCIATION	WRITING PRACTICE
ᚺ	HAGALAZ 'Haw-gaw-laws'	H	
ᚾ	NAUTHIZ 'Now-theez'	N	
ᛁ	ISA 'Ee-saw'	I	
ᛃ	JERA 'Yare-awe'	J, Y	
ᛇ	EYWAS 'Eye-was'	E	
ᛈ	PERTHRO 'Perth-row'	P	
ᛉ	ALGIZ 'All-yeese'	Z	
ᛋ	SOWILO 'Soe-wee-low'	S	

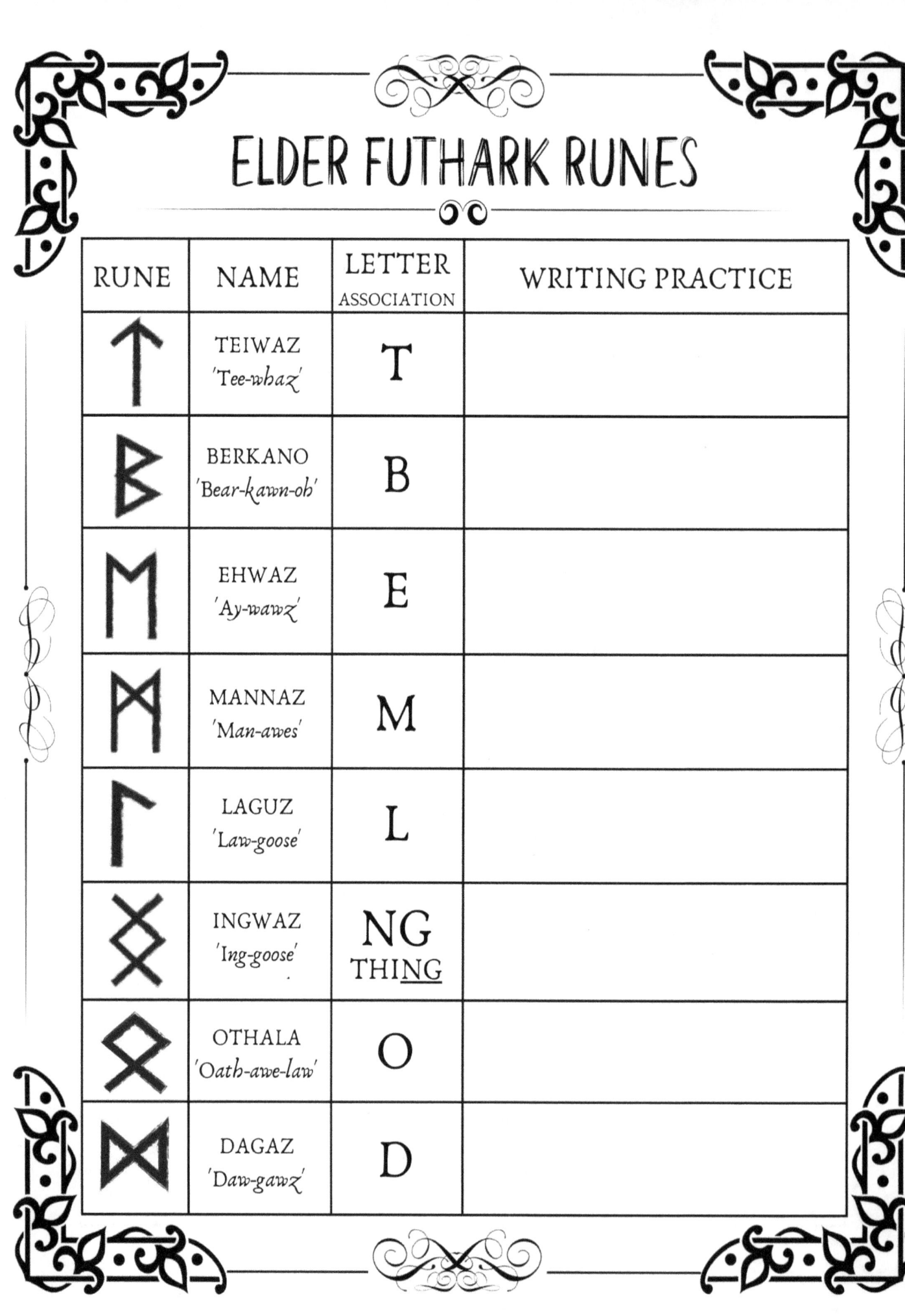

ELDER FUTHARK RUNES

Animals and Familiars

Animal Magick & Familiars

The notion of an animal familiar is incorporated into practice in several modern Paganism traditions, notably the many Wiccan paths. A familiar is frequently characterized nowadays as an animal with whom we have a magickal relationship, but the concept is a little more complicated than that.

During the European witch hunts, it is written in Rosemary Guiley's 'Encyclopedia of Witches and Witchcraft,' that familiars were gifted to witches from the devil himself during this time. They were essentially little demons that could be summoned to fulfil a witches bidding. Demons usually used cats, especially black cats, but sometimes they also used dogs, toads, and other small animals to possess.

Familiars were affiliated with spirits of the earth and nature in various Scandinavian nations. Faeries, dwarves, and other elemental entities were thought to possess animal bodies. With the advent of the Christian church, this practice became prohibited since any spirit other than an angel was presumed to be a demon. Due to their association with recognized witches and heretics, many domesticated animals were killed during the period of witch-hunting.

There is limited evidence of animal familiars being used during the Salem witch trials, however one man was accused with enticing a dog to attack by magickal methods. Surprisingly, the dog was tried, convicted, and executed. In shamanic activities, the animal familiar is a thought-form or spiritual entity rather than a material being. It frequently travels astrally or acts as a magickal protector against anyone who would attempt to psychically assault the shaman.

Many neopagans have interpreted the term to refer to a real, live animal. Even though this is not how the word 'familiar' was originally used, many pagans have an animal companion that they think of as their familiar. Society has matured since those times, and no longer think of these animals as possessed demonic spirits. Instead, they form an emotional and psychic relationship with the cat, dog, or whatever animal is receptive to the powers of its human companion.

Not everyone has, need, or even desires a familiar. If you have a pet animal, such as a cat or a dog, focus on strengthening your psychic bond with that animal. If an animal has unexpectedly emerged in your life, such as a stray cat who appears on a regular basis, it's conceivable that it was drawn to you psychically. However, first rule out any commonplace explanations for its occurrence, such as leaving food out for the neighborhood kitties, or seeing an influx of birds in the spring time, when the ground thaws and makes food more readily available to them. Not all animal guests are magickal; some just come to visit.

Animal Magick & Familiars

Some traditions believe that you can bring a familiar to you through meditation. Find a peaceful, undisturbed spot to relax and let your mind roam. As you wander, you may come across numerous persons or things. Concentrate on meeting an animal acquaintance and see if you come across any.

Aside from familiars, some people perform magickal work with what is known as a power animal or a spirit animal. A power animal is a spiritual protector with whom some individuals have a connection. However, like other spiritual beings, there is no law or rule requiring you to have one. If you chance to connect with an animal entity while meditating or astral travelling, it may be your power animal, or it could simply be inquisitive about what you're up to.

Animal Correspondences

ANTS - Energy, organization, patience, perseverance, planning, self-discipline, stamina, teamwork.

BATS - Ability to observe the unseen, accessing past lives, changes for the better, initiation, moon magick, new ideas, rebirth, transition, understanding grief.

BEARS - Astral travel, change, communication with spirit, death and rebirth, defense, earth magick, facing fears, gentle strength, grounding, healer, healing and inner knowledge, inner energy of the soul, introspection, power, revenge, solitude, strength, transformation, unconscious mind, wisdom.

BEAVERS - Building, gathering, persistence, shaping, structure.

Animal Correspondences

BEES - Ability to focus, assisting earth-bound spirits move on to their right place, association to the Goddess Diana, communication with the deceased, community, female warrior energy, gathering, prosperity, reincarnation, service, wealth.

BIRDS - Associated with death and transitions, freedom, individuality, unity.

BUTTERFLIES/CATERPILLARS - Balance, grace, reincarnation, transformation.

CATS - Balancing of energies, cleansing, cleverness, grace, guardians, independence, moon magick, mystic powers, purification, seeing the unseen, understanding mystery, wholeness.

CHICKENS - Hearing your inner voice, language, power of voice, protection of family and community, seeking answers, sunrise magick.

CHIPMUNKS - Ability to see both light and shadow, frugal living, gathering, mobility.

COWS - Connection to the earth, economy, patience, wealth and prosperity.

DEER - Alertness, body awareness, earth magick, gentleness, gracefulness, innocence, kindness, peace, recognition of outside influences, sensitivity, unconditional love.

Animal Correspondences

DOGS - Companionship, earth magick, faithfulness, family, loyalty, moon magick., protection, warnings, wisdom.

DONKEYS - Ability to make decisions, intuition, stubbornness.

DUCKS - Logic, water energy, water magick.

ELK - Agility, freedom, majesty, nobility, power, pride, stamina, strength.

FERRETS - Information, seeing truth behind the façade.

FISH - Abundance, children, fertility, harmony, love, mind/emotion balance, regeneration.

FOX - Agility, cleverness, cunning, discretion, elusiveness, feminine courage, fire magick, intelligence, slyness, subtlety.

FROGS - Cleansing, connection with water element, healing, transformation, understanding emotions.

GOATS - Abundance, agility, confidence, diligence, flexibility, healing and sun magick, independence, tenacity.

HORSES - Astral travel, earth magick, freedom, moon magick, power, protection, stability and courage, travel.

MICE - Details, earth magick, faith, innocence, quietness, scrutiny, shyness, trust.

Animal Correspondences

OWLS - Air magick, darkness, deception, insight, patience, truth, wisdom.

PIGS - Cunning, earth magick, intelligence, past life knowledge, truth.

RABBITS - Alertness, conquering fear, faith, fear, fertility, innocence, luck, moon magick, movement, nurturing, safety, sensitivity.

RATS - Abundant reproduction, adaptability, defense, earth magick, restlessness, shrewdness, social, stealth, success.

SHEEP - Abundance, assurance, balance, confidence, courage, fertility, new beginnings.

SNAILS - Determination, perseverance.

SNAKES - Power, primitive or elemental energy, sensuality, sexual potency, shrewdness, transformation, transmutation.

SPIDERS - Creativity, divine inspiration, fate, feminine energy, illusion, industrious, shape-shifting, wisdom.

SQUIRRELS - Activity, awareness, balance in giving and receiving, change, discovery, earth magick, energy, playfulness, preparation, resourcefulness, sociability, trust.

Animal Correspondences

WOLVES - Earth magick, freedom, guardianship, guidance, independence, instinct, intelligence, loyalty, moon magick, perseverance, protection, shadow work, spirit, stability, success, wisdom.

Animal Magick & Familiars

The Elements

In many modern pagan religions, the four primary elements are quite essential. A few Wiccan traditions incorporate a fifth element, referred to as spirit or self, however this is not common across all pagan paths.

The four-element concept is nothing new. Empedocles, a Greek philosopher, is credited with developing the cosmogenic hypothesis, which states that these four elements are the foundation of all existent matter. While most of Empedocles' literature has been lost, his concepts have survived and are largely embraced by many pagans.

For thousands of years, our forefathers and mothers thought that the elements—Earth, Air, Fire, and Water—were the universe's building blocks, and that their inherent characteristics and energies could be harnessed to produce desired outcomes. As part of the Western Mystery Tradition, this idea flourished and became altered over time. This is a set of beliefs that had a big impact on wicca, which is based on nature and is quite versatile. Wiccans speak to the ancient powers of the elements in different ways through rituals and magick. They consult these forces for help in changing their lives, just like ancient shamans did.

You may already know what the role of the elements are in wicca. You may know that the pentacle represents Earth, the wand represents Air, the cup represents Water, and the athame represents Fire. The pentagram represents all five elements, respectively. Did you know that each elements psychic energy is located within every human on the planet? Or that spiritually connecting with an element might assist heal an imbalance in your life? Not to mention Akasha, which means "spirit," or the fifth element. It embodies the other four elements, but in its own regard, is an element on its own.

Watchtowers are related with the four elements and directions in several faiths, notably wiccan. These are occasionally summoned for protection when casting a magickal circle, depending on who you ask.

However, if you've never heard of any of this before, don't worry - it doesn't matter how much about wicca or the elements you've learnt so far. Elemental magick can help both new and experienced witches.

The element-centered practice is a wonderful way to connect to the goddess, god, nature, the universe, or whatever name your belief system assigns to the energy of 'All That Is.'

Earth

The earth is believed to be the ultimate feminine element because of its connection to the north. The goddess is identified with the soil because it is fertile and stable. The globe itself is a ball of life, and as the wheel of the year spins, we may witness all of life's phases unfold: birth, life, death, and, eventually, rebirth. The ground is nourishing and stable, robust and sturdy, and full of endurance and strength, much like the people who live on it. Both green and brown are associated with the earth in color correspondences, which is understandable given the nature of the colors. Depending on the deck, the suit of pentacles or coins is linked to the earth in tarot readings.

CORRESPONDENCES

Gender: Feminine **Planet:** Venus, Saturn **Time:** Midnight **Season:** Winter
Direction: North **Tarot Cards:** Pentacles, Coins **Zodiac:** Taurus, Virgo, Capricorn
Symbolism: Animals, compassion, death, grounding, healing, knowledge, money, moral courage, nature, principles, procreation, prosperity, reincarnation, reliability, resilience, strength, success.
Nature Spirits: Dwarves, elves, faeries, faun, pixies, trolls, wood nymphs.
Colors: Black, brown, gold, green.
Food and Drink: Beer, bread, butter, garlic, nuts, oats, onions, potatoes, rice, salt, vodka, whiskey.
Herbs: Alfalfa, barley, cedar, comfrey, corn, cypress, grains, honeysuckle, ivy, lichen, lilac, magnolia, moss, nuts, oak, patchouli, primrose, roots, sage, vetivert.
Crystals and Gemstones: Amethyst, azurite, bedrock, coal, emerald, fluorite, granite, iron, jasper, jet, lead, moss agate, onyx, peridot, quartz, rutilated quartz, salt, slate, tigers eye, tourmaline, tree agate.
Deities: Adonis, Arawn, Athos, Ceres, Cernunnos, Cerridwyn, Cybele, Demeter, Dionysus, Epona, Gaia, Herne, Houtu, Jord, Leimarel, Mah, Marduk, Mat Zemlya, Mother Earth, Nephtys, Opes, Pachamama, Pan, Persephone, Proserpina, Ptithivi, Rhiannon, Sidabi, Sif, Tammuz, Terra, Thoth, Umay.
Animals: Ant, bear, bison, bull, cow, deer, dog, gopher, grubs, horse, moles, snake, stag, voles, wolf, worms.
Symbols: Canyons, caves, fields, forests, gardens, plains, rocks, soil, stones, trees.

Earth

Air

Known as "the element of the east," air is associated with the soul and the source of life's breath. You should concentrate on the element of air if you are working on something that has to do with communication, wisdom, or mental skills. Troubles are carried away by the wind, contention is blown away by the wind, and positive ideas are carried to people who are far away. Air is related with the colors yellow and white, and it has a connection to the suit of swords in the tarot card deck.

CORRESPONDENCES

Gender: Masculine   **Planet:** Mercury, Jupiter   **Time:** Dawn   **Season:** Spring
Direction: East   **Tarot Cards:** Swords   **Zodiac:** Gemini, Libra, Aquarius
Symbolism: Communication, creativity, intelligence, intuition, inspiration, knowledge, logic, memory, thought, truth, wisdom.
Nature Spirits: Spirits, sprites, sylphs, winged faeries, zephyrs.
Colors: Gold, light blue, pastels, white, yellow.
Food and Drink: Beans, cabbage, carbonated beverages, chickweed, dates, grains, leafy greens, lentils, lingonberries, popcorn, puffed rice, rice cakes, toast, tofu, vinegar.
Herbs: Anise, aspen, bergamot, bluebell, clover, dandelion, dill, frankincense, lavender, lemongrass, marjoram, myrrh, peppermint, pine, primrose, sage, vervain, violets, yarrow.
Crystals and Gemstones: Agate, alexandrite, amber, amethyst, citrine, clear quartz, fluorite, jasper, mica, pumice, topaz.
Deities: Aeolus, Aradia, Arianhod, Boreas, Cardea, Enlil, Eurus, Hermes, Kheoheva, Merawrim, Mercury, Morrigan, Notus, Nuit, Shu, Thoth, Urania, Zephyrus, Zeus.
Animals: Bats, birds, flying insects, spiders.
Symbols: Bell, breath, breeze, broom, censer, clouds, feather, incense, pen, sky, staff, sword, wand, wind, wind chimes.

Air

Fire

Fire is a cleansing, masculine element linked with the southern hemisphere and related with determination and willpower. Fire is both a source of creation and a source of destruction, and it represents the fertility of the god. Fire has the ability to heal or hurt. It has the ability to breathe new life into the dead and rotting or to demolish the old and worn. In the tarot, the suit of wands is linked to fire. Fire connections are represented by the colors red and orange in color correspondences.

CORRESPONDENCES

Gender: Masculine **Planet:** Sun, Mars **Time:** Noon **Season:** Summer
Direction: South **Tarot Cards:** Wands **Zodiac:** Aries, Leo, Sagittarius

Symbolism: Achievement, action, anger, courage, creativity, desire, destruction, energy, loyalty, lust, movement, new beginnings, passion, power, protection, sexuality, strength, transformation, war, will, willpower.

Nature Spirits: Chimera, djinn, dragon, phoenix, salamander.

Colors: Crimson, gold, orange, red, white, yellow.

Food and Drink: Beans, beef, chili, cider, cinnamon, cloves, coffee, curry, garlic, garlic bread, ham, lemon, lemonade, lime, limeade, marmalade, onion, orange juice, oranges, spicy foods, tea, wassail.

Herbs: Allspice, basil, cacti, chilis, cinnamon, cloves, coffee, coriander, cumin, garlic, ginger, heliotrope, hibiscus, jalapenos, juniper, lemon, lime, marigold, mustard, nettle, onion, orange, poppies, red pepper, saffron, thistle.

Crystals and Gemstones: Agate, bloodstone, brass, carnelian, fire opal, garnet, gold, lavastone, pyrite, red jasper, rhodochrosite, ruby, tigers eye.

Deities: Aed, Agni, Alaz, Alpan, Amaterasu, Arshi Tengri, Belenus, Brigid, Cacus, Chantico, Dazhbog, Eate, En, Freya, Fuji, Gerra, Gibil, Grannus, Hephaestus, Hestia, Horus, Huilu, Iansa, Ishum, Jowangsin, Kamar, Kojin, Kresnik, Logi, Mariel, Mixcoati, Morrigan, Nantosuelta, Nuska, Odgan, Ogun, Oya, Peklenc, Pele, Prometheus, Ra, Sekhmet, Sethlans, Shapash, Svarog, Vesta, Vulcan, Vut-Ami, Xiuhtecuhtli, Yal-Un Eke, Zhurong.

Animals: Bee, coyote, fox, horse, ladybug, lion, mantis, scorpion, shark, snake, tiger.

Symbols: Athame, candles, dagger, flame, heat, lamp, lava, stars, sun, swords, volcano, wands.

Fire

Water

Water is a feminine force associated with the goddess. Water is tied to the west and associated with passion and emotion. Consecrated water is used in various religions, including Catholicism where holy water is merely plain water with salt added, generally with a blessing or prayer. Some wiccan covens use this water to consecrate the circle and their tools.

CORRESPONDENCES

Gender: Feminine   **Planet:** Moon, Neptune, Pluto   **Time:** Twilight   **Season:** Fall
Direction: West   **Tarot Cards:** Cups   **Zodiac:** Cancer, Scorpio, Pisces
Symbolism: Curses, death, deep feelings, Emotion, fertility, intuition, love, lunar energy, psychic abilities, reflection, self-healing, unconscious mind.
Nature Spirits: Banshee, bean-nighe, Cailleach, faeries associated with wells, finfolk, kelpie, lake ladies, mermaid, nymph, or lakes, ponds, streams, undine, washerwoman, water cows, water horse, water maidens, white woman.
Colors: Aquamarine, black, blue, bluish-silver, gray, indigo, seafoam, silver, white.
Food and Drink: Apple, coconut, pear, strawberry, tea, water, watermelon.
Herbs: Aloe, apple, birch, cabbage, catnip, cattail, chamomile, coconut, comfrey, cucumber, eucalyptus, fern, gardenia, geranium, gourd, grape, kelp, lettuce, licorice, lilac, lotus, moss, pear, seaweed, strawberry, tomato, water lily, willow.
Crystals and Gemstones: Amethyst, aquamarine, beryl, blue topaz, blue tourmaline, coral, fluorite, lapis lazuli, moonstone, opal, pearl, silver.
Deities: Achelous, Aegir, Alpheus, Anuket, Ap, Brizo, Cerridwen, Ceto, Coventina, Danu, Davy Jones, Doris, Enki, Eurybia, Fontus, Ganga, Gonggong, Graeae, Grannus, Hapi, Hebo, Juturna, Lir, Llyr, Marduk, Mazu, Mokosh, Nammu, Nehalennia, Nephthys, Neptune, Nerites, Nerthus, Nerus, Nix, Oshun, Poseidon, Salacia, Satet, Selkie, Sinann, Sirsir, Sobek, Suijin, Sulis, Susanoo, Tefnut, Tethys, Thetis, Tiamat, Tiberinus, Veles, Yami
Animals: Alligator, ammonite, barnacle, beaver, coral, crab, crane, crocodile, dolphin, dragonfly, dragons, duck, eel, fish, frog, geese, heron, jellyfish, koi, lobster, manatee, manta ray, nautilus, octopus, penguin, salamander, sea otter, seahorse, seal, serpents, shark, snake, starfish, swan, turtle, water birds, whale.
Symbols: Bowl, cauldron, chalice, creek, cup, driftwood, fog, hag stones, lake, mist, ocean, pond, rain, river, sea glass, seaweed, shell, spring, trident, well.

Water

Spirit

Modern pagan traditions include the element of spirit, which is also known as Akasha or the Aether, as a fifth element in their classification of the elements. The spirit serves as a link between the physical and the spiritual worlds, and is typically symbolized as a circle or spiral of some sort.

Also referred to as Quintessence, (meaning 'the fifth element' in Latin), and Manas. However you choose to title it, Spirit, Ether, or Soul is the element of self-awareness, completeness, and transcendence.

Spirit's beginnings date back to Aristotle, who thought the moon divided earth and the spirit realm. The four elements were connected to the earth, however Aether is spiritual.

The spirit element was considered to be the source of all elements and the natural cycle to which they will return. Body and soul are linked through the Aether, or spirit.

Because spirit is not earthbound, it lacks comparable correspondences. Feel free to use any correspondences that speak to you. Here are some popular correspondences or meanings, but remember there are no rules, so do what seems right to you.

CORRESPONDENCES

Gender: Non-Binary **Planet:** The Universe **Time:** Infinite **Season:** The Wheel in motion
Direction: Central **Tarot Cards:** The Major Arcana **Zodiac:** All
Symbolism: Ascension, harmony, hope, joy, mystery, self-awareness, selflessness, transcendence, transformation, unity, wholeness.
Nature Spirits: Sphinx, World Tree.
Colors: White (A mixture of all colors).
Food and Drink: Beer, cacao, chocolate, eggs, honey, liquor, pound cake, sweets, tea, wine.
Herbs: Apple, ash, cannabis, chestnut, lotus, mistletoe, oak, poplar, resurrection fern, tobacco.
Crystals and Gemstones: Amethyst, opal, pearl, quartz.
Deities: All.
Animals: Cat, deer, dove.
Symbols: Helix, infinity, light, spiral, the universe.

Spirit

Candle Magick

BONUS: Color Magick

Candle Magick

In religious and spiritual rituals around the world, fire is common. However, one might argue that fire plays a central role in Wiccan and Pagan traditions, whether it be a ritual bonfire, tall candles commemorating the Goddess and God, or modest tea lights indicating the perimeter of the sacred circle. Candle magick is one of the most fascinating methods to work with the transformational element of fire. Candles, which are simple, beautiful, and very symbolic, make it easy to harness this power in the shape of a single, entrancing flame.

Candle magick is a way to channel the unseen energy of the universe into specific thoughtforms that work to change the physical world, whether that change is something you can see, like more money in your pocket, or something you can't see, like a more hopeful outlook on a situation that seemed hopeless before. Candle magick is not only a powerful kind of magick, but it is also considered the simplest and easiest form of magick for beginners to master. This makes it a great starting place for anybody interested in beginning to practice witchcraft.

Although candle magick might seem wonderfully straightforward, there is more to it than lighting a votive and reciting a few phrases. As with any other art form, there are technical and safety considerations that you should keep in mind.

When you use candles for magick, you should always use a new one for each spell. Candles retain the vibration of their previous use. Before performing any ceremony, cleanse and charge the candle(s) with your intention to increase their power. Some prefer to anoint the candles with specific oils, mixes, or herbs, or to carve runes, phrases, or symbols into the wax.

Think about what it is you would like to bring to fruition in your life as you light the candle. Sit and reflect about your objective as the candle burns down. When you feel like you're done, either blow out the candle or sit with it until it goes out.

NOTE: NEVER LEAVE BURNING CANDLES UNATTENDED

If the candle still has use left and you desire to re-perform the same spell, always store the unlit candle in a secure location to treat your intent with care. Every time you light the candle, reaffirm your purpose. When the candle extinguishes itself, or you have completed with its use, dispose of the wax in a safe manner. Alternatively, you may bury the remaining wax outdoors.

Candle Magick
COLOR USES

Color magick is a component of many magickal traditions due to the connections that colors hold. Bear in mind, however, that certain traditions may establish their own correspondences that differ from those listed here.

When it comes to implementing these correspondences, be inventive and think outside the box. Keep a variety of candles, colored paper, altar cloths and fabric, ribbons, and even ink on hand to employ in various magickal workings. Spells and incantations should be written in the proper color or printed on the correct color paper. You may also use stones, flowers and plants in your desired color if you like. If you meditate or perform any chakra energy work, you can even envision yourself surrounded by the color of light required for your magickal activity. Only your imagination limits the possibilities.

Colors are composed of various vibrational frequencies. Due to the fact that the universe is vibrating and we are vibrating, we interconnect on subtle levels, sometimes without even realizing it. While some spells specify the color to use, if this is not accessible to you or if you are performing your own spell, the following is a list of colors and their magickal correspondences.

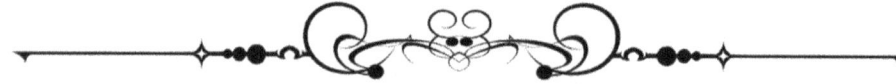

WHITE - Attraction, balancing, clarity, cleansing, consecrating and blessing magickal tools, divination, grounding, guidance, healing, higher self, hope, innocence, optimism, peace, protection, purification, spirituality, truth, workplace magick.

CAN BE USED AS A SUBSTITUTE FOR ALL OTHER COLORS IF THEY ARE NOT AVAILABLE TO YOU.

BLACK - Absorbing, acceptance, anger, banishing, binding, break hexes, challenges, death, determination, endings, grief, justice, karma, loss, magick, negativity, patience, persistence, rebirth, release, secrets, security, self control, spirituality, strength, the afterlife.

Candle Magick
COLOR USES

RED - Action, assertiveness, business, change, courage, creativity, desire, energy, love, loyalty, motivation, overcoming obstacles, passion, power, romance, strength, survival.

YELLOW - Action, business, communication, friendships, happiness, inspiration, intellect, intuition, knowledge, learning new skills, loans and credit, pleasure, stimulation, travel, wisdom.

PINK - Acceptance, affection, beauty, children, compassion, family, femininity, fidelity, friendship, healing abuse, kindness, love, marriage, nurturing, passion, reconciliation, sensuality.

GREEN - Abundance, acceptance, action, agriculture, beauty, change, creativity, environment, family, fertility, harmony, healing, longevity, luck, nurturing, partnerships, peace, prosperity.

PURPLE - Addiction, astrology, authority, emotions, enlightenment, imagination, independence, influence, overcoming fears, power, psychic protection, spiritual development, spirituality, truth, wisdom, writing.

ORANGE - Abundance, adaptability, ambition, celebration, confidence, courage, creativity, discipline, freedom, goals, independence, justice, money, pleasure, positivity, reconciliation, stimulation, strength, travel, vitality (energy).

BLUE - Career, communication, dreamwork, honesty, interviews, justice, leadership, marriage, mental obstacles, pregnancy, sleep, study, trust, wisdom.

BROWN - Animals, balance, courage, endurance, finding lost objects, grounding, hard work, material matters, material protection, stability.

Candle Magick
COLOR USES

SILVER - Awareness, divination, feminine energy, fertility, healing, hidden potential, intuition, money, moon and star magick, psychic powers, purification, sea, stability, success, the goddess.

GOLD - Abundance, ambitions, creativity, divination, fame and fortune, happiness, influence, luxury, masculine energy, money, positivity, power, sun magick, the god.

VIOLET - Balancing sensitivity, devotion, divination, enhancing nurturing qualities, idealism, peace, spirituality, wisdom.

INDIGO - Clarity of purpose, emotion, expressiveness, fluidity, insight, meditation, self-mastery, spiritual healing.

GRAY - Binding negative influences, complex decisions, contemplation, neutrality, reaching compromise, reserve, stability.

What type of candles should you use?

Generally speaking, chime candles or tea light candles are the best choice for one-time spells. Taper candles enhance spells that are done over many days. Pillar and jar candles offer the longest burn duration for spells lasting a week or more. Quality jar candles are often only available in white or a few choice colors. By tying a colored ribbon around the base of the candle jar or writing your intention on a corresponding colored piece of paper and safely burning it, you can help draw in the energies of the desired color.

Candle Magick

Candle Magick

Candle Magick

Herb Magick

Herb Magick

The Magick of Plants & Herbs

Plants and herbs are a great way to magnify your intentions during spellwork and rituals, by using their properties and energy to your benefit. Although it is not absolutely necessary to have an entire apothecary with a variety of herbs at your disposal, you can make do with just a select few herbs and still be able to achieve your desired outcome or intention.

Herbs have been utilized medicinally and ritually for thousands of years. Each herb has its own distinct qualities, and these traits are what identify the plant and make it special. There are hundreds, if not thousands of different plants and herbs on our planet, some of which have not yet been discovered, so I would encourage you to research and grow your knowledge as you progress and develop your own path within the craft. You will find extra space at the end of this section to start recording your own findings.

Pagans, wiccans, and witches employ magickal plants and herbs to strengthen their spells and rituals. Herbs with magickal properties may serve a number of purposes. If you are working with prosperity, for instance, you must use plants connected with prosperity. Due to the identical qualities of many plants, you can combine them to increase their effectiveness of your rituals or spells.

Herbs have planetary and elemental associations. These correspond to your herbs properties and/or functions. Knowing the five elements and how to blend compatible herbs is vital for the practice of magick. For example, several love herbs are associated with water, and several are associated with the planetary correspondence of Venus. If it feels right to you, then feel free to combine herbs to help boost spells.

Herbs can be worn on the body, carried as an amulet, placed in sachets, added to baths, burnt on charcoal, or used in infusions. Similarly, you may stuff poppets with your herbs. In witchcraft, the word "herb" is all-encompassing and refers to wood chips, spices, flowers, and, more broadly, to plants employed for their magickal characteristics by wiccan and witchcraft adepts.

Included in this Book of Shadows are the top 32 popular herbs that are used in the craft for magickal purposes. The majority of these herbs can be found at your local grocery store, which also ensures that they will be genuine and real. If you wish to purchase herbs online, please do your research to be sure you know how to spot fake herbs or to find a reputable retailer.

WARNING

SOME HERBS HAVE POISONOUS QUALITIES AND MAY PRODUCE TOXIC FUMES WHEN BURNED. ALSO, DO NOT INGEST ANY HERBS THAT ARE NOT MEANT FOR CULINARY OR FOOD PURPOSES. PLEASE EXERCISE EXTREME CAUTION WITH HERBS.

Herb Magick

Allspice

- Money, luck, healing.
- Burn crushed allspice to attract luck & money.
- Adds determination & energy to spells and charms.

Planet: Mars | Element: Fire

Basil

- Love, wealth, sympathy & protection.
- Wear or carry to help attract wealth and success.
- Removes harmful spirits.

Planet: Mars | Element: Fire

Herb Magick

Bay Leaf

- Protection, good fortune, success, purification, strength, healing & psychic powers.
- Write wishes on the leaves & burn them to make come true.

Planet: Earth | Element: Fire

Blessed Thistle

- Purification
- Hex breaking.
- Protection from negativity & evil.
- Carry for strength & protection.
- Renews vitality in a room.

Planet: Mars | Element: Fire

Herb Magick

Calendula

- The 'Luck' herb.
- Happiness & Harmony.
- Healing, cleansing & protection.
- Scattered under the bed will help make dreams come true.

Planet: Sun | Element: Fire

Chamomile

- Great for attracting money, love & prosperity.
- Removes curses & hexes.
- Great for purification purposes.
- Healing & reducing stress.

Planet: Sun | Element: Water

Herb Magick

Cinnamon

- Healing, love, luck, power, prosperity, protection, spirituality, strength, success.
- When burned raises protective vibrations & draws money.

Planet: Sun | Element: Fire

Cloves

- Love, money & protection.
- Helps with divination & psychic abilities.
- Can be used to bring mental clarity & cleansing the aura.

Planet: Sun/Jupiter | Element: Fire

Herb Magick

Cumin

- Fidelity, protection & exorcism.
- An object containing a cumin seed will prevent theft.
- Burn with Frankincense for protection.

Planet: Mars | Element: Fire

Dill

- Money, protection, luck & lust.
- Used in love & protection charms.
- Use dill seeds in money spells.
- Adding dill seeds to a bath will make men irresistible on a date.

Planet: Mercury | Element: Fire

Herb Magick

Echinacea

- Powerful healing properties.
- Use to increase the power of other herbs, potions & spells.
- Great for attracting money.
- Used as an offering to spirits.

Planet: Mars | Element: Earth

Eucalyptus

- Healing properties.
- Use leaves to heal a room of negative energy.
- Oil is great for cleansing tools.
- Great for moon magick.

Planet: Moon | Element: Water

Herb Magick

Fennel Seed

- Use in spells for protection, healing & purification.
- Provides help & strength when facing danger or dire times.
- Hang in window to repel evil.

Planet: Mercury | Element: Air

Flax Seed

- Used for money spells & healing rituals.
- Burn for divinatory powers.
- Placed in a shoe, pocket, wallet or purse will ward off poverty.

Planet: Mercury | Element: Fire

Herb Magick

Garlic

- Used for healing, protection, exorcism, repulsion of vampires, purification of spaces & objects.
- Used to invoke Hecate.
- Helps keep willpower strong.

Planet: Mars | Element: Fire

Honeysuckle

- Draws money, success & quick abundance.
- Crushed flowers rubbed onto forehead enhances psychic powers.
- Helps sharpen intuition.

Planet: Venus/Mercury | Element: Earth

Herb Magick

Lavender

- Love & fertility.
- Protection & cleansing.
- Attracting love.
- Enhance clairvoyance, awareness & intuition.

Planet: Mercury | Element: Air

Motherwort

- Increases peaceful energies & protects the home.
- Place on altar to raise spiritual vibrations.
- Promotes inner confidence.

Planet: Venus | Element: Water

Herb Magick

Mugwort

- Powerful protection.
- Used for spiritual cleansing, healing & divination.
- Stimulates psychic abilities.
- Promotes prophetic dreams.

Planet: Venus | Element: Earth

Mustard Seed

- Courage, faith & endurance.
- Carry a few grains in a small bag to guard against injury.
- Oldest known good luck charm when used in an amulet.

Planet: Mars | Element: Fire

Herb Magick

Oregano

- Joy, strength, vitality & added energy.
- Plant around your home to ward against negative magick and energies.

Planet: Mercury | Element: Air

Pennyroyal

- Protection, protection & healing.
- Brings peace to your home & protects from domestic abuse.
- Protects against evil.
- Breaks hexes & curses.

Planet: Mars | Element: Fire

Herb Magick

Red Clover Blossoms

- Brings good luck for money.
- Helps with love & matters relating to a marriage.
- Add to a bath to ensure a successful financial transaction.

Planet: Mercury | Element: Air

Red Rose

- Love & romance.
- Rose petals are powerful in attracting love.
- Use in spellwork for clairvoyance, healing and prosperity.

Planet: Venus | Element: Water

Herb Magick

Rose Hips

- Attracts loving energies & peace.
- Brings good luck.
- Promotes psychic power, divination & healing.
- Calls in positive spirits.

Planet: Jupiter | Element: Water

Rosemary

- Use to improve health in healing poppets.
- Use for love spells, improved memory & purification.
- **SUBSTITUTE FOR ALL HERBS**

Planet: Sun | Element: Fire

Herb Magick

Sage
- Purification, gets rid of negative energies
- Promotes emotional, mental, physical health, spiritual health.
- Purify spaces with sage smudge.

Planet: Jupiter | Element: Air

St. Johns Wort
- Powerful protection herb.
- Placed in a jar and hung by doors keeps the devil away.
- Protects from all forms of black magick & witchcraft.

Planet: Sun | Element: Fire

Herb Magick

Thyme

- Attracts affection & loyalty.
- Boosts good opinion from others.
- Banishing, purification & to attract good health.
- Use if you need more time.

Planet: Venus | Element: Air

Valerian Root

- Used to ward off enemies.
- Increases effects of curses & hexes.
- Sprinkle powdered Valerian Root around the home to protect from evil & unwanted visitors.

Planet: Venus | Element: Water

Herb Magick

Willow Bark
- Enhances creativity & fertility.
- Excellent protection against evil & negative energies.
- Spiritual healing, divination & enhancing intuition.

Planet: Moon | Element: Water

Yarrow
- Purification & spiritual protection.
- Increases psychic awareness.
- Protects from psychic attacks.
- Wards off negative energies.

Planet: Venus | Element: Water

Herb Magick

Herb Magick

Herb Magick

Herb Magick

Crystal Magick

Crystal Magick

It is realistic to assume that people have been fascinated by stones and crystals for as long as our species has existed. It is not known how crystals and stones were used in earlier times, but it is safe to say that amulets and talismans have been popular for as long as the human species have been around. Numerous early pieces and works were derived from natural sources.

The Ancient Sumerians used crystals in magick recipes, making them the first recorded usage of crystals. Stones utilized by the Egyptians included lapis lazuli, turquoise, carnelian, and emerald. These very same stones were crafted into burial amulets. Their primary uses were protection and health. Chrysolite (later topaz and peridot) was used to treat insomnia and ward off bad spirits. Egyptians also utilized gemstones for beauty. Galena (lead ore) was powdered and used as kohl (eye shadow). Similarly, malachite was also used in the same way. Green stones were used to represent the heart of the deceased and was typically buried with them.

The name "crystal" is derived from the Greek word for ice, since it was formerly thought that pure quartz was water that had been frozen so deeply that it would stay solid forever. Amethyst, which means 'not drunken,' was worn as an amulet to ward off both intoxication and hangovers. Hematite is derived from the Latin word for blood, owing to the crimson coloration that occurs when it oxidizes. The ancient Greeks associated hematite, a kind of iron ore, with Ares, the God of War. Greek troops rubbed hematite on their bodies prior to battle, presumably to render themselves invulnerable. Additionally, Greek sailors carried a variety of amulets to ensure their safety at sea.

It's worth noting that there are several examples of gemstones having identical meanings in various civilizations. Numerous crystals are utilized in rituals, jewelry creation, healing, and daily living. If you are unfamiliar with crystals or how to utilize them, they might be daunting. The following are some of the most popular crystals, along with brief descriptions of their healing properties, physical characteristics, and, of course, their magickal uses.

Each crystal and stone contains its own unique energy. Their energy can be channeled for personal use or to boost your magick. Utilize a gemstone whose magickal attributes correspond to your intentions. Please remember that you must cleanse, charge (with moonlight or sunlight), and activate your crystals before using them. Please note that some crystals may dissolve in water or may be damaged by direct sunlight, so be sure to research and find out how best to care for your crystals.

If you feel attracted or drawn to a specific crystal or stone, it is important that you follow your intuition, obtain the crystal, and work with it, as this is a divine sign that you were meant to be connected with its energy, vibration and properties.

Crystal Magick

Agate ag·ate /aɡət/

Agate is a form of Chalcedony that may be found in a wide range of colors and shapes. Jewelry is often adorned with this stone. Agates are frequently striped or speckled in appearance, and they are generally somewhat translucent. Because there are many different types, their magickal properties vary depending on which type of Agate you may have.

If you are drawn to Agate:

This signifies that you are anxious or neglected. Agate can assist you in developing energy of security and happy feelings.

Magickal Uses:

Black Agate: Courage, healing, peaceful energy, success.
Brown Agate: Courage, healing, home, money, setting goals, success.
Red Agate: Action, healing, love, protection. Boosts determination and helps with overcoming obstacles.
Green Agate: Family ties, fertility, healing, love, personal growth. Boosts the energy of spells.
Moss Agate: Abundance, balancing of emotions, creativity, harmony, optimism, strength.
Tip: Can be used to help with plant growth and health.
Snakeskin Agate: Animals, sexuality. **Tip:** This stone is excellent for connecting with animals and generating energy for animal magick.
Tree Agate: Stone of abundance, contemplation, personal well-being, and knowledge.

Element: EARTH	Zodiac: VIRGO/GEMINI
Birthstone: SEPTEMBER	Chakra: THIRD EYE/CROWN

DRAW OR PRINT A PICTURE OF AGATE
FOR THE SPACE ABOVE

Crystal Magick

Agate

NOTES - RESEARCH
SPELLWORK & RITUALS

Crystal Magick

Amethyst am·e·thyst /aməTHəst/

Likely the most noticeable and recognized crystal in the world. Amethyst comes in a range of violet and purple tints, which varies the appearance of the stone. Amethyst is a member of the quartz family and has many healing properties such as lowering stress and strain, regulating mood swings, reducing irritability, dispersing wrath, fury, fear, and worries, and alleviating sadness and grief. Amethyst stimulates spiritual consciousness, broadens intuition, and improves psychic powers. Amethyst is also a protection crystal against bad energy and spirits, transforming them into love and light.

If you are drawn to Amethyst:

It indicates your desire for a deeper knowledge and a calming of your senses in order to hear your inner voice. This may be accomplished by meditating with this stone, whether as a bracelet or by holding a piece of amethyst.

Magickal Uses:

Awareness, calming, divination, dreamwork, focus, growth, harmony, intuition, justice, love, powerful healing, spirituality, wisdom. **Tip:** Keep a piece of amethyst at your desk to inspire motivation and self-expression, and work with the grounding energy of amethyst before or after performing ritual magick.

Element: WATER/AIR   **Birthstone:** FEBRUARY
Chakra: THIRD EYE/CROWN
Zodiac: VIRGO/SAGITTARIUS/CAPRICORN/AQUARIUS/PISCES

DRAW OR PRINT A PICTURE OF AMETHYST
FOR THE SPACE ABOVE

Crystal Magick

Amazonite am·a·zon·ite / ˈa-mə-zə-ˌnīt

Amazonite is a feldspar stone with a distinctive blue-green hue. We adore it for its benefits to the Throat and Heart Chakras. It is typically found around the Amazon River and is occasionally referred to as Amazon Stone or Amazon Jade. Amazonite will help you to move past fear, judgement, and prior trauma, by giving you the courage to search deep inside yourself to find the truth. Setting boundaries and creating personal space in relationships is helped by Amazonite. It can also promote seeing all sides of a problem. Use it for meditation and clarity. It also balances male and female energies.

If you are drawn to Amazonite:

It may signal that you are experiencing low self-esteem or are having difficulty communicating with someone. Amazonite helps you overcome this by balancing your Throat Chakra and your confidence to move on from feelings of judgement from others.

Magickal Uses:

Aids communication, good luck, intuition, repels negativity, sharpening of the mind, stability, the opening of psychic channels, trust. **Tip:** Great for personal growth and goal-setting when used as an amulet or good luck charm.

Element: WATER/EARTH
Chakra: THROAT/HEART

Birthstone: SEPTEMBER
Zodiac: VIRGO

DRAW OR PRINT A PICTURE OF AMAZONITE
FOR THE SPACE ABOVE

Crystal Magick

Amazonite

NOTES - RESEARCH
SPELLWORK & RITUALS

Crystal Magick

Black Tourmaline   tour·ma·line / ˈtur-mə-lən

Black Tourmaline is a hexagonal aluminum borosilicate crystal that is frequently black in color. Black tourmaline is an excellent stone for energy cleansing. Often referred to be a protective stone, black tourmaline is one of the best crystals for both novice and experienced crystal collectors. Tourmaline is frequently seen in necklaces, bracelets, and gem elixirs, as well as near front doors and as trip companions. Given its simplicity, you may be wondering why everyone gravitates toward it. Black tourmaline, in its purest form, is one of the most potent grounding, purifying, and protection stones. This statement neatly summarizes black tourmaline: "I remove negativity; I am protected on all levels."

If you are drawn to Black Tourmaline:

This stone is very beneficial for individuals who are dealing with significant levels of stress in any area of their lives, as it is very powerful for grounding chaotic energies. Also very protective if you are an individual who is overly generous.

Magickal Uses:

Helps to get energy moving which is good for spellwork and rituals. Promotes inner confidence and independence. Promotes acceptance and enhances psychic abilities.

Element: EARTH
Chakra: ROOT

Birthstone: OCTOBER
Zodiac: PISCES

DRAW OR PRINT A PICTURE OF BLACK TOURMALINE
FOR THE SPACE ABOVE

Crystal Magick

Black Tourmaline

**NOTES - RESEARCH
SPELLWORK & RITUALS**

Crystal Magick

Citrine cit·rine /ˈsi-ˌtrīn

Citrine is a translucent coarse-grained form of the silica crystal quartz that is often light yellow or orange in color with a brownish undertone. Citrine is believed to be connected to the solar plexus. It aids in the support of your power chakra by instilling confidence and strength in you. Citrine is frequently used to promote happiness and optimism. It is frequently utilized to aid in manifesting financial prosperity and opportunity. Additionally, citrine stimulates the digestive system by cleaning and eliminating the blocked region in order to cleanse it. Citrine is a gemstone that may be used as jewelry or used to decorate your home. Citrine is frequently included in abundance rituals to attract money and fortune.

If you are drawn to Citrine:

It implies that you might benefit from a "Vitamin C(itrine)" boost in the following areas of your life: Energy, Happiness, Joy, and Light.

Magickal Uses:

Abundance, hope, optimism, success, manifesting change, strengthening of will power. Invites happiness and harmony into the home. Useful for interpreting dreams and raising energy. Protection, creativity, good luck. Widely used in spells to attract or manifest money or financial abundance.

Element: FIRE   **Birthstone:** NOVEMBER
Zodiac: ARIES/GEMINI/LEO/LIBRA
Chakra: SACRAL/SOLAR PLEXUS/ROOT

DRAW OR PRINT A PICTURE OF CITRINE
FOR THE SPACE ABOVE

Crystal Magick

Clear Quartz 'kwôrts

The term "Clear Quartz" is also used to refer to Rock Crystal. It is a colorless kind of quartz and a naturally occurring type of silicon dioxide. Perhaps the most plentiful mineral on the planet is clear quartz. Containing high vibrations, clear or crystal quartz boosts the healing abilities of the stones it surrounds. It can collect, distribute, and regulate energy, especially negative energy. When you have "brain fog" or require clarity, this stone aids with focus and memory recall. Additionally, these translucent crystals serve as 'manifestors.' They are the ones that make things happen in life! If you're on a new road or in need of change in your life, Clear Quartz is the ideal stone for you. It aids in decision-making, offers stability and foundation, and thus aids in making sensible decisions.

If you are drawn to Clear Quartz:

It is a signal that you must reclaim control of your life. Regain your composure, brush yourself off, and go for it!

Magickal Uses:

Purification of any kind, provides protection, good for shamanic work. Aids with decision making, amplifies energy. Raises awareness, lifts spiritual practice to new heights, purifies the aura, strengthens family bonds. **SUBSTITUTE FOR ALL CRYSTALS IN SPELLWORK AND RITUALS.**

Element: EARTH	Birthstone: APRIL
Zodiac: ARIES/LEO/VIRGO	Chakra: ALL

DRAW OR PRINT A PICTURE OF CLEAR QUARTZ
FOR THE SPACE ABOVE

Crystal Magick

Clear Quartz

NOTES - RESEARCH
SPELLWORK & RITUALS

Crystal Magick

Green Aventurine ə-ˈven-chə-ˌrēn

Simply put, Aventurine is a quartz crystal with mica inclusions. Aventurine is a stone representing wealth and good fortune due to its metaphysical characteristics. Aventurine is a stone associated with abundance. Indecisive? Aventurine is an excellent crystal for decision-making. Additionally, it fosters leadership, perseverance, optimism, and innovation. It broadens the mind to consider various options and paths. It encourages compassion and empathy as a heart chakra stone. It alleviates and calms rage and irritability.

If you are drawn to Green Aventurine:

Attraction to Aventurine may signify that you require a boost in your confidence. By incorporating or wearing Aventurine, you may foster confidence in your decision-making, which will ultimately result in prosperity and success.

Magickal Uses:

Attracts money, success and luck. Calming, supportive, healing. Fosters compassion and friendship. Tip: use aventurine for spellwork around heartbreak.

Element: AIR/WATER
Zodiac: LIBRA/VIRGO

Birthstone: APRIL
Chakra: HEART

DRAW OR PRINT A PICTURE OF GREEN AVENTURINE FOR THE SPACE ABOVE

Crystal Magick

Green Aventurine

NOTES - RESEARCH
SPELLWORK & RITUALS

Crystal Magick

Howlite   how·lite / ˈhaʊˌlīt

Howlite has a white marble-like look and is veined with grey, black, or brown. However, in its raw and purest form, the stone is pure white. Howlite is a porous stone that is excellent at absorbing dye, which is why it is frequently used to mimic other gemstones, and Howlite itself can be seen in a multitude of different colors. When this stone is used as a meditation tool and spiritual ally, you may have a sense of being transported to snow-covered mountain ranges, where soul and nature are intertwined in a blanket of white. As with many white sacred gemstones, Howlite can promote mental clarity and tranquility; nevertheless, its black lines indicate that the mind is still active, attentive, and not turned off.

If you are drawn to Howlite:

Howlite, as a stone of awareness, may signify that you desire a greater understanding of yourself, others, the world, and life itself.

Magickal Uses:

Stone of emotions. Supports showing of emotion in a healthy manner. Encourages creativity and self-expression. Aids with memory.

Element: WATER

Zodiac: CANCER/SCORPIO

Birthstone: JUNE/JULY

Chakra: THIRD-EYE

DRAW OR PRINT A PICTURE OF HOWLITE
FOR THE SPACE ABOVE

Crystal Magick

Howlite

NOTES - RESEARCH
SPELLWORK & RITUALS

Crystal Magick

Jade 'jād

Jade is a silicate stone that is frequently associated with East Asian art. It is a mineral belonging to the Jadeite group and has a monoclinic crystal structure. Although jade is most often identified from its green hues, it is also available in brown, lavender, orange, purple, red and white. Jade signifies assurance, acceptance, and good health. Jade is a famous healing gem recognized for bringing luck to those who wear it. While the world commonly associates Jade with Chinese medicine and healing, its origins extend well beyond one continent. Jade has been present for millennia, and its effect on humans may be traced in numerous tribes, villages, and tributaries across the planet.

If you are drawn to Jade:

If you're experiencing emotional pain as a result of love difficulties, whether it's love of or for another person or self-love, Jade can help restore balance and tranquility.

Magickal Uses:

Receptive energy, provides guidance and inspiration. Attracts luck, abundance, success. Repels negative energy. Protection. Associated with fertility, justice, peace, harmony and well-being.

Element: WATER **Birthstone:** AUGUST
Chakra: HEART **Zodiac:** TAURUS/GEMINI/LIBRA/ARIES

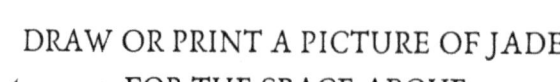

DRAW OR PRINT A PICTURE OF JADE
FOR THE SPACE ABOVE

Crystal Magick

Jade

NOTES - RESEARCH
SPELLWORK & RITUALS

Crystal Magick

Lapis Lazuli *la·pis la·zu·li / ˌla-pəs-ˈla-zə-lē*

Lapis Lazuli is a stunning heavenly deep blue stone that is regarded semi-precious due to its vibrant color display. It is composed of deep blue lazurite, iridescent pyrite, foggy white calcite, and several other minerals. Lapis Lazuli is said to attract good fortune and luck. It symbolizes good luck, and anybody who wears it will benefit from the energies that may transform any negative energy into a positive one. Lapis lazuli is revered as 'The Wisdom Stone' due to its healing properties. With its traditional style, it was favored by Egypt's pharaohs thousands of years ago. The Lapis Lazuli crystal absorbs the majority of your truth, knowledge, and spiritual wonder, and transforms it into your inner peace.

If you are drawn to Lapis Lazuli:

If you are considering major life changes such as job or profession or relocation, Lapis Lazuli will be a powerful stone for you. The Lapis Lazuli crystal will encourage you to live life for yourself if you are unsure of what is best for you, rather than letting other peoples opinions steer you in a different direction.

Magickal Uses:

Stone of wisdom, enhances psychic abilities and intuition. Good for divination, attracts love.
Tip: Wear Lapis Lazuli when travelling, seeking justice and to protect and boost courage.

Element: AIR
Chakra: THIRD-EYE/THROAT

Birthstone: SEPTEMBER
Zodiac: TAURUS/LIBRA

DRAW OR PRINT A PICTURE OF LAPIS LAZULI FOR THE SPACE ABOVE

Crystal Magick

Lapis Lazuli

NOTES - RESEARCH
SPELLWORK & RITUALS

Crystal Magick

Malachite mal·a·chite / ˈma-lə-ˌkīt

Malachite is a well-known mineral due to its bright green color and lovely banded masses. Densely banded examples are frequently cut and polished to enhance their exquisite coloration. The bands may be composed of concentric rings with unusual designs; such examples are quite valuable. For thousands of years, polished, banded Malachite has been carved into ornaments and worn as jewelry, and in certain ancient cultures, it was believed to provide protection against evil. Malachite is the essence of joy and is referred to as the "stone of transformation" due to its ability to unveil and cure emotional anguish through its absorption of the pain. It is particularly useful to provide the information essential for personal development during times of uncertainty.

If you are drawn to Malachite:

Malachite, as a stone of transformation, promotes change and emotional risk-taking. It identifies the obstacles to spiritual development, unearths buried emotions and psychosomatic causes, and then enables you to sever undesirable bonds and outworn behaviors.

Magickal Uses:

Stone of Transformation. Aids with personal and business success. Bings peace and hope. Banishes negativity and provides protection, especially for those travelling. **Tip:** Use Malachite in spellwork to increase luck, money and prosperity. Carry a piece of Malachite to provide protection when travelling.

Element: EARTH   Zodiac: TAURUS/CAPRICORN/SCORPIO

Birthstone: APRIL/MAY   Chakra: SOLAR PLEXUS/HEART

DRAW OR PRINT A PICTURE OF MALACHITE
FOR THE SPACE ABOVE

Crystal Magick

Malachite

NOTES - RESEARCH
SPELLWORK & RITUALS

Crystal Magick

Moonstone

Moonstone is made up of two different kinds of feldspar minerals. It is an opalescent crystal that changes in color depending on the stone. Additionally, it is described as grey, colorless, brown, yellow, or green. Moonstone promotes personal growth and fresh beginnings, as well as calming emotional instability and relieving stress. Moonstone is a naturally occurring crystal mineral believed to capture the moon's energy, which represents yin's quiet and soothing strength. Similarly, this stone boosts your intuition and promotes positive well-being and harmony. Moonstone can improve luck, intuition, and creativity. Moonstone is commonly utilized in meditation and self-growth.

If you are drawn to Moonstone:

If you've ever felt as if you were losing your mind under a full moon, that is one indication of how profoundly the Moon influences our emotional balance. The Moonstone is here to illuminate the darkness, to elevate all those emotional states, and to bring all those wild feelings back in check.

Magickal Uses:

Lunar energy and magick. Aids in strengthening psychic abilities, contacting of spirits, divination and dreamwork. Promotes healing, calming, unites body and spirit. Aids those seeking wisdom, good for spells focused on fertility and abundance.

Element: WATER   Zodiac: CANCER/LIBRA/SCORPIO/PISCES
Chakra: SACRAL/HEART/CROWN/THIRD-EYE
Birthstone: JUNE

DRAW OR PRINT A PICTURE OF MOONSTONE
FOR THE SPACE ABOVE

Crystal Magick

Moonstone

NOTES - RESEARCH
SPELLWORK & RITUALS

Crystal Magick

Obsidian   ob·sid·i·an / əb-ˈsi-dē-ən

Obsidian is created when felsic lava cools quickly with little crystallisation. Also known as volcanic glass, Obsidian is naturally black and has a glassy texture and beautiful sheen. Obsidian is found in several hues, such as gold, mahogany, snowflake and rainbow. Obsidian is a hard, brittle stone that was frequently utilized for tools. Obsidian is associated with safety and grounding. As a very protective stone, Obsidian is always prepared to keep your entire body ready for action, which includes detoxifying every inch. Obsidian is helpful for maintaining a healthy circulation.

If you are drawn to Obsidian:

Obsidian provides you the confidence to face the unknown, accept who you actually are, let go of previous traumas, and let go of what no longer serves you.

Magickal Uses:

Protection, connection, communication. Good for binding spells. Attracts luck and fosters peace. Brings clarity to divination. Helps to provide balance during times of transformation.

Element: EARTH/FIRE   Zodiac: SCORPIO/SAGITTARIUS

Chakra: SOLAR PLEXUS/THIRD-EYE/ROOT

Birthstone: OCTOBER/NOVEMBER

DRAW OR PRINT A PICTURE OF OBSIDIAN FOR THE SPACE ABOVE

Crystal Magick

Obsidian

NOTES - RESEARCH
SPELLWORK & RITUALS

Crystal Magick

Pyrite py·rite / ˈpī-ˌrīt

Often called fool's gold, Pyrite is frequently a metallic cluster or a brassy yellow mineral with a gold-like appearance, hence the 'golden' appearance. Pyrite repels bad energy and wards off negative entities and spirits. Pyrite boosts the memory, assisting you in recalling critical information. Ancient Incas meditated and utilized this stone in their divination practices. Pyrite activates the body's nourishing energy, regulating and harmonizing one's emotional state and general well-being. Pyrite may be used in home decor for the purpose of activating universal energy, cleansing and clearing the mind in order to recall one's true self.

If you are drawn to Pyrite:

Pyrite is all about ensuring your strength and stability, as well as your everlasting freedom from the shackles of control. It seems to possess an intuitive quality that protects you on a spiritual and emotional level.

Magickal Uses:

Focusing energy, grounding, divination, psychic work. Helps to strengthen willpower, aids with manifestation. Aids those seeking the truth, provides protection from deceit. Great for feng shui.

Element: FIRE   **Zodiac:** LEO   **Birthstone:** JULY/AUGUST
Chakra: SOLAR PLEXUS/THIRD-EYE

DRAW OR PRINT A PICTURE OF PYRITE
FOR THE SPACE ABOVE

Crystal Magick

Pyrite

NOTES - RESEARCH
SPELLWORK & RITUALS

Crystal Magick

Rose Quartz 'kworts

Rose Quartz, like the quartz family, is a silicon dioxide mineral. The color of rose quartz is due to the mineral's titanium, iron, or manganese content. Rose quartz emits pinkish tones that vary according to the piece of quartz. Rose quartz is associated with love and compassion, which makes it an excellent crystal for the heart and throat chakras. The therapeutic benefits of rose quartz include loving energy, abundance, joy, and the ability to heal emotional issues. Additionally, rose quartz is utilized to enhance fertility, kindness, affection, and self-love. Put this stone in strategic places around your house, like in your bathroom for a ritual bath or for added self-love in the bedroom.

If you are drawn to Rose Quartz:

Also known as the Heart Stone, if your heart chakra is blocked, you may exhibit undesirable relationship behaviors. Maybe you're more co-dependent or prone to jealousy. If you are struggling to feel connected and open to the bountiful opportunities that come with a happy life, Rose Quartz has the ability to align your heart once more with those desires.

Magickal Uses:

Associated with romance, love, sex and fertility. Aids with emotional healing and reconciliation. Dispels loneliness, opens the heart to compassion. Removes negative energy, releases stress. Strengthens faith, brings closeness to the power and wisdom of the divine.

Element: WATER
Birthstone: JANUARY
Zodiac: TAURUS/LIBRA
Chakra: HEART/THROAT

DRAW OR PRINT A PICTURE OF ROSE QUARTZ
FOR THE SPACE ABOVE

Crystal Magick

Rose Quartz

NOTES - RESEARCH
SPELLWORK & RITUALS

Crystal Magick

Selenite sel·e·nite / ˈse-lə-ˌnīt

Selenite is a popular healing and ceremonial crystal. Selenite is a crystalline form of gypsum with a silvery-white luster. Selenite gets its name from Selene, the Greek goddess of the moon. Selenite is also known as Desert Rose and Satin Spar. Selenite is an excellent crystal for meditation, reiki, or any other spiritual or divinatory practice. Assists in gaining insight from the source, clarifying judgement and assisting with seeing the bigger picture. It clears bad energy and purifies your environment. During a ceremony, hold selenite in your hands and breathe. You can also grid your house for protection by placing in multiple areas like windows.

If you are drawn to Selenite:

If you feel stuck, Selenite will help you get things moving again. If you tend to have negative or anxious thoughts, or think critical of yourself, hold a piece of selenite inches from your body, and moving it slowly up and down, you can invite the stone to soak up all of your negative unwanted energy.

Magickal Uses:

Lunar associations. Great for moon magick. Use for love spells, draws on the energy of renewal. New beginnings, purification, justice, clarity, harmony. Wards off negativity. Charges other stones and crystals that are nearby, great for a crystal grid formation.

Element: AIR *Zodiac:* PISCES/TAURUS/CANCER
Birthstone: APRIL to JULY *Chakra:* THIRD EYE/CROWN

DRAW OR PRINT A PICTURE OF SELENITE
FOR THE SPACE ABOVE

Crystal Magick

Selenite

NOTES - RESEARCH
SPELLWORK & RITUALS

Crystal Magick

Smoky Quartz 'kwòrts

Smoky Quartz is a greyish or brown quartz. Like its other quartz counterparts, this crystal is a wonderful grounding stone. Smoky Quartz dispels anxieties and brightens the mood. Smoky Quartz dispels bad energy, promoting emotional stability and alleviating stress and anxiety. This stone encourages positive thoughts and behaviors. It is linked to the root chakra and helps keep your energy grounded and your life stable. Smoky Quartz is an excellent choice in rituals to let go of something.

If you are drawn to Smoky Quartz:

Smoky Quartz is here to protect your wonderful energies from being drowned out. A great stone for individuals tired of bad energy and emotions weighing them down. If you are an empath who struggles maintaining boundaries or just need a little push to start on a new path, Smoky Quartz may be the stone for you.

Magickal Uses:

A powerhouse of energy. Use to cleanse negative energy, aids in raising awareness, helps us to tap into subconscious wisdom. Enhances creative expression. Good for dreamwork. Attracts luck and abundance, provides protection, removes obstacles.

Element: EARTH **Birthstone:** APRIL **Chakra:** ROOT/CROWN
Zodiac: SCORPIO/SAGITTARIUS/CAPRICORN

DRAW OR PRINT A PICTURE OF SMOKY QUARTZ
FOR THE SPACE ABOVE

Crystal Magick

Smoky Quartz

NOTES - RESEARCH
SPELLWORK & RITUALS

Crystal Magick

Tigers Eye

Tiger's Eye is also a type of quartz. It is a mineral made of silicon dioxide and a great deal of iron, which contributes to its striped appeal. A protective stone that also brings luck, this eye-catching stone aids in problem-solving and clearing muddled emotions. Tigers Eye aids in calming fears and anxiety, and also increases activity, boldness, and self-confidence. This stone's many applications and advantages make it a great gift!

If you are drawn to Tigers Eye:

Tigers Eye invites riches, success, and good fortune into your life. Additionally, the stone will boost your confidence and attract prosperity. These golden stones are ideal if you're looking for financial achievement, business growth, and opportunities.

Magickal Uses:

Working and communicating with animals. Empowers psychic abilities, supports learning. Aids in divination. Provides protection and security. Fosters strength and confidence. Abundance, money, the repayment of debts owed.

Element: FIRE **Birthstone:** JUNE to AUGUST
Chakra: SACRAL/SOLAR PLEXUS
Zodiac: GEMINI/LEO/CAPRICORN

DRAW OR PRINT A PICTURE OF TIGERS EYE
FOR THE SPACE ABOVE

Crystal Magick

Tigers Eye

NOTES - RESEARCH
SPELLWORK & RITUALS

Crystal Magick
The Power of the Crystal Grid

Crystal Grids are a beautiful and powerful way to bring your dreams, goals, and intentions into the world. They also have the power to heal. The energy of the crystals you use, how you set them up, and what you want to happen gives a crystal grid its power. A crystal grid utilizes sacred geometry along with your crystals to manifest your desires. Keep in mind that the universe will likely grant us the things we NEED, not the desires we WANT. So, if you want it to happen, it's best to focus on what you need instead of what you want. Most of the time, people use crystal grids to bring about health, wealth, healing, and protection.

Crystal grids have several uses and methods. They are the best high-vibe decorations in any room, but they are also so much more. They can be used for healing (both in person and from afar), making things happen, ritual work, meditation, setting intentions, or just being creative. Crystal grids don't really have any set rules.. It's best to go with your gut and do what you feel led you to work with the crystals. Anyone can Google a crystal grid 'how-to,' but manifesting and healing become more effective when you trust your instincts and do what feels right. That's where the true magick comes from.

People choose stones depending on their attributes and what they want to manifest. Others choose crystals spontaneously and research their attributes afterwards. Don't worry if your options are limited. You may work with what you have, but your intentions are the most powerful here. Crystals operate with your inner magick and strength, and have mystical capabilities. There are an unlimited number of choices for crystal grids, but the most essential aspect is to trust your instincts and emotions.

Using a Crystal Grid

1. Remember to cleanse your stones and the working area before you begin.
2. Decide what your intentions are for your crystal grid and write them down.
3. Choose your crystals; either intuitively or by choice.
4. Place your written intentions in the middle of your working space.
5. Begin placing crystals on the grid by following your intuition.
6. Activate your grid with a larger stone, a Clear Quartz point or tower, or simply speak out loud that it has been activated.
7. Leave your grid to draw in power, or dismantle when you are finished.

USE THE CRYSTAL GRIDS ON THE FOLLOWING PAGES

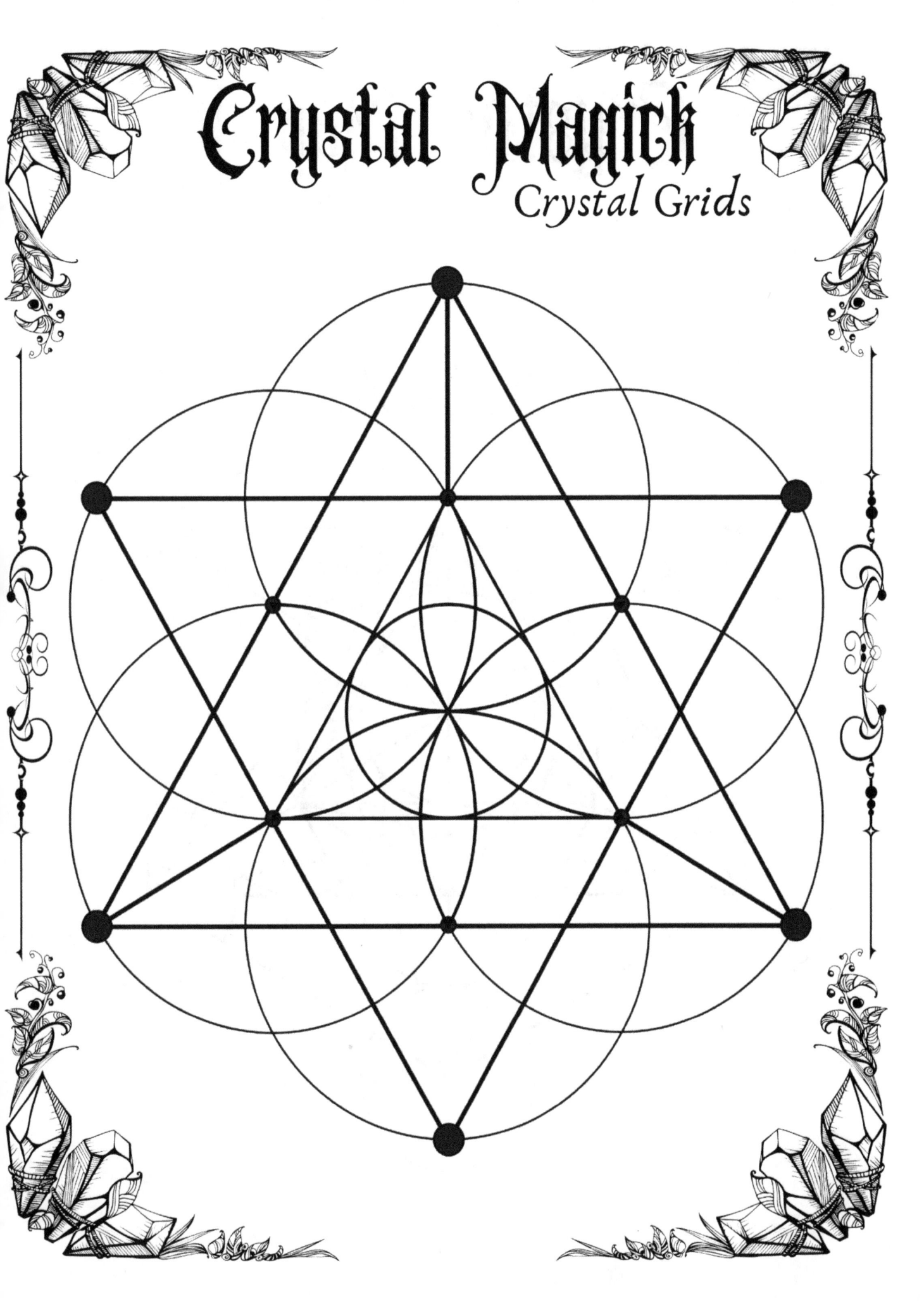

Crystal Magick
Crystal Grids

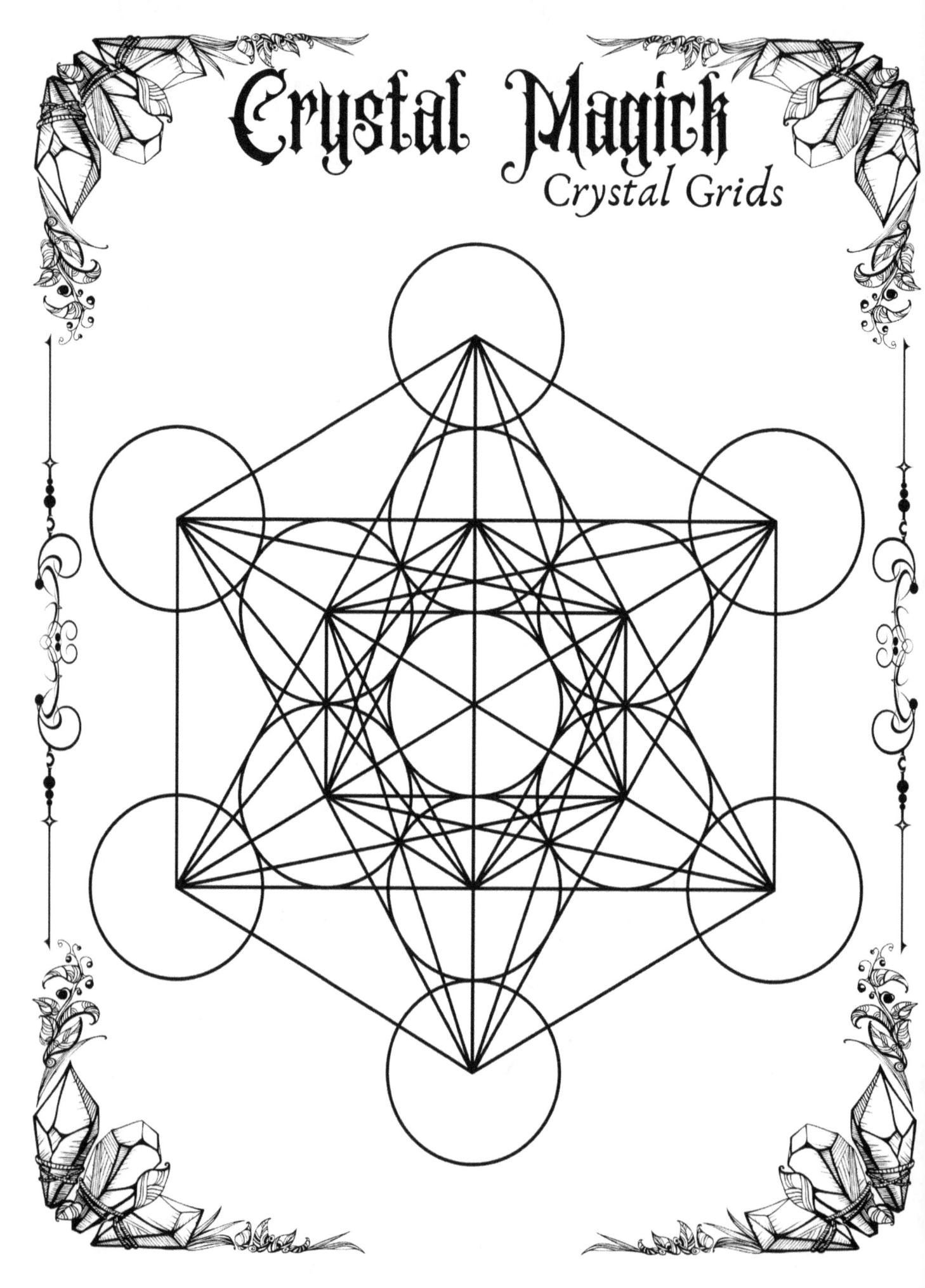

Crystal Magick
Crystal Grids

Crystal Magick

NAME:

If you are drawn to _____:

Magickal Uses:

Element: Birthstone:
Chakra: Zodiac:

DRAW OR PRINT A PICTURE OF YOUR CRYSTAL
FOR THE SPACE ABOVE

Crystal Magick

NOTES - RESEARCH
SPELLWORK & RITUALS

NAME:

Crystal Magick

NAME:
_____
_____
_____
_____
_____
_____

If you are drawn to _____ :
_____
_____
_____

Magickal Uses:
_____
_____
_____
_____

Element: Birthstone:
Chakra: Zodiac:

DRAW OR PRINT A PICTURE OF YOUR CRYSTAL
FOR THE SPACE ABOVE

Crystal Magick

NAME:

NOTES - RESEARCH
SPELLWORK & RITUALS

Crystal Magick

NAME:
_____
_____
_____
_____
_____

If you are drawn to _____:
_____
_____
_____

Magickal Uses:
_____
_____
_____

Element: Birthstone:
Chakra: Zodiac:

DRAW OR PRINT A PICTURE OF YOUR CRYSTAL
FOR THE SPACE ABOVE

Crystal Magick

NOTES - RESEARCH
SPELLWORK & RITUALS

NAME:

NEED MORE SPACE TO RECORD YOUR THOUGHTS AND NOTES?

You will be happy to know that there is a Book of Shadows Companion Journal that compliments this book. It is available on Amazon, and has over 200 blank pages for you to record more notes, thoughts, spells, rituals and any other information you desire. It also has all the same templates and charts.

GET YOUR MAGICKAL COMPANION TODAY

On Amazon:

Book of Shadows Companion Journal by J.C. Marco

Number Magick & Numerology

(BONUS: Angel Numbers)

Number Magick

Numerology is practiced in many pagan spiritual systems. According to the fundamental principles of numerology, numbers have a tremendous degree of spiritual, vibrational and magickal importance. Some numbers are stronger and more powerful than others, and number combinations can be created for magickal usage, such as, creating a sigil.

Numerology in itself is very extensive, so I encourage you to do some research. For now, I will go over the basics so you can have a better understanding of numerology and how the numbers can help in your spellwork and practice.

In a typical numerological reading, the chart below can be used to associate the individual numbers to each of the letters of the alphabet, same as if you were creating a sigil. You can then use this combination of numbers, or the reduced single digit, as a boost to your magick.

1	2	3	4	5	6	7	8	9
A	B	C	D	E	F	G	H	I
J	K	L	M	N	O	P	Q	R
S	T	U	V	W	X	Y	Z	

This chart is used for numerology and sigils.

Numbers become a part of our everyday lives as soon as we begin to speak, pulsing in the backdrop of existence. You have your birth date, social security number, address, shoe sizes, phone number, bank accounts; the list is endless.

The increasing prevalence of numbers alone conveys a feeling of their spiritual as well as mundane importance. Both ancient seers and present-day lightworkers perceive unique vibrations in numbers, a type of mathematical language that unlocks other symbols, signs, omens, and patterns in the universe.

Understanding the significance of these numbers allows us to better appreciate the profound messages they bring us, especially when they appear in our astrological chart or throughout our life. Almost every calculation in numerology is reduced to a single digit. And, with the exception of Master Numbers or Angel Numbers, we will always reduce until we reach one of these single digits. Lets take a look at some of the numbers you can use in your practice.

Number Magick
Life Path Number

When we are calculating our Life Path number, we will use our full birthdate in this example.

- If you were born on July 13, 1982 we will start by breaking down each individual section.
- JULY is the seventh month, so this number is 7
- 13 reduced to a single digit: 1 + 3 = 4
- 1982 added together to get a single digit: 1 + 9 + 8 + 2 = 20
    - 20 reduced to a single digit: 2 + 0 = 2
- So now we have our three separate numbers of 7, 4 and 2
- Adding these together we get: 7 + 4 + 2 = 13
- Reduced again to a single digit, we get: 1 + 3 = 4
- The LIFE PATH NUMBER IS 4.

Your Life Path Number

YOUR BIRTHDATE: /   /

MONTH (*Reduced to a single digit*):

DAY (*Reduced to a single digit*):

YEAR (*Reduced to a single digit*):

Add all three and reduce to a single digit:
(*With the exception of Master Numbers, do not reduce 11, 22 and 33.*)

YOUR LIFE PATH NUMBER IS:

Your Life Path Number will remain constant for the rest of your life because your birthdate does not change.

Number Magick
Life Path Meanings

1. The path of 1 is full of enthusiasm and motivation as an innovator and pioneer. These folks are natural leaders who can create opportunities for themselves. The lesson of 1 is to develop true self-confidence and practice trusting others.
2. This is the path of the modest yet significant leader. These individuals are composed, cooperative, and recognize the value of partnership. They must, however, learn to advocate for themselves when their demands are not addressed.
3. A 3 person has a young vitality that others find appealing since they are creative and expressive. These joyful folks have limited knowledge of the world. Accepting and exploring challenging issues and feelings might aid them on their journey to personal growth.
4. The fourth Life Path is one that is primarily focused on hard work and service. These individuals are strong and consistent, and they serve as a rock in the lives of others. Their lesson is to relax their minds, and recognize that love and happiness are equally vital as responsibility.
5. Anyone with a Life Path 5 will see life as an adventure. They are inquisitive people who enjoy diversity and thrive in lively social circumstances. What needs to be learned is dedication. A persistent drive to change their circumstances may lead to an unfulfilling life.
6. These are the nurturers, the lovers, and the guardians. The 6 path is gifted with a big heart, which allows these individuals to help others a great deal. People must learn to love themselves and understand that their needs are just as important as those of others in this life.
7. The goal of the 7 path is to find out what life's secrets are. These are extremely curious individuals who have an insatiable need to dive into any issue in pursuit of answers and facts. Still, they're withdrawn and have much to learn about relationships and vulnerability.
8. People with a number 8 Life Path frequently achieve tremendous success in life which is not due to luck; rather, it is due to the consistent focus, intent, and time they put into their work. While they flourish professionally, their ego may benefit from some practice in working nicely with others.

The 9 Life Path is concerned with mankind and devotes their heart and soul to serving the greater good. These people are kind, patient, and in touch with their inner wisdom. In this life, the path of 9 must learn to meet their own wants and ideals in order to let go of past traumas.

Number Magick
Destiny Number

When we are calculating our Destiny Number, we will use our full name given to us at birth, as recorded on our birth certificate. Avoid using nicknames for this process. This will include your first, middle and last names. If you have multiple middle names, these should be included as well. For this example, we will use the name JOHN JACOB SMITH. We will utilize the number chart mentioned earlier to find out the numerical value of all the letters in this name:

1	2	3	4	5	6	7	8	9
A	B	C	D	E	F	G	H	I
J	K	L	M	N	O	P	Q	R
S	T	U	V	W	X	Y	Z	

JOHN: 1 + 6 + 8 + 5 = 20 and 2 + 0 = 2
JACOB: 1 + 1 + 3 + 6 + 2 = 13 and 1 + 3 = 4
SMITH: 1 + 4 + 9 + 2 + 8 = 24 and 2 + 4 = 6
Adding the three values (2 + 4 + 6) we get a total of 12, and by reducing that number further (1 + 2), we get a Destiny Number of 3.

Your Destiny Number

YOUR FULL NAME:

FIRST NAME:
NUMERICAL VALUE:
  Added and reduced:

MIDDLE NAME(S):
NUMERICAL VALUE:
  Added and reduced:

LAST NAME:
NUMERICAL VALUE:
  Added and reduced:

Add all three and reduce to a single digit:
(With the exception of Master Numbers, do not reduce 11, 22 and 33.)

YOUR DESTINY NUMBER IS:

Number Magick

Correspondences

ZODIAC: Aries, Leo
TAROT: The Magician
PERSONALITY TRAITS: Ambitious, freedom-loving, independent, innovative, motivated, pioneering, proactive, reckless, self-centered, uninhibited.

This single-digit number has a great deal of drive and momentum. It is a real trailblazer, ready to break new ground and lead the way for others to follow. It is both a natural leader and a formidable force. The number one symbolizes newness, mobility, and the possibilities that await us. Spiritually, it symbolizes the divine creation of the cosmos, life and birth of all things.

The number 1 is the foundation of our life's opportunities. It denotes confidence, strength, and action. It forces us to examine our existing circumstances and recognize that we have the ability to transform them into anything we choose. Even when we are terrified, the number 1 motivates us to take charge of our destiny and welcome fresh beginnings.

Strengths

INDEPENDENT: The number 1 is the most self-sufficient in numerology, needing nothing but itself and its own energy to flourish. Instead of waiting for opportunities to reveal themselves, it generates them by capitalizing on circumstances that others are reluctant to examine. Going at it alone gives you more freedom and allows for faster, more efficient movement.

GOAL-ORIENTED: This number excels at setting and attaining goals because of its optimistic outlook and unwavering self-determination. It has difficulty remaining motionless because it senses a world brimming with possibilities just waiting to be discovered. It's not that the number 1 can't be happy; rather, it gets its satisfaction from staying busy and always evolving. Simply said, why remain still when you can go forward?

Number Magick

INNOVATIVE: There are no obstacles for the determined 1, not that they don't experience them, but because this number's imaginative intellect is capable of coming up with fresh ideas and ingenious methods to avoid them. Instead of being frightened by obstacles, the 1 sees them as a challenge that must (and will) be overcome. Seeing a door while others perceive a wall is a huge advantage for the 1.

Weaknesses

FORCEFUL: While this number may appear ambitious, its all-or-nothing approach may make it appear indifferent or demanding as it drives its way forward. It is more physical than spiritual, does not need anyone's help, and is too absorbed with its own objectives to realize when it has offended. In the name of movement and advancement, softer impulses such as collaboration and patience are pushed aside.

RISKY: The number 1 might describe itself as courageous and fearless, yet a lack of forethought may quickly lead to problems that could have been avoided. The 1's tunnel vision and excessive sense of invincibility cause it to be so concentrated on the path ahead, that it misses warning flags in its peripheral vision.

DOUBTFUL: Self-doubt is the Achilles' heel of a person with such a tremendous will to succeed and accomplish. Though it may not show it on the surface, the number 1 is terrified of making errors or falling short of its aim. Even mild criticism is taken seriously, yet it is eventually used as encouragement to grow.

Number Magick

2 Correspondences

ZODIAC: Taurus, Cancer
TAROT: The High Priestess
PERSONALITY TRAITS: Cooperative, empathetic, inclusive, influential, intuitive, protective, sensitive, supportive, tactful.

Numerologists see the number 2 as a feminine force that embodies both elegance and strength. It is collaborative, always seeking to restore harmony and balance to a relationship or circumstance. This number has the greatest intuition of all the numbers; it is very instinctive and sensitive. It can perceive currents and sentiments automatically and then use these cues to empathically connect with others.

The number two represents partnerships or the uniting or balancing of two diverse people, ideas, or things. While it wields immense power in any scenario, it does it with such subtlety and tact that the end effect is harmony and togetherness rather than control and authority. It is able to see both sides of an issue objectively and guide people towards the centre ground.

Strengths

INTUITIVE: On a very deep and subconscious level, this number may detect energy that can only be felt and not seen. This attribute enables the number 2 to be instinctively aware of sentiments, ideas, hopes, and anxieties that others haven't even acknowledged, and then use them to bring support and compassion to the relationship.

UNIFYING: The 2 is a peacemaker who understands the need of collaboration and teamwork. It is polite in its interactions since anything less would result in an imbalance. Even when confronted with opposing energies, this number recognizes how the contrasts may be combined to produce something whole and well-rounded.

Number Magick

INFLUENTIAL: The 2 has enormous power over circumstances and relationships (love and otherwise), but does so with such care that its influence might go unnoticed. It's as though it's occurring behind the scenes: no one sees it, but the effects are apparent. It does not need to coerce or pressure others to follow its leadership since its immense compassion and cooperative attributes urge others to follow it.

Weaknesses

INDECISIVE: In attempt to continue in the middle ground, the number 2 has difficulty identifying biases, making large and small judgments difficult. When a preference cannot be identified in any manner, this number becomes inactive.

EASILY HURT: The desire to create peace within itself and with everyone else is so great that even the smallest annoyance or offence may knock the number 2 off kilter and into a great deal of pain. There are highly sensitive energies present here. After putting so much effort into achieving oneness, anything that compromises or pushes against these attempts is very difficult for the 2.

UNASSERTIVE: In order to maintain the peace, the number 2 will set its own wants aside. Things may linger in an uncomfortable situation for much too long, quietly laboring to make it better on its own, rather than being more straightforward and efficient in its efforts. It will frequently prefer its existing experience over a fresh and alternative course.

Number Magick

Correspondences

ZODIAC: Gemini, Sagittarius
TAROT: The Empress
PERSONALITY TRAITS: Artistic, communicative, curious, jovial, naïve, optimistic, scattered, social, youthful.

The 3 tends to thrive in an optimistic and stimulating environment. It emits a youthful and enthusiastic outlook on life, as well as a huge zest for living. It goes from event to event, hoping to meet new friends along the way. The prized talent of the number 3 is communication, which it uses to develop a broad and engaging group of connections, partners, and best buddies.

The 3 is very original and values intelligent thought and creative expression. This number's creative, inquisitive attitude enables it to express abstract thoughts and discover answers that others may overlook. The number 3 is a kid at heart, and it never misses an opportunity to have fun, interact with people, and convey all the love and pleasure it symbolizes.

Strengths

COMMUNICATIVE: The 3 is a natural communicator who excels in all types of expression. It is overflowing with thoughts, plans, desires, and musings that must be shared with the rest of the world. The number 3 is an 'ideas person,' and by expressing these ideas, it draws supporting energies that can help it convert its thoughts into actual plans.

ARTISTIC: Color, music, creativity... everything that stimulates the senses has the number 3 stamped all over it. It understands that the written and spoken word can only get us so far. Words may transmit ideas, but art has the unrivalled ability to portray our emotions.

Number Magick

CHARMING: The number 3's magnetic personality makes it simple to attract others. Its upbeat mood and strong communication skills combine to generate a natural charm that captures and holds the attention of others. Without any attempting, the number 3 is the center of attention.

Weaknesses

NAIVE: Because of its youth and innocence, the number 3 is completely oblivious of the world's reality. Because it hasn't had the opportunity to get this mature knowledge via experience, it is prone to making poor judgments, placing itself in dangerous circumstances, and being burnt by others.

UNFOCUSED: This number is unfocused due to shiny-object syndrome. It is enthralled by everything it sees and will not stay focused in one direction for long before moving its attention elsewhere. It is so full of enthusiasm that it only wants to live, love, laugh, and create... which means that real-life objectives and progress go by the wayside.

SHALLOW: The 3 loves to live somewhat superficially in life and relationships. Going deeper would involve exposing oneself to possible negative and having to relate to emotions and situations with which it is unfamiliar. This number prioritizes enjoyment above progress; if something isn't playful and entertaining, the 3 would prefer not to engage at all.

Number Magick

Correspondences

ZODIAC: Cancer
TAROT: The Emperor
PERSONALITY TRAITS: Dependable, hard worker, loyal, organized, patient, practical, strict, strong, traditional.

Number 4 comes to the rescue when strength and efficiency are required. The 4 is a simple number that takes a straight-forward approach to life and business. It is incredibly reliable and provides a lot of steadiness to a person or situation. The 4 is committed to progress, albeit in a more conservative rather than progressive manner. It sticks to what has worked in the past instead of trying out new things.

In some Asian countries, the number 4 is even worse than the number 13 when it comes to bad luck. Tetraphobia is the word given to the dread of the number four. However, the number 4 carries a smart and reasonable energy that may provide us with a sense of stability and consistency. It knows right from wrong and sees everything in black and white, with no shades of grey. The number 4 leads with its intellect, not its emotions, and uses this cerebral fortitude to create a life of service and satisfaction.

Strengths

PRACTICAL: The 4 has a practical view on life and is not persuaded by the newest or shiniest product, event, or concept. This reason enables it to make sound judgments and devise strong approaches that can truly shift the needle. For the 4, rationality is the foundation of productivity.

LOYAL: The number 4 likes being reliable, and it will work hard all day to show how dedicated it is. It requires a firm foundation to feel at ease, therefore it will go to considerable lengths to establish secure, long-term connections, opportunities, and agreements.

Number Magick

SERVICE-ORIENTED: Service comes easily to the 4 because of its diligent character. It understands that time and effort are required to get the greatest outcomes, thus acts of service in relationships, employment, friendships, and at home are required to keep things moving smoothly. It's just another way the 4 generates stability, and it's willing to put in the effort.

Weaknesses

DOGMATIC: The number 4 has a highly conservative and rigid personal belief system. Once it has formed an opinion, it regards it as reality and has no qualms about teaching it to others. Unfortunately, this rigid method of thinking offers little opportunity for alternative viewpoints. While the 4 thinks it is being true to itself, it is actually restricting itself.

DULL: When it comes to choosing work over pleasure and adhering to established interests and pastimes, the number 4 might be a little monotonous. It might be a straight-edged person who isn't readily enthused and isn't interested in exploring or trying new things. It is completely content with its way of life; it is simply that others find it uninteresting.

RIGID: Because the number 4 is so rigid, it is difficult for it to be a team player. It's confident to the point of arrogance, always believing it's right and never permitting itself to be influenced. In some situations, this promise makes sense, but the 4 still has a lot to learn about giving and taking and working together.

Number Magick

Correspondences

ZODIAC: Leo, Virgo, Gemini
TAROT: The Hierophant
PERSONALITY TRAITS: Adventurous, energetic, flexible, inconsistent, independent, outgoing, restless, social, unpredictable.

Curiosity and the desire for a range of fascinating experiences are essential characteristics of the number 5. It yearns for freedom and adventure and isn't scared to let the wind take it wherever it desires. For the 5, life is about getting out there and experimenting, not establishing objectives and making plans. Anything that stimulates the senses captivates the 5's attention, and it eagerly awaits the opportunity to participate.

The number 5 is a leader of change, able to adapt and do well in a wide range of situations and with different people. Things are most enjoyable when they are fresh, vibrant, and full of potential. The 5 will turn to something more captivating the instant an activity becomes too normal or predictable. The only thing this number is genuinely attached to is the fact that it is unattached.

Strengths

CURIOUS: Unlike tunnel vision, the number 5 has 360-degree perspective and finds everything appealing. This inquisitive temperament leads to a range of intriguing and illuminating new encounters that few people have. Experimenting is the best technique to learn for the 5.

ADAPTABLE: Because this number does not stay with any one concept, career, relationship, or scenario for long, flexibility is essential. Its unattached emotions enable it greater mobility. Whether by choice or by circumstance, this number may readily shift gears and focus its attention and energy on its new situations.

Number Magick

SOCIAL: The 5 is an explorer who understands that interacting with others is one of the finest ways to learn about the world. This number thrives in social situations and never misses a chance to interact with and learn from a new person, whether in a dynamic one-on-one or group setting.

Weaknesses

NON-COMMITTAL: The number 5 is particularly non-committal due to an irrepressible craving for freedom and perpetual change. Committing, according to the 5, implies being bored and tied down, which contradicts all it stands for. Because this number lacks the focus to see things through, it is difficult to form lasting connections and become proficient in life skills.

UNRELIABLE: Easily distracted and sometimes too inquisitive, the number 5 has difficulty focusing long enough to follow through on tasks and promises. This inconsistency is harmful to all commitments and relationships, and it may make the 5 appear inept and careless.

NO DIRECTION: This number is content to merely go with the flow of life. However, since it lacks direction, the 5 consumes a lot of time on activities that do not really serve a purpose while passing up possibilities that may help it succeed. The 5 may have realized in retrospect that they should have planned more thoroughly.

Number Magick

6 Correspondences

ZODIAC: Virgo, Taurus, Libra
TAROT: The Lovers
PERSONALITY TRAITS: Caring, compassionate, harmonious, healing, idealistic, nurturing, protective, romantic, warm.

Representing the heart, a 6 has the capacity to nurture, care for and heal through unconditional love. A force of kindness and understanding, it may be the beacon of hope we all need in our lives. It is responsible for using its heart and soul to assist others.

The 6 shines in all types of relationships, but especially in emotional ones. Its empathy helps people feel comfortable letting their guard down and being honest and transparent about their feelings, allowing it to comprehend and give the necessary assistance. Everyone could use someone who exemplifies the 6's dedicated enthusiasm.

Strengths

SUPPORTIVE: When a shoulder is required, the number 6 will be the first to come, armed with a compassionate, soothing presence and sincere guidance. It does not merely wait to speak, but listens and attempts to understand so that it might target its compassion and healing where it is most needed.

PROTECTIVE: The 6's unconditional love extends to all beings and enables it to speak up for those who lack a voice. When it comes to family, though, this defense becomes even more ferocious. Anything that undermines the emotional or spiritual equilibrium of its loved ones will infuriate the 6.

Number Magick

ROMANTIC: The number 6 is the most romantic of all. It works hard to foster calm, cooperative partnerships and speaks all love languages fluently. The number 6 is only content when its other half is content, thus it will devote all of its time, support, and dedication to making this happen.

Weaknesses

PASSIVE: In order to satisfy others and preserve the peace, the number 6 may frequently allow itself to be taken advantage of. More aggressive, commanding energies may easily dominate the 6, who would sooner accept an unfavorable decision than speak up and cause a stir.

SELF-SACRIFICING: While compassion is a virtue, the number 6 is so eager to sacrifice itself for the benefit of others and harmony, it completely ignores its own needs and well-being. There are only so many hours in the day, and this number frequently misses the self-care that would make it seem more balanced. As the proverb goes, it is impossible to pour from an empty cup.

IDEALISTIC: The 6 wants everyone to treat others the same way it does, which it believes would result in a flawless world. However, that is not how the actual world works, and when this number finds its goals are unreachable, it may experience tremendous distress and imbalance.

Number Magick

Correspondences

ZODIAC: Libra, Pisces
TAROT: The Chariot
PERSONALITY TRAITS: Analytical, intellectual, introspective, mysterious, perceptive, reserved, skeptical, solitary, spiritual.

The number 7 is both profound and intelligent. Simple explanations and superficial understanding are inadequate; this is trivial information. It knows the true gold is hidden deeper and will not stop digging until it finds it... and then it will dig some more. The 7 employs a variety of particular talents in its quest for knowledge, including questioning, investigating, listening, and perceiving.

Though spirituality is extremely important to the number 7, it prefers an intellectual rather than an emotional approach to life. It is a number that likes accumulating and sifting information in order to discover answers. Nonetheless, it has a stronger intuition than you may imagine, which it employs as a guide. This mix of conscious and subconscious thinking enables the mind of number 7 to shine a light into the most inaccessible places in order to uncover hidden truths.

Strengths

SPIRITUAL: There always seems to be something unseen on a deeper level, and because of this, the 7 tends to be more spiritually inclined. While religion is too confining for this limitless number, a highly intimate, intellectual relationship to the spiritual realm adds wonder and depth to its experiences.

CURIOUS: With a limitless amount of unanswered questions, the universe is a fascinating place for the number 7. It seeks to get as much knowledge and insight as possible and is interested in a variety of topics. Whether feasible or theoretical, the 7 always has an inquisitive mind.

Number Magick

ANALYTICAL: The number 7 is more than simply a sponge for information. While it is driven to gather as much information as possible, its greatest strength is analyzing what it learns. The ability to distinguish what is beneficial from what is pointless, and to distinguish reality from fiction aids the 7 in staying on track and following the most important wisdom.

Weaknesses

RECLUSIVE: Spending much of its time deep in meditation and research, and does not value the lighter side of life. A lack of social connection progressively pulls the number seven inside, limiting its life experiences and making it difficult to create new friendships and love connections.

SECRETIVE: This number prefers to keep its cards close. The 7 is not trying to conceal harmful information; it just does not feel the need for everyone to know everything about itself. It is difficult to connect with individuals on a genuine level if you never let them see your actual self.

SUSPICIOUS: Due to its insatiable need to delve under the surface, the number 7 may destroy a positive situation by leaping to conclusions and accusations or searching for solutions where none exist. It's constantly assuming there's more to the tale when there isn't.

Number Magick

Correspondences

ZODIAC: Scorpio, Capricorn
TAROT: Strength
PERSONALITY TRAITS: Accomplished, authoritative, balanced, dedicated, goal-oriented, materialistic, professional, prosperous, strong.

The number 8 is the achiever in numerology, and it assesses life based on its achievements. It possesses sound business judgement, a commanding presence, and a strong desire to succeed. The number 8 is also a sign of equilibrium, as seen by its symmetrical form. It returns one blessing to the universe for every one it gets. When things are harmonized, they seem solid, regulated, and supported, which creates the most productive working environment for the 8.

The number 8 is regarded the luckiest number in Chinese culture, and it is purposely incorporated into marital dates, birth dates, residences, and money. People have been known to modify their names to add additional 8s to their numerology chart in an attempt to reach the same level of success as this number. The number 8 signifies the pinnacle of success, which many people will strive for their whole life.

Strengths

AMBITIOUS: It would be an understatement to say that the 8 is ambitious; they thrive on success! This number seeks to accomplish as many goals and attain as much success as possible. It adopts strategic methods and is dedicated to its mission. The wonderful sentiments that come from achievement provide the 8 with all it requires to continue ascending.

KARMIC: The number 8 is all about giving back in a spiritual way. It recognizes that its triumphs are not solely due to its own efforts and will consciously acknowledge and appreciate any assistance received. It balances achievement with thankfulness, which may then be rebalanced with further achievement — the 8 is always generating a cycle of success.

Number Magick

ENDURING: Even when the odds are against it, the 8 demonstrates a high level of persistence. It is aware that it is competent, but that capability isn't always the only element at work. The 8 is confident that with perseverance and work, the situation will improve. It is willing to endure adversity because it knows that success lies on the other side.

Weaknesses

MATERIALISTIC: The 8 enjoys celebrating its achievements by surrounding itself with lovely things. This is seen as a reward for the individual and a chance to start the cycle of manifestation over again. Others might think that the number 8 is shallow or pretentious because of this trait. It may also attract fraudsters who misunderstand the aim of the 8.

AUTHORITATIVE: It is hardly surprising that all of this success has gone straight to the head of number 8. The person has adapted to being in charge, which makes them feel like it has power over others. However, with a 'my way or the highway' attitude, the 8 tends to disregard the efforts and ideas of others, and therefore losing the trust faster than it was gained.

ENTITLED: The 8 isn't looking for permission or apologies. Its goal for success may make it oblivious to laws and regulations, but ignoring these limits and putting issues into one's own hands makes cooperation impossible and drives a wedge between partnerships. The number 8 has become used to achieving its goals and now expects to do so.

Number Magick

Correspondences

ZODIAC: *Sagittarius, Aries*
TAROT: *The Hermit*
PERSONALITY TRAITS: *Accepting, aware, compassionate, experienced, humanitarian, kind, sacrificial, spiritual, wise.*

The number 9's energy implies completeness but not an end. Consider it in a cyclical sense; it's about the conclusion of one cycle and the opportunity for another to begin. In numerology, the number 9 functions as an usher in this process of change or transformation, leading and empowering us with its knowledge. It receives answers from a divine source and then transmits them to us in the physical realm.

This number is compassionate at heart. It is caring, kind, and determined to make the most possible good. The number 9 has been through a lot and as a result is wiser, stronger, and more conscious. Because of these firsthand experiences, they are more empathetic of those who are hurting and eager to give essential help.

Strengths

AWAKENING: The number 9 has discovered the worth and significance of its inner wisdom via life experience. It is now capable of awakening people to their own higher self. The 9 demonstrates how to manage adversity with grace and empathy, teaching others to do the same.

TOLERANT: Unlike other numbers, which only perceive black and white, the number 9 sees the limitless shades of grey in between. It does not distinguish between races, faiths, or ways of life; instead, it provides everyone room and respect. A healthy absence of prejudice and judgement allows the 9 to regard everyone as valued and deserving of its support.

Number Magick

SUPPORTIVE: The number 9's warm heart draws many souls seeking assistance. Regardless of its own circumstances, it acknowledges its need to aid others on their path. It understands how the world works and what it takes to survive difficult circumstances, making it a useful source of wisdom, comfort, and healing for others.

Weaknesses

RESENTFUL: The number 9 has been through a lot that has left a deep impression on its heart. When the 9 does not allow itself to analyze and heal these traumas, it puts a shadow on its spirit and severely effects its current connections.

SACRIFICING: This number is sacrificing to a fault. It believes it is performing a responsibility by being available in whatever way is needed to the people around them, yet this is a sacrifice attitude. The 9 is so concerned with caring for someone else that it neglects to care for itself, laying the groundwork for an unbalanced and distracted existence.

SUFFERING: As a result of the difficulties the number 9 has faced, it may come to believe that life is a painful experience. It may prioritize moments of hardship over those of ease, or stormy partnerships over balanced ones. The more 9 accepts adversity, the more frequent it may become.

What are Master Numbers?

Master Numbers like 11, 22, and 33 can mean both good and bad things. Most people notice single-digit numbers, but double-digit numbers have all the power. A Master Number, according to numerology, might indicate trouble, but it can also indicate tremendous power, thus possessing one is a real blessing. You may have a happy and prosperous life if you are able to cope with the unexpected events that the numbers throw your way.

Because the numbers are rooted in the digits 1, 2 and 3, the only Master Numbers in numerology will be 11, 22 and 33. The Triangle of Enlightenment is made up of these numbers. These profound energies represent the three stages of creation: visualizing, constructing, and sharing. Number 11 is the visionary, 22 is the builder or architect of that vision, and 33 introduces it to the world.

Master Numbers appear in our life in various ways. They may appear in your numerology charts as core numbers derived from your Life Path Number or name. This is why it is critical to be in sync with all elements of our numerology in order to discover where these powers may be lurking.

Master Number Meanings

11 The Master Intuitive

The number 11 symbolizes your emotions, subconscious, sensitivities, and intuition. Although Master Number 11 contains vibrations from number 2 (1 + 1 = 2), it is greatly affected by leadership, cooperation, and support.
Your intuition, gut feeling, and indirect signals from the universe are extremely significant to you. This might result in tremendous anxiety and a lot of restless energy. You most likely have an issue with being skeptical and cautious for no apparent cause.

If you aren't focusing on something precise, your energy will be scattered. But when you channel all that anxious energy into something tangible, you may easily create something magickal. Of course, if you don't keep this power in check, you can end up overthinking.

If you ignore your instincts, you might do more harm than good. Because Master Number 11 is so focused on trust, following your intuition rather than seeking for physical evidence is more crucial.

What are Master Numbers?

When your intuition is multiplied by 11, it might be tough to overcome these obstacles, but the most essential person to trust in you is yourself. Take chances, follow your heart, and enjoy life in the spur of the moment. And if you get a terrible feeling about anything, trust yourself.

22 The Master Builder

The 22 Master Number represents balance, confidence, innovation, and intellect. In numerology, Master Number 22 also denotes power in terms of productivity, bringing huge ideas to reality.

Master Number 22 is inspired by the number 4 (2 + 2 = 4), which signifies mental stability, patience, and determination, and it also contains energy from the number 11.

You have little trouble accomplishing tasks if you are a Master Number 22. You have a strong character trait that makes you efficient in bringing your dreams to fruition.

However, "with great power comes great responsibility." You have a history of pushing yourself too far and, as a result, not fully using the immense strength that comes with Master Number 22.

Life would be simpler if you took the time to trust in your skills rather than beating yourself up for not meeting your goals on time. You're already grounded, sensible, and a diligent worker.

Having those three attributes is fantastic, and you don't have to deliver results all of the time to demonstrate your worth.

It is known as the Master Builder and most influential number in numerology since it has the ability to make any dream a reality.

What are Master Numbers?

33 The Master Teacher

Master Number 33 is the most spiritually advanced of the Master Numbers and is regarded as the Master Teacher. It amplifies the powers of previous numbers to new heights and has the potential to impart knowledge and truth on others.

Number 6 transmits humility, care, and compassion to Master Number 33. It is Life Path Number 6's higher vibration and is quite uncommon. Master Number 33 combines the abilities of both 11 and 22, bringing them all together in this number.

However, guess what? That implies they have twice as many disadvantages. Because of their powers, it is one of the hardest things to stay in control.

If your Master Number is 33, you are an exceptionally creative and pleasant person who, if not balanced, may be quite judgmental and critical. You can make your ideas come to life and help other people do the same. You could say you have Saint Joan of Arc's spirit within you.

People with Master Number 33 frequently lack personal ambition; their primary aims are related to the greater benefit of humanity and what they can do to improve society as a whole.

Because 33 is so uncommon, even if it occurs in your chart, it isn't always necessarily regarded a Master Number. If 33 is discovered in your core numbers (Life Path, heart's desire, personality, maturity, or personal expression numbers), the Master Number direction can only be applied to those; otherwise, it should be viewed as two different numbers and joined together to produce 6.

Angel Numbers

Angel Numbers

Angel numbers are series of numbers (usually three or four) that repeat and/or follow patterns (such as 111 or 4444, and 321 or 8787). Even though these numbers can show up in the most unexpected places, they usually catch our eye and make us wonder, even if only for a short time. People are drawn to these sequences, though, because of what they mean. People think that these numbers are messages from the spiritual universe that give people direction, wisdom, and knowledge.

Angel numbers can tell you if you're on the right path, give you important information about a complicated situation, or even explain the powerful, mysterious meaning of recurring themes in your life, whether you think they come from angels, guides, ancestors, spirits, or just a higher level of your own consciousness.

If you can believe it, people have known for hundreds of years that numbers that repeat have power and meaning. The ancient Greek philosopher Pythagoras was a gifted mathematician who believed that human existence is a tangible manifestation of the vibrational energy of numbers.

During the previous two decades, this idea has swept the metaphysical community. Whether you think angels are providing you hyper-specific messages or that your subconscious is verifying your awareness, angel numbers have left an everlasting impression on human psyche.

Angel numbers aren't related to your birthday, unlike other esoteric pursuits. Angel Numbers aren't based on your birth date, time, or location like zodiac signs, astrological birth charts, or numerology life path numbers. While your zodiac sign shows your likes, dislikes, interests, and preferences, your angel number shows how you interact with the world, not who you are.

Another important thing about angel numbers is that they change all the time. You might see the same angel number for years, or you might only see it once. There is no order to how you find this mystical signature, so a long-term connection is not more important than a one-time observation. What matters most is that you pay attention and notice.

Numerology, Angel Numbers and any other divinatory method is all subjective. Resources should not be prescriptive, but rather provide context — the more you study, the more at ease you will be growing your own thoughts, impressions, and interpretations. Because your understanding and experiences are unique to you, don't be afraid to dig into your own life as you get closer to spirituality.

Angel Number Meanings

In numerology, every number means something different, and angel numbers are no exception. As you start to build your own relationship with angel numbers, you can use the strong spiritual meanings of numbers to figure out what certain sequences mean.

000 or 0000

The number zero is connected with fresh opportunities. When you see a zero in a group of three, four, or in a pattern, it could be a sign of a new start. You are at the start of a new cycle, which means you may create whatever your heart wishes. At this stage in your journey, don't be hesitant to make large, bold decisions.

111 or 1111

One is a significant manifestation figure. If you see the number one as an angel number in groups of three, four, or in a pattern, you should be aware that the universe is giving you a 'green light' to plant a seed, manifest your intentions or wish for something. You are getting a lot of help from your ancestors and guides at this time, so the present and the future are connected in a very active way.

222 or 2222

The number two signifies equilibrium, trust, and alignment. Seeing two consecutively in a set of three, four, or inside a pattern, might signify that someone on the physical or spiritual level is helping you reach your goal. When you see twos, it may be prudent to call your most reliable ally to see whether divine cooperation is possible.

333 or 3333

Three indicates creative magnetism. If the number three shows up in a sequence, or in a set of three or four, this angel number signifies that there is a situation that you may be part of that could use one of your special skills. Furthermore, the presence of three signifies that by tapping into your natural talents, you will find greater worth in whatever situation you are in. Your artistic expression is really important!

Angel Number Meanings

444 or 4444

Stability is what the number four means. Seeing four as an angel number in a set of three, four, or in a pattern, means that you are in the process of anchoring, digging in, and building a very long-lasting infrastructure. Don't be hesitant to ask for guidance or assistance while engaging with four, especially if you're managing long-term tasks that demand unique skills. This is really about creating trust, which will allow you to advance to greater levels.

555 or 5555

The existence of five indicates that significant changes are possible. If you've been feeling stuck, stifled, or inspired, seeing the number five as an angel number in a set of three, four, or in a pattern, means that big changes are coming. For now, these changes are happening behind the scenes, which means that important people are still weighing their options. However, if you see the number 5 as an angel number, it means you're heading in the right direction.

666 or 6666

Some people are afraid of the number six (especially in a triplet) because they believe it is related to the devil or other demonic figures. However, in angel numbers, the number six is helpful, kind, and understanding when it is part of a set of three, four, or in a pattern. Six might serve as a comforting and much-needed reminder to treat oneself with kindness and compassion. With angel number six on your side, you understand that you have the ability to choose how you see a situation and that everything unfolds for a purpose.

777 or 7777

Seven is a lucky number in angels just like it is in casinos! The appearance of seven as an angel number in a group of three, four, or inside a pattern, implies good fortune, especially financial good fortune. Because new financial chances may appear, seven encourages you to expand out and seek options outside of your comfort zone.

Short-term engagements may turn into rich, reliable revenue streams, thus merging your faith and ideals is the ideal embodiment of this energy.

Angel Number Meanings

888 or 8888

The number eight is one of the most heavenly in numerology, and perceiving it as an angel number (either inside a group of three, four, or within a pattern) might signify a deep link to the spiritual realms. Those who believe in an afterlife may interpret the number eight as a sign that they are getting supernatural assistance from loved ones who have passed on. Fundamentally, the number eight represents infinity — the never-ending cycle that transcends any single lifetime — so don't be hesitant to follow your intuition when this angel number emerges.

999 or 9999

The presence of nine, as the final digit in numerology, indicates that a chapter is drawing to a close. Witnessing nine as an angel number (either inside a set of three, four, or within a pattern) indicates that an important cycle is coming to an end, and you'll soon be embarking on a new adventure. Similarly, it is a good moment to get out of your comfort zone, broaden your horizons, and explore new territory. Whether you want to start a new job or go back to school, the spiritual realm will undoubtedly support your bold decisions.

One of my favorite elements about angel numbers is that their significance is unique to each individual. For example, one individual may interpret "333" as a sign that they are on the correct path, whilst another may interpret "333" as confirmation of intuition. When you see an angel number, stop, get a pen and paper (or the notes app on your phone), and scribble down any thoughts, ideas, or impressions that come to mind. That way, you may develop a unique relationship with that angel number, and if it appears in the future, you will already know what that sequence symbolizes in your life.

On the following pages, you will find an angel number tracker so you can keep a record of all the times you see these numbers to start understanding their message more clearly.

Angel Numbers Record

ANGEL NUMBER	TIME & PLACE	SIGNIFICANCE

Angel Numbers Record

ANGEL NUMBER	TIME & PLACE	SIGNIFICANCE

The Seven Magickal Days

Moon phases are an effective tool for timing rituals and witchcraft. However, did you realize there are other substitutes? What if you can't wait for the full moon? Can you utilize another day of the week? Of course. In this section, we'll look at the magickal days of the week as an alternative and quicker method to timing your rituals.

In several pagan traditions, the days of the week are integral components of spellcasting. For instance, spells promoting richness or success may be performed on Thursday, as the day is connected with wealth and desire. Due to the days connotations, it may be best to work on a business or communication-related spell on a Wednesday. While not all traditions adhere to this principle, if you conduct any magickal activity, always document the day of the week on which the spell is performed. You may be shocked to find some connections in the future!

Every day is magickal; thus, rather than waiting for a planet to move or for the moon to cycle, you may harness the energy of a specific day of the week. Understanding how to employ the daily energies can be a significant boost to your magickal practice. As a result, this will assist you in increasing the energy force of your spellwork. Additionally, understanding the associated correspondences of each day can assist you in selecting the optimal day to maximize your magickal intentions in a variety of ways. In essence, incorporating this information into your practice will enable you to more precisely manifest your wishes with greater focus.

Each day of the week is associated with a certain planet, connected with a masculine or feminine energy, a deity or deities, earth elements, stones, crystals, and so forth. When utilizing these magickal energies, begin by identifying the magickal weekday that best suits your objectives. Following that, when you prepare your spellwork or ritual, consider the many parts of that day that you might be able to include into your efforts. This considerably increases the effectiveness of your intentions.

You may feel pressed for time to add to your magickal practice. Between work, cooking, having a social life and trying to catch every curveball that comes your way, you have maybe around twenty minutes to practice magick - sure, no problem. Magick doesn't have to be complicated to work. The most potent magick is simple, practical, and heartfelt.

And whether you're a seasoned hand or a beginning practitioner, you'll always want to learn more. Observing daily correspondences with fresh, realistic, and an open-minded view allows you to expand your knowledge and give you opportunities to find new skills.

Sunday

Sunday is linked with our closest star, the sun. This day is brimming with enchantment and all manner of fantastic possibilities for success, fortune, and fame. Sundays are for personal accomplishments of any form, such as pursuing a promotion at work, pursuing fame and fortune, or receiving recognition for a job well done. All of these objectives are influenced by the sun.

Correspondences

Element: Fire   **Zodiac:** Leo   **Planet:** Sun

Colors: Gold, orange, yellow.   **Energy:** Masculine

Crystals:
Amber, carnelian, citrine, diamond, quartz, sunstone, tigers eye, topaz.

Herbs & Incense:
Amber, calendula, cedar, chamomile, cinnamon, cloves, frankincense, heliotrope, marigold, sunflower.

Deities:
Amaterasu, Apollo, Aurora, Bastet, Belenos, Bridget, Freyr, Helios, Ra, Sekhmet, Sulis, Sunna.

Magickal Intentions & Associations:
Abundance, enlightenment, fame, growth, healing, miracles, promotion, prosperity, strength, success, wealth.

Sunday

NOTES | SPELLWORK | RITUALS | THOUGHTS

Monday

This weekday is dedicated to our lunar satellite the moon, and all of her enchantment and mystery. Mondays are dedicated to the mysteries of women, illusion, prophetic dreaming, feelings and emotions, travel, and fertility. Monday would be a great day if you need to do any sort of Moon Magick, but cannot wait until the appropriate phase or cycle comes around.

Correspondences

Energy: Feminine

Element: Water   **Zodiac:** Cancer   **Planet:** Moon

Colors: Light blue, light grey, pearl, silver, white.

Crystals:
Amethyst, aquamarine, fluorite, moonstone, opal, pearl, quartz, sapphire, selenite, silver.

Herbs & Incense:
Catnip, chamomile, comfrey, gardenia, jasmine, lotus, mint, moonflower, sage, white rose, willow, wintergreen.

Deities:
Artemis, Diana, Hecate, Kalfu, Luna, Phoebe, Selena, Selene, Thoth.

Magickal Intentions & Associations:
Dreaming, emotional balance, femininity, fertility, friendship, illusion, intuition, justice, peace, psychic abilities, shadow work, sleep, spirituality, women's mysteries.

Monday

NOTES | SPELLWORK | RITUALS | THOUGHTS

Tuesday

Tuesday is a Mars day, and similar to the god of war, today is an excellent time to invoke magick to summon power and courage. This weekday is set aside for rebels and fighters. Tuesday is the best day of the week if you are facing any form of challenge, need a boost of courage, or want to strengthen your passions.

Correspondences

Element: Water & Fire   **Zodiac:** Aries & Scorpio   **Planet:** Mars

Colors: Black, orange, pink, red.   **Energy:** Masculine

Crystals:
Bloodstone, carnelian, flint, garnet, red jasper, rhodonite, ruby.

Herbs & Incense:
Dragon's blood, hawthorn, nettle, red flowers and plants associated with Mars, thistle, thorns, wormwood.

Deities:
Any war or justice deity, Apollo, Ares, Bran, Kali, Lilith, Maeve, Mars, Sekhmet, The Morrigan, Tiu, Tiwaz, Tyr, Valkyries.

Magickal Intentions & Associations:
Banishing, binding, conflict, courage, justice, legal matters, protection, rebellion, reversal, self confidence, strength, success, war.

Tuesday

NOTES | SPELLWORK | RITUALS | THOUGHTS

Wednesday

Wednesdays are outlandish and bizarre days. They are used for communication, adaptation, cunning, and the arts. This is a Mercury day, and being the patron deity of mysteries, change, and excitement, this day is brimming with them.

Correspondences

Element: Earth **Zodiac:** Virgo **Planet:** Mercury

Colors: Magenta, orange, purple, yellow. **Energy:** Masculine

Crystals:
Agate, aventurine, citrine, emerald, hematite, lapis lazuli, sodalite.

Herbs & Incense:
Apple, aspen, cherry, chervil, eucalyptus, fennel, fern, lavender, licorice, lilies, mugwort, plantain, poppy, rosemary.

Deities:
Athena, Hermes, Lady Fortuna, Lugh, Mercury, Odin, Woden.

Magickal Intentions & Associations:
Business, chance, communication, contracts, creativity, debt, education, fortune, healing, music, the arts, transportation, wisdom.

Wednesday

NOTES | SPELLWORK | RITUALS | THOUGHTS

Thursday

Thursday is the day of Jupiter. This is the weekday of wealth, abundance, and health. Thursday is designated as "Thor's day." This Norse god bestowed upon the day his name and other characteristics, including power and abundance.

Correspondences

Energy: Masculine

Element: Water & Fire

Zodiac: Pisces & Sagittarius

Colors: Green, purple, royal blue.

Planet: Jupiter

Crystals:
Amethyst, lapis lazuli, lepidolite, sapphire, sugilite, turquoise.

Herbs & Incense:
Beech, cedar, cinnamon, cinquefoil, clove, honeysuckle, melissa, nutmeg, oak, pine, saffron, sage.

Deities:
Juno, Jupiter, Thor, Zeus.

Magickal Intentions & Associations:

Abundance, business, career success, cleansing, consecration, education, good luck, harvest, healing, honor, legal matters, loyalty, merchants, military, prosperity, protection, storms, travel, wealth.

Thursday

NOTES | SPELLWORK | RITUALS | THOUGHTS

Friday

Venus' day is Friday, both as a planet and as the Roman goddess of love. This day is also sacred to a number of other gods and goddesses of love, including Eros, Venus, Aphrodite, and the Norse goddess Freyja, who bestowed the day's name. On this day of the week, subjects such as love, birth, fertility, and romance are discussed.

Correspondences

Energy: Feminine

Element: Air & Earth

Zodiac: Libra & Taurus

Colors: Aqua, grey, pink, white.

Planet: Venus

Crystals:
Coral, emerald, jade, lapis lazuli, malachite, moonstone, peridot, pink tourmaline, rose quartz, ruby.

Herbs & Incense:
Apple blossoms, birch, blue lotus, cardamom, feverfew, ivy, jasmine, red hibiscus, rose, rosemary, saffron, sage, strawberries, violet.

Deities:
Aphrodite, Freya, Frigg, Venus.

Magickal Intentions & Associations:
Alliances, balance, beauty, birth, bringing the new into your life - new energy, fertility, friendship, grace, harmony, love, music, new people, new projects, passion, pregnancy, prosperity, romance, sex, the arts.

Friday

NOTES | SPELLWORK | RITUALS | THOUGHTS

Saturday

Named after the god Saturn, this deity was the keeper of karma and time. This day, of course, is related with Saturn and is our final day of the week. Saturdays are traditionally excellent days for protection, expelling a negative circumstance, and generally cleaning up whatever magickal messes you've been ignoring.

Correspondences

Element: Earth, Air, Fire & Water

Colors: Black, dark purple, grey, red.

Energy: Masculine

Zodiac: Capricorn & Aquarius

Planet: Saturn

Crystals:
Amethyst, apache tear, black onyx, hematite, jet, obsidian, serpentine, smoky quartz.

Herbs & Incense:
Black poppy seeds, cypress, ivy, mandrake, mullein, myrrh, oak, thyme, wolfsbane.

Deities:
Cronus, Hecate, Oshun, Saturn, Set, The Norns, Yemaya.

Magickal Intentions & Associations:
Banishing, binding, cleansing, completion, duty, family, knowledge, locating lost items, manifesting, meditation, protection, psychic defense, self transformation, self-discipline, spirituality, time, values & morals, wisdom.

Saturday

NOTES | SPELLWORK | RITUALS | THOUGHTS

Magickal Times of the Day

Magickal Times of the Day

In addition to the days of the week, you also have the option to perform your spellwork or rituals at specific times throughout the day to enhance the success rate.

1 AM - Focus on self, new beginnings, banishing any shadows, quiet stillness.

2 AM - Banishing negativity and toxicity, especially between two people.

3 AM - Thoughts, determination, will-power, focus.

4 AM - Earth energies, success, improved luck. Best time for meditation and connection to the divine.

5 AM - Activity, spiritual growth, health, psychic insight.

6 AM - Beginnings, devotion, perseverance, tenacity, decision making, wisdom.

7 AM - Hope, awareness, improved insight, perspective, memory.

8 AM - Personal transformation through the conscious mind.

9 AM - Seeking, helping or assisting others, focus.

10 AM - Awakening, resolution, better decision-making, confidence, work related matters.

11 AM - Vision, law of attraction, transformation for things that may have seemed impossible.

1 PM - Cycles, personal security, self image, personal refuge.

2 PM - Progress, sexual symmetry, understanding, movement in relationships.

3 PM - Symmetry of the mind, body and spirit.

4 PM - Timely work, magick to boost intentions, goal-oriented energy.

5 PM - Knowing yourself, messages from the spirit realm.

6 PM - Creative achievements, safety, completion, protection magick.

7 PM - Kindness, empathy, diversity, making amends through love, healing.

8 PM - Putting thoughts into action, taking on a key role.

9 PM - Seeing the big picture, the souls contract.

10 PM - Clear goals, clear mindedness, sensibility, recognition.

11 PM - Communication, positively coping with change, receiving.

Magickal Times of the Day

DAWN: Beginnings, hope, the season of Spring.

MORNING: Conscious mind, authority, keen perception.

NOON: Sun magick, fire magick, reason, banishing darkness, the season of Summer, karma.

DUSK: Completion, closure, endings, the season of Fall.

NIGHT: Rest, health, moon magick, star magick, the season of Winter.

MIDNIGHT: The Witching Hour, spirit communication, astral travel, faery magick, glamour magick.

Magickal Times of the Day

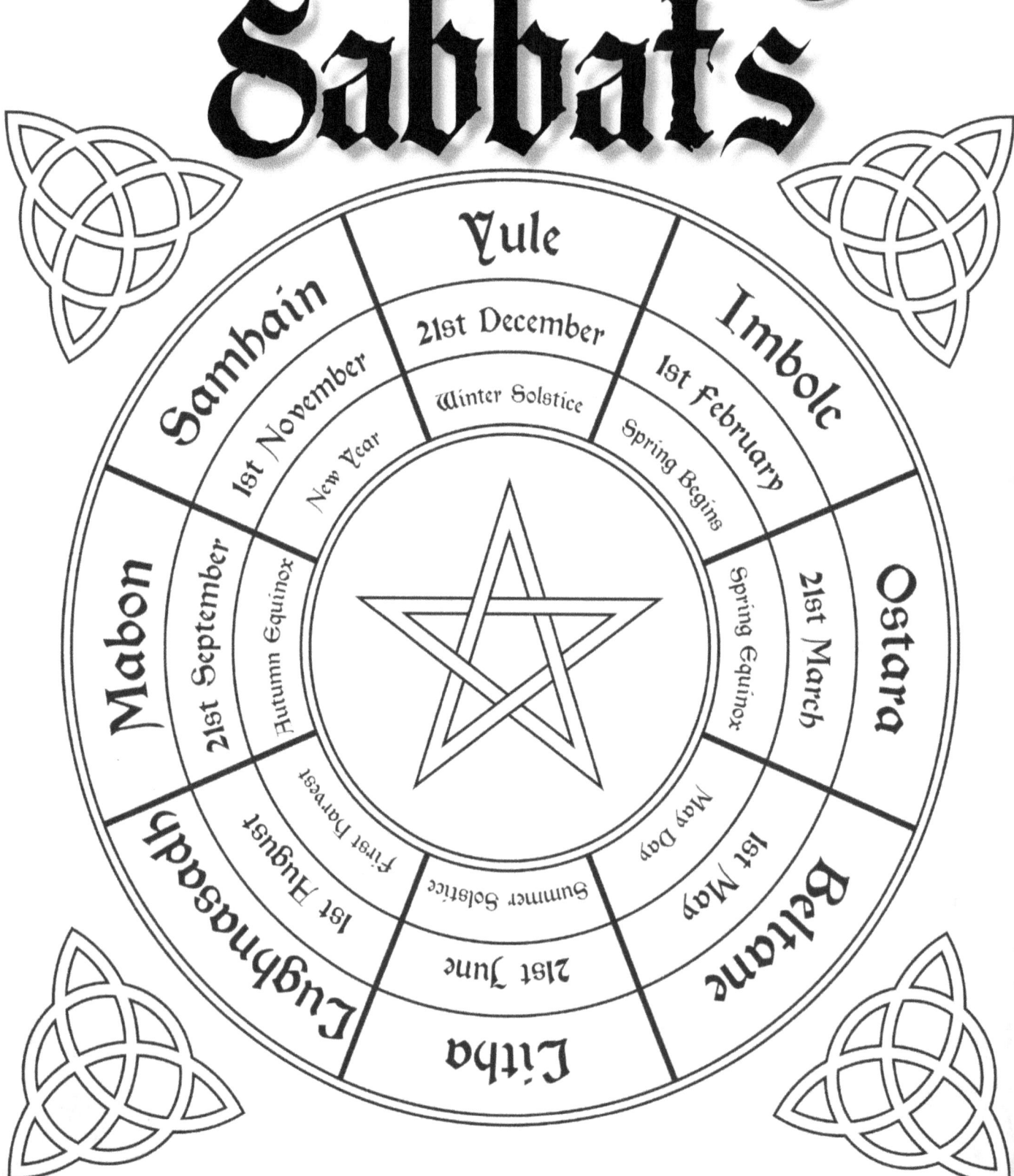

What are Sabbats?

Numerous modern pagan traditions are founded around eight sabbats, or seasonal celebrations. While each sabbat has a unique history, they are always honored by interacting with nature in some way. From Samhain through to Mabon, the Wheel of the Year, the yearly cycle of seasons, has been influenced by tradition, history, and magick.

Sabbats (pronounced sab-bats) are the eight major annual festivals observed by Wiccans and many other Pagans. These are chances for Pagans to realize the fundamental connection between the spiritual and physical realms, between the earth (and its seasonal changes) and the supernatural. The Sabbat holidays go from sunset to sunset, and the majority of ceremonies and magick occur at night.

It is common to refer to four of the celebrations as "the greater Sabbats" and four of them as "the lesser Sabbats," depending on their origins in ancient Celtic or Western European traditions. In the Wheel of the Year, there is a rotation between a festival dedicated to solar events and a festival dedicated to earth-centered events. One can worship gods and goddesses, celebrate changes in the natural world and call on spiritual abilities to apply healing magick in each of these occasions. It is not uncommon for pagans to gather during the sabbat to participate in community rituals.

In addition to the two Equinoxes (Spring and Fall), the four seasonal Sabbats contain two solstices (Winter and Summer). All four of these festivals are dedicated to celebrating the passage of time and light, among other things. The Equinoxes represent points of equilibrium between darkness and light, whereas the solstice marks a change from light to darkness or darkness to light. The Winter Solstice, or Yule, is the first sabbat, since the Wheel of the Year begins on November 1.

The sabbats are celebrated as holidays by witches from all walks of life, regardless of their religious affiliation. The cornerstones of nature's never-ending cycle of life are found in these occasions. The sabbats are commonly shown by putting them around the Wheel of the Year.

Known as the sun sabbats or lesser sabbats, Yule, Ostara, Litha, and Mabon are the celebrations that mark the start of each season. These are often referred to as the solstices and equinoxes. The four greater moon sabbats are Imbolc, Beltane, Lammas, and Samhain. Each season has a halfway point marked by these holidays, which always happen on the same day regardless of the year.

Yule

Dates: December 20 - 23

Winter Solstice - December 21st *Festival of Light*
Yuletide *Shortest day of the Year*

In the Northern Hemisphere, people know the Winter Solstice as Yule. It is a time for contemplation, storytelling, honoring friendship, and greeting the return of the Horned God (Cernunnos or Kernuno), as symbolized by the return of the light, during the shortest day and longest night of the year.

During the winter solstice, people of all religions, faiths and backgrounds get together with their families and friends. The season of rebirth and renewal is celebrated by Wiccans and Pagans around the solstice, known as Yule, when the sun returns to the earth. When the traditional new year starts is a good time to do magick. Embrace the dormant season of the soil by welcoming sunshine and warmth into your dwelling.

Yule is the time of year when some people believe that the sun deity is reborn, bringing light back to the world. It also symbolizes the never-ending cycle of the seasons, as the Holly King passes his authority to the Oak King.

Reflection takes precedence over activity throughout the winter months. At Yule, it's customary to reflect. It's a good time to reflect on the year that's passed and share stories about the adventures you've had. During this holiday season, we remember our loved ones who have passed on and offer them a special place to celebrate with us.

The burning of the Yule log, which symbolizes the light that may be discovered in the darkness, is one of the most essential components of Yule. The log is typically kept burning all night to serve as a reminder that no matter how dark things become, we can always endure. The tradition of saving a chunk of the Yule log for the following year's fire is a metaphor for nature's cyclical existence.

Yule

Correspondences

Themes — Longest night of the year, hope after the darkness, transformation, rebirth, new beginnings, new life, honoring the triple goddess, welcoming the sun child.

Symbols — Yule log, mistletoe, evergreens, pinecones, bells, holly, ivy, wreaths, poinsettias, lights, gifts, yule tree, bayberry candles.

Colors — Red, Green, White, Gold, Silver.

Food — Cookies and cakes, gingerbread, apple cider, baked apples, eggnog, turkey, nuts, roast beef, pears, fruitcake, mulled wine, ham, bread, pork.

Herbs — Holly, mistletoe, pine, oak, fir, birch, hazel, sandalwood, myrrh, frankincense, cinnamon, nutmeg, cloves, cedar, balsam, blessed thistle, sage, rosemary, valerian.

Crystals — Ruby, garnet, emerald, diamond, bloodstone, tiger's eye, cat's eye, citrine, green tourmaline, alexandrite, pearls.

Spells — Happiness, goal-setting, hope, peace, strengthening bonds, celebrate the longest night, spells for success, personal and family blessings, cleansing home and altar.

Animals — Cardinal, dove, bear, stag, reindeer, squirrel, bull, goat, wren, robin, trolls, yule elf, phoenix, yule gnome, sacred white buffalo.

Incense — Cedar, pine, bayberry, cinnamon, ginger, rosemary, frankincense, myrrh, nutmeg, wintergreen, saffron.

Deities — Great Mother, Befana, Holda, Isis, Triple Goddess, Mary, Mother Earth, The Snow Queen, Sun Child, Saturn, Cronos, Horus/Ra, Jesus, Santa Claus/Odin, Holly King, Old Man Winter.

Energy Focus — Introspection, transformation, strengthening bonds of family and friends, generosity, yule tree decorating.

Yule

Yule

Abundance Jar Ritual

You will need:

- Small glass jar with lid
- Holly
- Bayberry
- Cinnamon Sticks
- Juniper Berries
- Dried peppermint leaves
- Cedar essential oil
- Green candle
- Fir Incense

For the following weeks, months, and year, this jar is dedicated to manifesting abundance. Take care to include every step of the process as an integral part of your ritual, from acquiring your supplies to installing your jar.

To Begin:

Assemble your supplies, take a seat in your chosen place, and light your candle and incense.

Get rid of any thoughts that do not pertain to your end goal. Consider the different facets of your life. Where would you like to have more of what you desire? What parts of your life do you want to grow and flourish?

Fill your jar gradually with the items listed, in whatever order you like. Concentrate your efforts on that energizing sensation of improvement. A new year is approaching, which offers several opportunities for improvement and progression. Throughout the ceremony, attempt to maintain only pleasant thoughts. Visualize your dream year; anticipate progress and abundance. Clearly visualize the changes you wish to achieve within your life in the coming year.

You can take as much time as you need to do the process. Simply relax, breathe and really enjoy the experience. Once you're ready, seal your jar and place it in a prominent location. This might be on your altar or another significant location. The jar will serve as a reminder of the vision you have about yourself, and the light that surrounded you while you created it.

It may be an invaluable tool on days when you're not feeling well.
Looking at the jar and recalling the process of creation should bring a
smile to your face and a sense of hope for fresh beginnings to your thoughts.

Don't forget to write down your ritual, feelings, thoughts and the outcome.
This is a great way to see your progress and make any adjustments
in your future rituals or spellwork.

Yule

Imbolc

Dates: February 1st and/or 2nd
February Eve · Candlemas · Oimelc
St. Brigids Day · St. Brigits Day

Known as Candlemas, Imbolc celebrates the midway point of the winter season on February 1st and 2nd. Imbolc, which literally means "in the belly," is celebrated around the time when an ewe would normally become pregnant with her lamb. This idea of renewal, optimism, and fertility can be seen throughout the whole sabbat.

It's not uncommon for people to celebrate Brigid as a maiden at the time of Imbolc. She is linked to the land's fertility. Making and burning a sun wheel as a symbol of life's cyclical nature is common during this time of year.

This sabbat is ideal for spring cleaning. Imbolc is an excellent time to purge clutter and begin anew in preparation for the rapidly coming spring. Crops, animals, and even the equipment used in your practice get blessings. At Imbolc, everything should be refreshed.

Along with physical decluttering, Imbolc is a time for mental decluttering. This sabbat gives the right energy for releasing the old and embracing the new. The time for looking back is passed, and you should focus on the future, leaving room for any new chances that arise.

Imbolc takes place in early February. It marks the conclusion of winter and the onset of spring. In honor of the indications of spring, the holiday is connected with fertility and new life. It's also known as Brigid's Day. Brigid was a pre-Christian Celtic deity. Both the Pagan goddess and the Roman Catholic saint, St. Brigid of Kildare (approximately AD 451-525) have the same feast day (February 1), powers for healing, and responsibility for safeguarding domestic animals.

Imbolc

Correspondences

Themes — Growth and renewal, fertility, purity of life, the coming of light, a fresh start, continuity, first stirring of mother earth, honoring the virgin goddess.

Symbols — Candles, mirrors, snowflakes, brigid's cross, brigid's wheel, besoms, white flowers, sheep, sun wheel, daffodils, lanterns, acorns.

Colors — White, Red, Pink, Green, Pale Yellow, Blue, Brown, Orange, Lavender, Silver.

Food — Muffins, scones, dairy, herbal teas, cakes, poultry, ginger, lemon, braided breads, spicy food, spiced wine, cheese, yogurt, fish, raisins, poppyseed bread/cake, pancakes.

Herbs — Angelica, basil, bay leaf, blackberry, chamomile, rosemary, heather, rowan, dill, myrrh, willow, benzoin, celandine, clover, all yellow flowers.

Crystals — Amethyst, bloodstone, citrine, onyx, selenite, tourmaline, turquoise, garnet.

Spells — Candle magick, candle rituals, cleansing, luck, home blessings, fertility, protection, wishing, divination, initiation rituals, rid the home of stale energy.

Animals — Robin, sheep, lamb, cow, deer, burrowing animals, dragon, phoenix, owl, bear, firebird.

Incense — Basil, bay, cinnamon, vanilla, myrrh, jasmine, rosemary, frankincense, neroli, musk, olive, wisteria.

Deities — Virgin Goddess, Venus, Diana, Aradia, Athena, Inanna, Vesta, Brigid, Branwen, Selene, Young Sun Gods, Pan, Cupid/Eros, Dumuzi.

Energy Focus — Cleansing, grounding, renewal of good energy, renewal of light, seeking omens of spring, storytelling, cleaning house.

Imbolc

Imbolc

Imbolc Candle Ritual

You will need:
- 4 Tealight Candles
- Lighter or Matches to light the candles

Are you suffering from something in your life that needs to be healed? Are you stuck in a rut due to a lack of inspiration? Do you think that something in your life is harmful or toxic? During this ritual, visualize the candle light as a warm, embracing force that wraps itself around you, mending your diseases, sparking your creative spark, and cleansing whatever is broken within you.

Light the first candle, and say to yourself, or out loud if you choose:

> Despite the fact that it's still winter, there is a glimmer of hope amid the darkness.

Light the second candle and say:

> I summon the rising suns rays and its blazing heat.
> I rely on its ability to rekindle life even in the darkest places.

Light the third candle and say:

> Wisdom, inspiration, and fresh life — like the earliest stirrings of spring blossoms in the darkness — will always grow like fire.

Finally, light the final candle. While you are doing so, envision the four flames merging into one. As the light grows brighter, visualize the energy expanding in a cleansing glow, and say:

> During this season of rebirth, I ask these fires to cleanse and purify my soul.
> Fill me with the comfort of the fireplace and the bright sun's warmth.

Spend a few moments meditating on the light from your candles.
Consider this spiritual day a time of healing, inspiration, and cleansing.

After that, spend a few minutes writing down your thoughts and reflections.

Imbolc

Ostara

Dates: March 20th - 23rd

Spring Equinox - March 21st   **Lady Day**
Vernal Equinox   **First Day of Spring**

Ostara always occurs on or around March 21st, the first day of spring. As an equinox, it is a period when the light and dark are in perfect equilibrium. Ostara, named after the goddess Eostre, is a season of abundant fertility. The hopes that began during Imbolc are finally being realized.

Ostara's two primary emblems are the hare and eggs. The hare is considered to be a symbol of fertility and abundance. Eggs are a representation of limitless potential and the start of life. They are frequently connected with the entire cosmos, as though they encompass everything perfectly in equilibrium.

Ostara's days and nights are identical in length. The cycle is still waxing, and from now on, the days will begin to surpass the nights. Nature is truly blooming, rising from the winter to reintroduce life to the earth.

Easter became a Christian tradition as a result of Ostara. The hare was reincarnated as the Easter bunny, who left eggs for youngsters to discover. Easter, like Ostara, is a day of rebirth. Perhaps the most prominent example of a Christian festival derived from a pagan tradition is this one.

Ostara, or the Spring Equinox, occurs in March typically. As Pagans celebrate the arrival of spring and the end of winter, they incorporate several symbols of fresh life into their celebrations, such as eggs, flowers, and new plants.

Ostara

Correspondences

Themes — Balance, new life, abundance, fertility, equality between light and dark, cycles, resurrection, balance, youth, plant and animal fertility.

Symbols — Butterflies, rabbits, eggs, seeds, wildflowers, daffodils, tulips, baskets, ribbons, bees, sprouts.

Colors — Pastels, Cream, Light floral colors, Green, Pink, White, Yellow.

Food — Honeysuckle, carrots, chocolates, honey, eggs, fresh fruit, hot cross buns, green vegetables, sweet bread, lemonade, fish, honey cakes, leafy green vegetables.

Herbs — Acorn, celandine, crocus, daffodil, dogwood, Easter lily, ginger, hyssop, cinquefoil, honeysuckle, iris, jasmine, narcissus, peony, rose, violets, woodruff, forsythia.

Crystals — Moonstone, jasper, sunstone, rose quartz, aquamarine, bloodstone, red jasper, amethyst.

Spells — Fertility, sexuality, love and romance, renewal, nature rituals, house blessings, balance, growth, break away barriers, garden blessing, spell crafting.

Animals — Rabbit, hare, snake, chicks, robin, lamb, unicorn, dragon, swallow, pegasus, merpeople.

Incense — Jasmine, rose, strawberry, any floral incense, African violet, lotus, magnolia, ginger, sage, lavender.

Deities — Eostre, Ostara, Aphrodite, Athena, Cybele, Gaia, Isis, Persephone, Venus, Maiden, Pan, Cernunnos, Green Man, Adonis, Mars, Osiris, Thoth

Energy Focus — Balancing energy, starting something new, cleansing of negative stale energies, communication.

Ostara

Ostara

Build a Relationship with a Plant Spirit

If you've ever attempted to grow plants, you've probably found that you excel at growing certain plants but struggle with others. Spring is planting season, so why not spend some time getting to know the plants in your yard or home, and determine which plant is your ally?

Sit near the plant you desire to talk with, using a diary or your Book of Shadows to record the communication. Center and ground your energy, then closing your eyes, send it toward the plant. Determine whether you can sense its energy. Keep track of any feelings you experience and any pictures or colors you see. With your eyes closed, continue by saying the plant's name three times. This is like knocking on the plants door and informing it of your desire to communicate. Then, let the plant know who you are and what you're doing. After gaining the plant's attention and introducing yourself, you can attempt communication with it.

To quickly establish communication, try some of these example questions:
- How are you doing today?
- Tell me something interesting about yourself.
- What do you require to improve your health? Do you require more or less water?
- Are you receiving an excessive amount or a minimal amount of sunlight?
- Are you plagued by pests? If that is the case, how can I get rid of them?
- Do you enjoy music? What genres do you like listening to?
- Is there something else you want to communicate to me?

Ask one inquiry at a time and wait patiently for an answer. The plant may respond by displaying images or colors, messages in your mind, or by sending you sensations. Keep talking to the plant until the discussion concludes. Thank the plant for talking to you. Close the communication respectfully and ask if it would want a gift for cooperating with you. If it requests a gift or offering, do so to the best of your abilities.. They are usually for water or a precious stone, but this can be for anything, so keep an open mind.

Maintain regular communication with the plant to foster a deep bond.
A happy plant in your yard is likely to become a powerful plant friend
eager to guard or support you in magickal activity.
Use the following pages to record your communication.

Ostara

Beltane

Dates: April 30th – May 1st

Bealtaine   Roodmas   May Day

Beltane, observed on May 1, signifies the passage from spring to summer. This sabbat is brimming with vitality and passion. On the planet, light reigns supreme, and everyone embraces it. Beltane is a time to let go of worries and enjoy yourself.

Beltane is a period of abundant fertility, when the world is literally brimming with life. This sabbat is inextricably linked to love and sexuality. Hand-fasting ceremonies are popular at this time of year. A hand-fasting ceremony involves the exchanging of vows and the binding of the two people's hands to signify their commitment to one another. Hand-fasting is the wiccan equivalent to a marriage.

The bonfire is a popular Beltane custom. All other flames are extinguished during the celebration. Jumping the flames is a traditional technique to bring blessings or for lovers to declare their love for one another. It is believed that moving animals through the smoke protects them. At night's conclusion, everyone takes a piece of the flame and uses it to relight their own fires.

The maypole is a well-known Beltane emblem. It is adorned with foliage and ribbons and raised in such a way that it may be danced around by everybody. Couples who walk into the forest to express their desire often decorate their homes with greens found in the forest.

Beltane, which occurs on the first day of May each year, has Celtic origins; the name translates as "the fires of Bel." In Celtic religion, Bel was another deity. He was connected to summer, sexual development, procreation, and a celebration of life. People celebrate the start of summer with maypoles and dances, bonfires, and different ways to court. Many Pagans believe that this festival celebrates the wedding of the Horned God and the Goddess (of the moon or Mother goddess), which made it possible for new life to be born.

Beltane

Correspondences

Themes — Celebration of life, fertility, sexuality, love, passion, marriage of the goddess and god.

Symbols — Bonfires, flowers, music, garlands and vines, may pole, strings of beads or flowers, ribbons, butter churns, baskets.

Colors — Green, Red, White, Blue, Soft Pink, Yellow, Brown.

Food — Oatmeal, beef, dairy, honey, strawberries, cherries, green salads, wine, bread, cereals.

Herbs — Mint, rose, honeysuckle, clover, daffodil, dogwood, dragon's blood, ash, clover, elder, hawthorn, marigold, lilac, primrose, mugwort, thyme.

Crystals — Quartz, rose quartz, tourmaline, amber, garnet, emerald, malachite, orange carnelian, sapphire.

Spells — Fertility, creativity, prosperity, sex, love, banishing, protection, blessing of a new relationship.

Animals — Goat, honey bee, dove, swan, cat, leopard, rabbit, swallow, lynx.

Incense — Rose, jasmine, peach, vanilla, frankincense, lilac.

Deities — Flower Goddesses, Divine Couples, Deities of the Hunt, Aphrodite, Artemis, Bast, Diana, Faunus, Flora, Maia, Pan, the Horned God, Venus, and all Gods and Goddesses who preside over fertility.

Energy Focus — Shielding, protecting your energies, nurture and boost existing goals.

Beltane

Beltane

Setting up your Beltane Altar

Now that we've established that Beltane is a fertility celebration, how can we translate it into altar design? Because this spring festival is all about new life, fire, passion, and rebirth, there are several innovative ways to decorate for the occasion. Depending on the amount of space available, you may attempt some or perhaps all of these alternatives — clearly, someone who uses a bookcase as an altar would have less freedom than someone who uses a table, but do what speaks to you the most. Here are some Beltane altar layout ideas:

Colors of the Season

The soil is rich and green as young grass and trees emerge from winter slumber. Use lots of greens and vibrant spring hues like daffodils, forsythia, and dandelions, lilac purples, and robin's egg blue. Use these colours in your altar cloths, candles, or colorful ribbons.

Fertility Symbols

In some traditions, the masculine spirit of the god is strongest around Beltane. Antlers, sticks, acorns, and seeds are all signs of his fertility. Place any of these on your altar. You could also put a Maypole in the middle. Nothing looks more phallic than a big ole pole. Beltane honors both the god's passionate characteristics and the goddess' bountiful womb. She is the ground, warm and welcoming, eager to sprout seedlings. Add a goddess emblem like a statue, cauldron, or cup. You can also represent the goddess with a wreath or ring.

Flowers & Faeries

Beltane is the time of year when the earth becomes green again with life, and flowers bloom everywhere. Add daffodils, hyacinths, forsythia, daisies, and tulips to your altar, or make a floral crown to wear. To honor the Fae during this sabbat, include planting flowers and herbs. If you follow a faerie custom, leave gifts on your altar for the little spirits who help you around the house.

Fire Festival

In modern Paganism, Beltane is one of four fire festivals, so adding fire to the altar is a great way to celebrate the holiday. For those who cannot have a bonfire outside, candles (lots of them) or a table-top brazier might be used instead. Build an indoor fire in a small cast-iron cauldron on a heat-resistant surface.

Beltane

Litha

Dates: June 20th - 23rd
Summer Solstice - June 21st
Feast of the Sun   **Midsummer**

Litha, or Midsummer, is summers first day, and is held on or around June 21st and known as the longest day of the year. It is also the most illuminated day of the year. Litha is a time for productivity as well as play, encouraged by the longer days. But you should remember that it means that the days will no longer get longer.

This sabbat corresponds to the period during which the goddess is completely pregnant with the sun god, or when the sun god descends until his rebirth at Yule. It is the day on which the Oak King voluntarily relinquished authority to his twin brother, the Holly King, in order to maintain the natural cycle.

Litha is largely defined by bonfires. People frequently stay up all night before Litha to observe the dawn and greet the year's longest day. The blaze is symbolic of the sun's intensity at this time of year. The Litha bonfire is traditionally made by burning oak.

Litha is a joyful and celebratory season. It's the perfect time to think about what you've achieved during the first half of the year. Take advantage of the sun's brightness and warmth, since it will eventually give way to the moon's strength.

At the Summer Solstice, or midsummer, the sun is at its strongest. For many Pagans, Midsummer marks the culmination of the Horned God's (the masculine divine essence) maturation and the peak of the Goddess's strength since it is the longest day and the shortest night of the year.

Litha

Correspondences

Themes — Longest day of the year, celebration of nature, abundance, fulfillment, honoring the sun god, beginning of the harvest, honoring the pregnant goddess.

Symbols — Bonfires, oak, flowers, birch and fir branches, love amulets, the sun, flower door wreaths, sun dials, sun spiral, sunflowers, sea shells, witches ladder.

Colors — Blue, Gold, White, Brown, Green, Orange, Red, Yellow.

Food — Garden vegetables, summer fruit, honey, beef, lemons, oranges, pumpernickel bread, ale, carrot drinks, mead.

Herbs — Chamomile, lemongrass, honeysuckle, oak, lavender, vervain, star anise, mugwort, lily, fennel, elder, hemp, St. johns wort, pine, heather, yarrow.

Crystals — Sunstone, emerald, jade, lapis lazuli, diamond, tiger's eye, green agate, green fluorite, green jasper, bloodstone, amazonite.

Spells — Happiness, health and healing, protection, love, luck, relationships, fire and sun spells, burning oak rituals, divination, planet healing, nature spirit/fae magick.

Animals — Butterfly, bee, snake, horse, cattle, wren, robin, satyrs, faeries, firebird, dragon, thunderbird.

Incense — Lemon, myrrh, pine, rose, wisteria, heliotrope, saffron, frankincense, mint, sandalwood.

Deities — Mother Earth, Mother Nature, Venus, Aphrodite, Yemaya, Astarte, Freya, Hathor, Ishtar, Goddesses of love, passion, beauty and the sea. Father Sun/Sky, Oak King, Holly King, Hur, Gods at peak power and strength.

Energy Focus — Protection, healing, gathering herbs, celebrating with others, handfasting.

Litha

Litha

Celebrating the Summer Solstice

Wear Yellow or Gold
A simple method to celebrate the solstice? Look in your closet. You may get into the solstice mood by matching your attire to the sun's brilliant hues, much as you might wear green on St. Patrick's Day. Wear yellow or gold to honor the longest day of the year, and the sun at it's peak of power.

Meditate under the Sun
The sun is at its peak, bright and empowering during the summer solstice. With practice, meditation may be a powerful aid in cultivating a state of mindfulness and awareness. Even if you like to meditate while walking or praying, there are various methods to do it. Feel your feet on the grass; notice how the flowers smell; and listen to rustling trees if you'd like.

Do something that brings you Joy
Remember your bucket list? Now is the moment. Make a sandcastle, try a new hiking path, make up a TikTok dance, or visit a new town. The summer solstice invites you to follow your soul into what makes you happy. If you prefer a more low-key attitude, feel free to have a leisurely breakfast outside, tend to your plants, and soak in the sun.

Have an outdoor hangout
Picnics, bonfires, and barbecues are just a few of the many outdoor activities that you and a friend or two may enjoy together. Turn off your phone, be present in the moment and take in the warm energy emanating from nature and your fellow human beings when you do this.

Bring nature indoors
Nature is all around us, so carry a bit of it back with you after you're done playing. Your house may be refreshed by adding a touch of summer to it, whether you gather sand dollars from the beach, buy flowers at a market, or sort through leaves in your backyard.

Check in with yourself
Summer solstice is fun, energetic, and active. While out enjoying it, take some time to check in with yourself. Some methods include writing, tarot card readings, and examining your feelings and needs. After all, any spiritual exercise is a technique to improve inner connection.

Litha

Lughnasadh

Dates: August 1st - 2nd

Lammas August Eve Lunasa Garland Sunday

Lughnasadh (pronounced Loo-NAS-ah) is observed on August 1st and marks the transition from summer to autumn. Lughnasadh is the summer season's final celebration and a time to prepare for the tasks that must be done during the autumn to prepare for winter.

Lughnasadh is derived from a Celtic god. The feast was allegedly founded by Lugh to commemorate his mother Tailtiu. This sabbat is traditionally celebrated with bonfires, feasting, and dancing.

Most notably, Lammas marks the start of the year's first harvest. This harvest is often composed of grains and is critical to individuals who produce such crops. The first fruits of the season are presented to gods and goddesses to express thanks for their gifts and to assure the next year's rewards.

Often, the final sheaf of grain to be cut is preserved in the home until the next year's harvest. It will finally be restored to the land in order to carry on the gods' blessings from harvest to harvest. Occasionally, it is not cut at all and is just left in the field to retain its strength until the following harvest.

Immediately following the Midsummer Solstice or Summer Solstice, Pagans assemble for Lughnasadh, or Lammas. God Lugh was a formidable warrior who represented Earth's triumphs throughout the summer months. As the first of three harvest festivals, Lughnasadh celebrates thankfulness, the bringing of the early harvest, and the blessings of the summer that is drawing to a close.

Lughnasadh

Correspondences

Themes — The first harvest, coming of the dark, preparing for winter, change, honoring the parent deities.

Symbols — Cauldron, corn, cornucopias, scythe, sunflowers, corn dolls, sheaves of grain, spear, bonfires, god figures made of bread.

Colors — Gold, Green, Orange, Bronze, Red, Golden Yellow, Light Brown, Gray.

Food — Apples, corn, grains, breads, honey, nuts, potatoes, grapes, barely cakes, summer squash, wild berries, pears, elderberry wine, mead, cider.

Herbs — Mint, heather, blackberry, rose, sandalwood, goldenrod, rosemary, acacia, ginseng, fenugreek, frankincense, hollyhock, wheat, myrtle.

Crystals — Carnelian, cat's eye, citrine, marble, golden topaz, granite, aventurine, peridot, sardonyx, yellow diamonds.

Spells — Generosity, luck, prosperity, cleansing, renew your altar, refresh kitchen space, astrology, continued success, good fortune, abundance.

Animals — Crow, rooster, calves, squirrel, salmon, griffins, basilisks, centaurs, phoenix.

Incense — Rose, sandalwood, rosemary, chamomile, eucalyptus, safflower, frankincense.

Deities — The Mother, Dana, Tailltiu, Demeter, Ceres, The Barley Mother, Seelu, Isis, Luna, Lugh, Lleu, Dagon, Tammuz/Dummuzi, Dionysis, Taranis, Tina.

Energy Focus — Letting go of old habits, letting go of toxic relationships, renewal, cleansing, meditate and visualize completing a project.

Lughnasadh

Lughnasadh

Lammas Harvest Ritual

You will need:
- Orange, Red or Yellow Candle
- A few stalks of Wheat
- Un-Sliced Loaf of Bread
- Goblet or Chalice of ritual wine or non-alcoholic cider

Begin by lighting the candle and say:

*The Wheel of the Year has turned again,
and soon it will be time to harvest.
We have food to eat and fertile soil.
Nature has been bountiful, we have lots
in which to be thankful.
With your sickle and basket,
Mother of the Harvest,
bless me with your abundance.*

Holding the wheat stalks, think about what they represent: the earth's power, the impending winter, and the need to prepare ahead. Do you need assistance now? Are there current sacrifices that will produce future rewards?

Toss a few wheat grains off the stalks onto the altar. Give them to the earth as a gift. Say:

*I feel the strength of the Harvest within me.
The seed falls to the ground and comes back to life every year,
I too will be ever growing as the seasons change.
As the grain grows roots in the rich soil, I will also find my own roots to grow.
As a tiny seed grows into a strong stalk, so to will I grow where I land.
When the wheat is harvested and stored for the winter, I'll do the same with what I can use later.*

Take a piece and pass the bread around the circle so everyone gets a slice. When passing it around, say:

Of the first harvest gift, I pass to you.

When everyone has bread, acknowledge:

We are blessed to receive this beautiful bounty.

Everyone shares the bread together. Pass the ritual wine around the circle to wash the bread down. Once everyone has finished their bread, reflect on the cyclical nature of life and how it relates to you. If you casted a circle, you can now close the quarters, thanking them. If not, end the way you usually do.

Lughnasadh

Mabon

Dates: September 20th - 23rd

Fall / Autumn Equinox - September 21st   Second Harvest

Each year, Mabon coincides with the autumn equinox, which occurs on or around September 21st. It is once again a period of equilibrium. The lengths of the night and day are equal, and we are now entering the darker part of the year. From this point forward, the nights will become longer than the days.

Mabon, being the second harvest of the year, is a moment to rejoice in everything that has been bestowed upon us. Typically, it is a time of fruit and vegetable harvesting. At this time, a large feast is prepared to express appreciation for all of the benefits we have received during the year.

This sabbat is an excellent opportunity to reflect on the hopes and plans established at the start of the year and assess how they have manifested. It is when efforts are completed and relaxation may be taken from the effort expended in obtaining a rich crop. Everyone should have fun before the winter chill sets in.

During Mabon, people give thanks above all else. It is crucial to consider what you have received and what you have accomplished. During this time of year, it's a good idea to start thinking about projects you want to start in the new year. This will provide you with something to anticipate over the cold months.

The Autumn Equinox, or Mabon, embodies the fullness of autumn and harvest and is also a time of thanksgiving; a moment to show heartfelt gratitude for, and to share the summer's bounteous blessings. It is thought that by expressing appreciation and sharing, one might ensure the gods and goddess' graces throughout the potentially difficult winter months. Pagans utilize this time to contemplate the impermanence of all things and to accept the inevitable changes that life brings.

Mabon

Correspondences

Themes — The second harvest, balance and equality, gratitude, thankfulness, family and friends, rest, preparing for the winter and Samhain, celebration of wine.

Symbols — Acorn, apples, fallen leaves, gourds, pinecones, pomegranates, wheat stalks, sun wheel, all harvest symbols, ivy vines, horn of plenty.

Colors — Brown, Gold, Green, Orange, Maroon, Yellow, Russet, Purple, Violet, Indigo.

Food — Apples, bread, cider, squash, poultry, potatoes, carrots, nuts and grains, wine, corn, beans, dried fruit, ale.

Herbs — Cedar, cinnamon, pine, sage, honeysuckle, thistle, myrrh, yarrow, acorn, aster, ferns, hazel, ivy, marigold, milkweed, oak leaf, passionflower.

Crystals — Sapphire, lapis lazuli, yellow agate, peridot, gold, yellow topaz, amethyst, carnelian.

Spells — Reflection, changing what is not working, spell notes, new research, time for rest, protection, security, self-confidence, harmony and balance, prosperity.

Animals — Blackbird, stag, owl, eagle, dogs, wolf, salmon, goat, sphinx, minotaur, cyclops, andamans and gulons.

Incense — Autumn blends, myrrh, sage, pine, sweetgrass, apple blossom, frankincense, cinnamon, jasmine, oak moss, sage wood, patchouli, clove.

Deities — Modron, Bona Dea, Land Mother, Persephone, Demeter/Ceres, Morgan, Snake Woman, Epona, Pamona, The Muses, Sky Father, The Green Man, John Barley Corn, Thoth, Hermes, Hotei, Thor, Bacchus.

Energy Focus — Balance, confidence, reflection, rest and meditation, clearing clutter, offerings to the land, preparing for winter.

Mabon

Mabon

Balancing Meditation

You will need:
- Black and White candle - any size (If you prefer to use tealights, that's okay)
- Candle Holder or Bowl of Sand for the candles to sit in.

It's time for a fall version of Spring Cleaning. Remove whatever emotional baggage you may be holding. Accept that life has darker sides, but don't let them overwhelm you. Recognize that a healthy life is balanced. This rite should be done outdoors in the evening when the sun sets.

Adorn your altar with beautiful autumn leaves, acorns, and tiny pumpkins.

Lighting both candles, say:

> Day and night are balanced, light and dark is equal.
> Tonight, I desire symmetry in my life,
> as it is so in the universe.
> A black candle, ever reminding me of pain and darkness,
> such things I can remove from my life.
> A white candle for light and joy,
> all the good things I desire to manifest.
> The universe is in balance and harmony at Mabon,
> the time of the equinox, and so shall my life.

Focus your thoughts on the areas you want to improve.
Make an effort to eliminate the negative and reinforce the positive thoughts.
Toxic relationships should be left in the past and replaced with fresh, beneficial ones.
Let go of your worries and know that there will be a new day after every dark night of the soul. Remember to record your thoughts, feelings, emotions and ritual on the following pages.

Mabon

Samhain

Dates: October 31st – November 2nd

Halloween   *All Hallows Eve*   *Witches New Year*
Feast of the Dead   *Third / Final Harvest*

Samhain (sah-win) takes place on October 31, the same day as Halloween. The curtain or veil that separates the realms is at its thinnest during this sabbat. This powerful day is for remembering those we have lost to the spirit realm. Samhain commemorates the year's final harvest, a gathering of nuts and berries in preparation for the approaching winter.

It is not unusual to reserve an additional place at the Samhain feast for your ancestors. Discuss your departed loved ones, pay tribute to their memories, and serve them food. This is their opportunity to partake in the celebrations with you.

Other entities, like our ancestors, can enter our reality. It is prudent to avoid travelling alone at night during this time of year to avoid getting enticed by them. Samhain marks the culmination of the Wild Hunt. Going out alone might very well result in a meeting with the souls of the dead.

Samhain is considered the Witches New Year and the beginning of the year's cycle (like New Years Eve and New Years day). It is a time to reflect on and let go of the previous year and to finally rest from the harvest activity. Winter is rapidly approaching.

Samhain, otherwise known as All Hallows' Eve, and is likely the most well-known Pagan celebration outside of Pagan circles, as it coincides with the culturally famous Halloween.

As the Wheel of the Year's last celebration, it is a time to reflect on the circle of life, accept death, and honor ancestors. If invited, it is believed that the spirits of the deceased will attend rites on this Sabbat.

Samhain

Correspondences

Themes — End of summer, death and rebirth, spiritual reflection, honoring the dead, the veil between the spirit world and this one is at its thinnest, celebrate reincarnation.

Symbols — Apples, pumpkins, jack-o-lanterns, gourds, besoms, masks, cauldron, candles, colored leaves, death/dying, scarecrows, waning moon.

Colors — Black, Orange, Red, Gold, Silver, White.

Food — Apples, pumpkin, mulled cider, nuts, breads, beef, poultry, cakes for the dead, meats, pomegranates, potatoes, squash.

Herbs — Allspice, mint, mugwort, nutmeg, catnip, lavender, sage, rosemary, bay leaf, cinnamon, cloves, garlic, ginger, mandrake root, nettle, tarragon, wormwood.

Crystals — Aquamarine, jet, jasper, black obsidian, smoky quartz, amethyst, onyx, carnelian, bloodstone.

Spells — Divination, spirit contact, release, banishing, foreseeing the future, honoring/consulting ancestors, fire calling, past life recall.

Animals — Bat, stag, cat, spider, raven, crow, owl, jackal, elephant, ram, scorpion, goblins, medusa, beansidhe, harpies.

Incense — Mint, nutmeg, sage, copal, sandalwood, mastic resin, benzoin, sweetgrass, wormwood, mugwort, myrrh, patchouli.

Deities — The Crone, Hecate, Cerridwen, Arianrhod, Caillech, Baba Yaga, Bast, Persephone, Horned Hunter, Cernnunos, Osiris, Hades, Gwynn ap Nudd, Anubis, Loki, Dis, Arawn.

Energy Focus — Reflection, purification, renewal, paying debts, divination.

Samhain

Samhain

Ritual to honor your beloved Dead

Due to the fact that the veils between realms are sometimes regarded to be thinnest during Samhain, this is a potent time to communicate with and respect your ancestors or beloved deceased. Allow room and time for memories and tales to emerge and ground them by writing, painting, or sharing with others. This does not have to be exclusively for our human loved ones, it may also be pet companions or any other entity in your circle of beloveds.

There are so many ways to remember and celebrate the lives of your loved ones who have gone before you. To remember my loved one, I prefer to set up a tiny altar with a photo of them, a candle, and a sprig of rosemary. You may consider this a Samhain blessing for your loved ones who have passed away, honoring them in this sacred location.

Get creative honoring their memory

- Make a collage of photos.
- Gather special things or symbols that show how important they are to you. Create or recite a poem that captures the essence of the person or the uniqueness of your connection.
- Make a quilt in their memory, with each square honoring a different part of their life. You could also ask your friends and family to each make a quilt square in their memory.
- Write your deceased loved ones' recollections on little pieces of paper and place them in a bowl. While you read aloud, pull out one strip of paper at a time. Write, draw, or tell stories about how the memory made you feel.

Ensure that your altar stays up for a few days at least, or if you don't require the space right away, for as long as you like over the winter months. Take a few minutes every day to pause, think, and connect with the memories of your loved ones and ancestors who have passed away.

Create an Ancestor meal

It is a heartfelt gesture to prepare a special meal for your ancestors or loved ones. Taste and smell play a role in how we remember things. When we eat something that makes us think of our loved ones, it can bring back strong memories. During the meal, you might share recollections and tales of people who have departed. People sometimes crave foods they don't ordinarily eat, but were a favorite of a beloved one who passed.

Samhain

Esbats

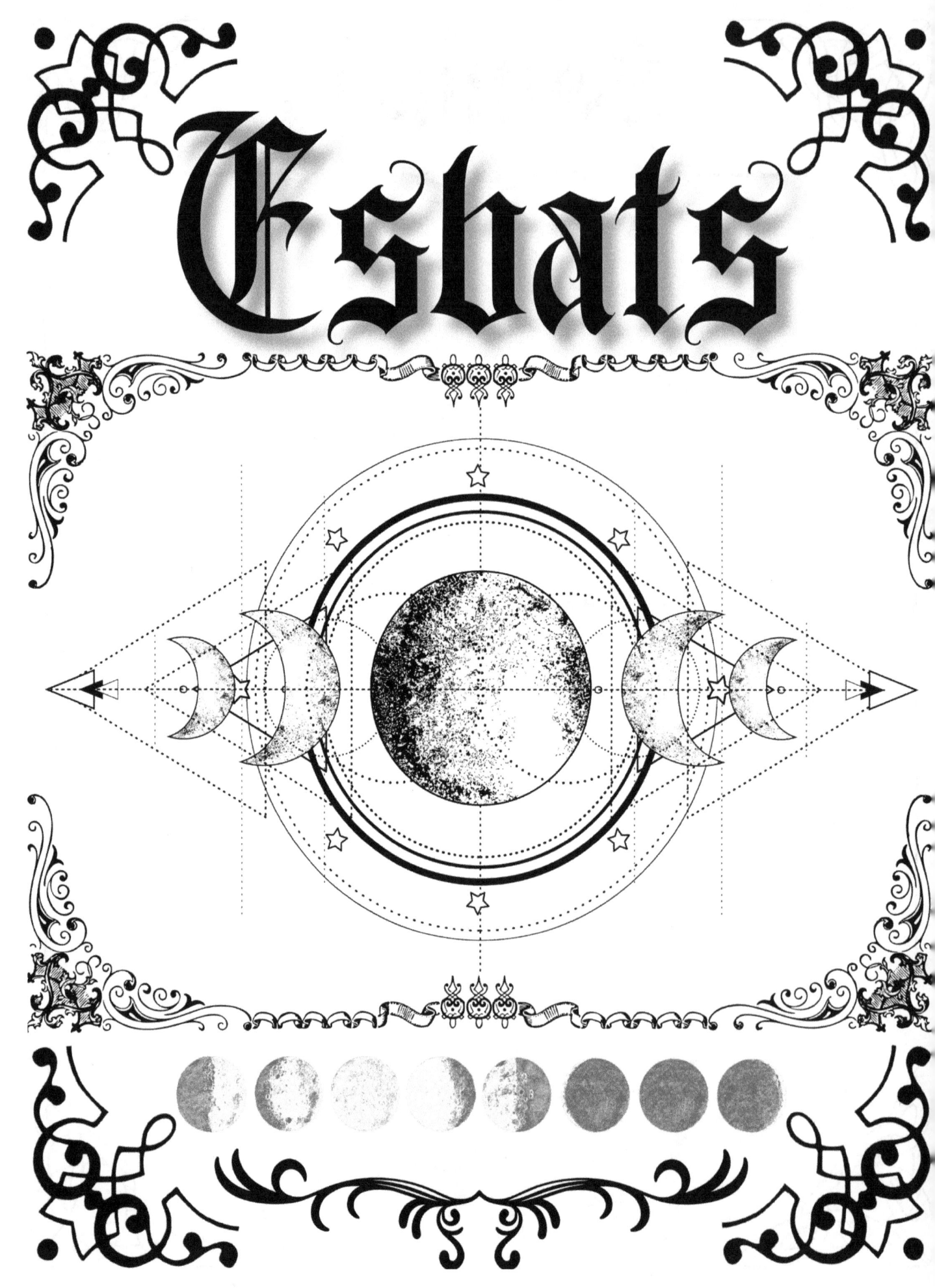

What are Esbats?

On Esbats, or Wiccan lunar spiritual days, people follow the moons journey around the earth. The Esbats provide a regular opportunity for wiccans to turn away from the mundane and devote time to spiritual thought or magickal practice. The attitude to sacred days is not universal. Certain cultures have specific rituals for each phase of the moon, and the Esbats can be observed by individuals or covens.

Wiccans commemorate the goddess once every four weeks, when the moon becomes full and illuminates the night sky. Esbats are sometimes thought of as the "second Wheel of the Year," because they are the polar opposites of the eight Sabbats, which commemorate the suns passage through the seasons and center on the god and his role in the earths life cycles.

The moon is the focal point of the Esbats, when covens gather to perform rituals, converse with the Triple Goddess, and practice magick in her sacred light. Solitary practitioners also observe the Esbats, fusing their energy with that of the millions of others staring upward at the same celestial body.

As with Sabbats, the nuances of Esbat festivities vary considerably between traditions, covens, and individuals. However, the goddess is always central, in one of her several manifestations. Many wiccans like to connect their Esbat focus with the season in which the full moon occurs. This implies they may honor a maiden aspect, such as Diana, during spring Esbats and a crone aspect, such as Hecate, during autumn and winter Esbats.

Alternatively, if a specific magickal goal is being worked on during your full moon ceremony, you may choose a goddess who is associated with that purpose. For instance, Aphrodite may be invoked for abundance-related magick. Many covens, on the other hand, are committed to a single aspect of the goddess throughout the year.

Ritual magick is frequently a component of Esbat procedures, and in certain cases, the major event. Covens and circles may be formed to benefit one or more of their members, the group as a whole, the larger community, or even the planet. Solitary practitioners may cast full moon rituals for more personal purposes, but they may also send forth broader wishes for world peace or environmental healing. Full moon magick is most effective when used to manifest good outcomes such as prosperity, a cheerful household, love relationships, and physical well-being.

Of course, there is always differing opinions, especially in wicca. Not all witches see ancient deities as goddess-like. Many just honor the goddess as an unidentified presence, or call her by her traditional name. Also, not everyone uses magick in Esbat rites. Many people use these special nights to simply offer gratitude for their blessings and to meditate, reflect and show gratitude for all they have.

What are Esbats?

According to our current Gregorian calendar, there are 12 or 13 Esbats every solar year. Approximately once every 2.5 years, we can experience two full moons in a single month. The second, a blue moon, is said to have an even stronger energetic quality than a full moon. Witches may sometimes hold special blue moon ceremonies and celebrations during these times.

In reality, not all wiccan traditions observe their Esbats on the full moon. Alternatively, some covens assemble during the new moon, believing that the beginning of the lunar cycle is the most perfect moment to celebrate the goddess.

As each quarter begins, you may also choose to honor our beautiful lunar friend in the sky with a small meditation or ritual. They pay attention to the full and new moons, as well as the waxing and waning half moons. Each of these actions is technically an Esbat, as the term refers to any ceremony that honors the goddess in her relationship with the moon.

We've all heard that if you gaze up at the full moon, a man's face will appear smiling back at you (the man in the moon). Some witches would undoubtedly argue the gender of such being! To be honest, seeing a face in the moon is frequently conceivable, however the expression varies from night to night and month to month.

When the next full moon comes around, be sure to look up at this beautiful friend in the sky. Raise your awareness to the goddess's energies all around you. What is her facial expression? What message may she be conveying to you? Gazing at the full moon during the height of its feminine energy gives you the chance to make a connection and make that strength your own, while also building a practice of observation for the Esbats.

Esbat derives from the French word 's'esbattre,' which roughly translates as "frolic joyfully." Along with having fun, this is a time to speak to the gods and goddesses of the pantheon(s) you follow. The Esbat ritual is followed by a cakes and ale celebration in certain groups.

If you prefer to practice in a secular manner, you can always utilize the Esbats as a time to cleanse, ground, and be thankful. This is a great time to think about your craft in all that it encompasses, and potentially start a new venture or journey, rather of honoring any sort of deities.

If you would like to include the Esbats into your craft, it should be made known that every month there is a specific name for the full moon, which in turn, also hints at what type of ceremony or ritual you can perform. The following page will have a list of all the full moon names throughout the year, and you can also do a quick google search to find dates for the moon phases to include as well.

Esbat Calendar

YEAR: ____

January — Full Moon Date: ___/___/____

WOLF MOON - In the middle of winter, starving wolves lament the lack of food and the cold weather by howling at the moon, giving us the name Wolf Moon in January. *AKA: (Old Moon, Ice Moon)

BEST MAGICK TO PRACTICE: Work with inner power, solidifying your path, protection, quiet contemplation and meditation.

February — Full Moon Date: ___/___/____

SNOW MOON - The full moon in February is known as the "snow moon" in North America because of the region's often frigid and snowy weather. *AKA: (Storm Moon, Hunger Moon)

BEST MAGICK TO PRACTICE: Confront truths, see your own darkness, cleansing and cleaning.

March — Full Moon Date: ___/___/____

WORM MOON - The worm moon was so named by the Native Americans because of the worm tracks that appeared in the recently thawed earth. *AKA: (Chaste Moon, Death Moon, Crust Moon, Sap Moon)

BEST MAGICK TO PRACTICE: Spring cleaning, light & dark balance, new growth, water magick.

April — Full Moon Date: ___/___/____

PINK MOON - After an early-blooming wildflower, Northern Native Americans refer to April's full moon as the "pink moon." *AKA: (Egg Moon, Fish Moon, Sprouting Grass Moon)

BEST MAGICK TO PRACTICE: Flow and change, growth, discovery, plant and flower magick.

May — Full Moon Date: ___/___/____

FLOWER MOON - Because of the many springtime blooms, May's full moon is known as the "flower moon." *AKA: (Hare Moon, Corn Moon, Milk Moon)

BEST MAGICK TO PRACTICE: Self love & care, fertility, faery magick, celebrating life, dancing.

June — Full Moon Date: ___/___/____

STRAWBERRY MOON - Named for the harvesting of strawberries in June *AKA: (Rose Moon, Hot Moon - signifying the start of summer)

BEST MAGICK TO PRACTICE: Sensuality of body, self care, nature magick, harvest magick.

*AKA - ALSO KNOWN AS

Esbat Calendar

July Full Moon Date: ___/___/____

BUCK MOON - Male deer re-grow their antlers in July, thus the Native American term for the July full moon. *AKA: (Thunder Moon, Hay Moon)
BEST MAGICK TO PRACTICE: Harvesting herbs, inner fire, sun & fire magick.

August Full Moon Date: ___/___/____

STURGEON MOON - The sturgeon moon was named by North American fishing tribes because the animal appeared in abundance in August. *AKA: (Green Corn Moon, Grain Moon, Red Moon)
BEST MAGICK TO PRACTICE: Storm and weather magick, harvesting and gathering, freedom.

September Full Moon Date: ___/___/____

HARVEST MOON - Named for the time of year that crops are gathered at the end of the summer. *AKA: (Full Corn Moon, Barley Moon)
BEST MAGICK TO PRACTICE: Celebrate the harvest, abundance, sharing, transformation.

October Full Moon Date: ___/___/____

HUNTERS MOON - Named for the optimal season in which to hunt animals that cannot yet hide in the winter snow. *AKA: (Travel Moon, Dying Grass Moon)
BEST MAGICK TO PRACTICE: Strength and endurance, protection, guidance, change, transition.

November Full Moon Date: ___/___/____

BEAVER MOON - The name of November's beaver moon is disputed. Some believe it's because Native Americans lay beaver traps during this month, while others claim it's because beavers are busy building winter dams. *AKA: (Frost Moon)
BEST MAGICK TO PRACTICE: Self reflection, divination, visualization, remembrance.

December Full Moon Date: ___/___/____

COLD MOON - Signifying the coming of winter. *AKA: (Long Night Moon, Oak Moon)
BEST MAGICK TO PRACTICE: Personal goals, renewal, reflection, rebirth, completion.

*AKA - ALSO KNOWN AS

Esbat Calendar

Esbat Ritual

What you need:

- Bowl of Water
- Moon Candle (This is traditionally a white pillar-style candle, unscented. Feel free to decorate or etch the candle with inscriptions or sigils that match the ritual or compliment your intent.)
- Adorn and decorate your altar with lunar symbols: Mirror, Silver ribbons, white crystals, etc.

If it is part of your tradition to cast a circle before beginning, you can do that now. If you do not normally cast a circle, it would be a good practice to at least take the time to cleanse the area, either with an incense or moon water, whichever works best for you. This ensures that there are no negative energies, and you have deemed your area a sacred space for the ritual.

Turn toward the altar with your arms extended out wide. Tilt your head skyward—this is, after all, a festival commemorating the full moon. Say:

Mother of the moon, Queen of the evening,
keeper of women's secrets, mistress of the waves,
you who are both ever-changing and ever-constant,
I implore you to lead me with your foresight,
help me flourish with your enlightenment,
and embrace me in your loving arms.

Ignite the moon candle. As it burns, remember that you have so much to be grateful for in your life. Take a moment to sit with the gratitude that comes with this reassuring feeling of calmness.

Esbat Ritual

To the sky, hold the bowl of water and say:

The moon symbolizing the mother,
she watches over me night and day.
Bringing the changing tide, the fluctuating night,
the movement that evolves women's bodies,
and the devotion of lovers to their cherished.
Her knowledge is great and wise,
and I celebrate her this night.
Watch over and protect me, great mother,
until returning the cycle once more,
and carry me to the next lunar phase,
the full moon is your light and love.

Since the last full moon, has there been any changes in your life? Are you grateful to have certain individuals in your life? Have you left a relationship that was bad or toxic? Have you had any instances of good fortune at work? Consider all the things for which you are grateful, as well as the changes you wish to see in your life by the next full moon. When you are finished, close the circle (however that may be to you) and complete the ritual. Remember to record your ritual, how it went, and the results you achieved so you can look back on it later.

Witchy Tip:

Use the moon water you just created during this ritual to water plants, make offerings, and complete spellwork until the next full moon comes back around.

Esbat Ritual

Esbats

Blue Moon

Blue Moon Date: ___/___/____

Not as uncommon as most people think, occurring approximately every 2.5 years, when there is a double full moon within the period of a month, the additional full moon is known as the blue moon.

Quite commonly, you may have overheard the expression "once in a blue moon," which is used to refer to events that are out-of-the-ordinary. Blue moons have a saying, a song, and even a line of cosmetic goods, but what are they precisely and what makes them so special? Blue moons are astrologically significant, and understanding how to harness their energy would be quite beneficial.

The current definition of a "blue moon" has become normal in our culture and society, so the implications are great that each blue moon will be just as powerful as the previous one. Magick is focused with raising energy. The more you focus your energy on something like a blue moon, the stronger it becomes.

How to harness Blue Moon energy

There is no need for an ancient book of spells transcribed in Latin. Simply state your intention clearly and take action to demonstrate to the universe that you mean business. How you attain your goal is up to you. Write on a piece of paper all the things that you don't need in your life that are no longer serving your greatest desires and goals, and burn it to release them. Alternatively, you may simply turn up the volume on your favorite song and dance as if no one is watching. Allow yourself to truly release. Blindfold yourself if you must.

Its important to consider taking some alone time and practice self-care at the end of a day during a blue moon. This can be however you desire it to be. Writing a letter of intent and reading it aloud has just as much value as searching up a spell that someone else has created. That being said, if you like to follow a ritual or spell that is 'ready-to-go,' then feel free to use the Blue Moon Ritual provided.

Did you Know?

- The word "blue moon" currently refers to the second full moon in a month, although it originally referred to an additional full moon in a season.
- Some modern magickal traditions equate the Blue Moon with a witches growth in knowledge and wisdom.
- The blue moon has no formal significance in current Wiccan and Pagan religions, yet many people see it as a special magickal occasion.

Blue Moon Ritual

What you need:

- The Empress tarot card (If you do not have a tarot deck available to you, you can simply Google and print an image of the Empress card to use). The Empress represents the goddess at her most fruitful and luminous, offering balance, self-love, and direction.
- Seasonal flowers.
- A candle that you feel will be suitable.
- A bowl of salt, placing inside any talismans, amulets, charms or crystals you would like cleansed.
- Incense such as Sandalwood, Sage or Palo Santo, which all have purifying qualities.

Set the items on your altar in whatever manner you deem appropriate, and after lighting the incense and candle, you can affirm aloud (or quietly):

> Empress of elegance, harmony, and truth,
> On this blue moon, I let go of any obstacles.
> Deliver them to Mother Earth
> and return to the ground,
> So I may be renewed for the
> approaching moon cycle.

There you have it: in true blue moon style, a ritual for letting go of what no longer serves you and accepting what does. Don't forget to record your ritual so you can come back and reflect on your manifestations at a later time.

Blue Moon Ritual

Moon Magick

It's a well-known fact that witches like the moon, and understanding how to harness the power of each moon phase may help you increase your abilities and conjure up some incredible spells. Indeed, regardless of whether one identifies as a witch or not, the majority of individuals sense a connection to Earth's natural satellite. Witches frequently refer to the moon as the mother energy, whereas the sun is referred to as the father energy.

Working and living according to the lunar cycles is one of the simplest and most effective methods to work with magick. We go through changes, waxing and waning like the moon. We are intimately and intuitively linked, and the moon has a profound impact on our emotions and magick. The moon is in charge of our emotional and subtle bodies; she is in charge of feminine secrets and the deep, dark recesses of our souls. Have you ever felt particularly over-sensitive around the time of the full moon? This is not coincidental. That is moon magick at work. Thankfully, this magick means that each month, just as the moon does, we have the chance to explore our spiritual cycles and dig into our shadows a little deeper.

Each moon phase corresponds to a certain kind of magick and intent, and each contains its own unique energy. Moon magick is founded on the concept of sympathetic magick, which is the practice of doing magick in the manner of the desired goal. In this situation, as the moon's light expands (waxing), so do we. As it diminishes or decreases (wanes), we become more focused on what we want to let go of. A simple technique to remember the moon phases is as follows: waxing (the moon is getting fuller and brighter until it reaches a full moon), waning (the moon is slowly getting darker and less bright culminating in a dark or new moon).

Another aspect to think about is the zodiac sign in which the moon currently resides when you are thinking about conducting spellwork. Each sign will have a unique effect on you, and if the moon is in your sign, you can expect to experience her energy more profoundly.

In ancient times, the moon was a magickal entity that few people understood, prompting the creation of stories and tales about this beautiful nocturnal orb. One example of this was the belief that a full moon drove you into a state of disorientation or insanity. It was claimed that at a full moon, all the insane individuals would appear, which is how the term 'lunatic' was coined. The word "luna," which translates to "moon" in latin, is where the name comes from. That is because lunatic originally meant 'someone who became insane with each lunar phase,' not to mention the urban legend of the Werewolf.

Moon Magick

For many Pagans, lunar cycles are critical to magickal workings. In certain traditions, it is suggested that ritual and spellwork be prepared and planned out for the four major phases (full, waxing, new and waning) due to their inherent magickal characteristics. If your tradition adheres to these guidelines—or if you wish to time your magick according to the lunar phase, a great place to start with learning moon magick is to focus on the Full Moon and New Moon first, then work your way into getting to know the other phases.

MOON TIP: Because of the moons rotation around the earth, the waxing and waning phases will always be the same. Here is an easy way to remember which is which; A waxing phase will always be illuminated on the RIGHT side of the moon, with the shadow on the LEFT, and a waning phase will always be illuminated on the LEFT side of the moon, with the shadow on the RIGHT.

[IN THE SOUTHERN HEMISHPERE, THE SHADOW & ILLUMINATION ARE OPPOSITE]

Focus on the Full & New Moon First

A perfect place to begin learning about lunar energy and how to harness it is to first focus your attention on the full and new moons. These two phases will assist you in developing a solid foundation of knowledge, and in fully using the energetic potential of these moon phases, you can unlock the magickal properties for your personal practice and manifestations. Once you have a solid understanding of the full and new moons, you can delve into the magickal properties of the remaining phases to fully round out your practice with moon magick.

Lunar cycles will have a significant role in your practice. The moon is viewed as the goddess, the sun as the god or father, and each of the three main phases is associated with a stage in the goddess' lifecycle. This is referred to as the 'Triple Goddess.' (Symbol pictured below)

TRIPLE GODDESS

Moon Magick

Maiden, Mother and Crone is what the triple goddess represents, or the stages of a woman's life. She represents the full moon, the waning moon, and the waxing moon. It symbolizes the cycle of birth, life, and death, reminding us that everything in our world has a beginning, middle, and end.

We already know that the moon is a vital component of our solar system, maintaining the earth's balance. The moon's gravitational pull has an influence on things like tides, and it is because of this that we can assume it has an effect on our physical self. If the waters and oceans can be influenced, surely we can be as well.

The lunar cycle, in a more spiritual sense, is the interaction between the sun and the moon, or goddess and god. A full moon, for example, is considered more potent since the goddess is illuminated by the god's full light and shines down on us. It is a beautiful event when the worlds two most powerful forces exchange energy in our skies. As the light diminishes, so does its powerful draw, until the new moon arrives and we have a chance to rest, recharge, and restart.

When discussing the lunar cycle, there are eight distinct phases. These are as follows:

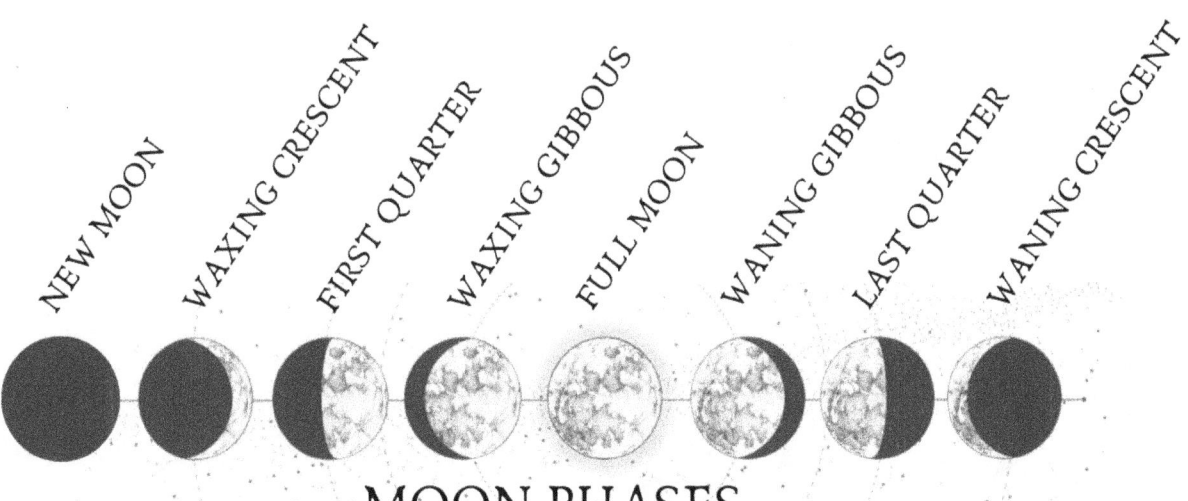

MOON PHASES

The cycle begins with the dark, new moon and gradually progresses into the waxing moon. It reaches its zenith during the full moon, before fading gradually into the waning moon and returning to a new moon. These stages all have distinct meanings and energies that we may utilize in our magick, and we will cover each of these phases and how you can utilize each one for different magickal needs in your practice.

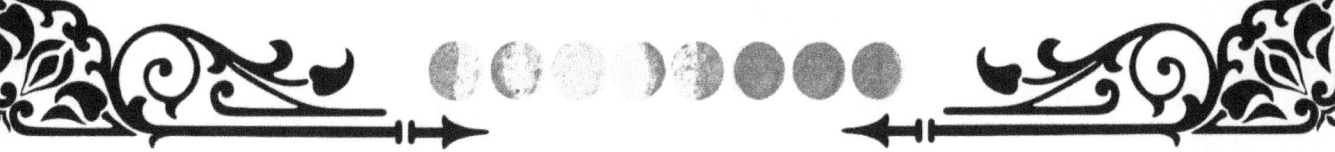

Moon Magick Correspondences

Although each moon phase itself has different intentions attached to them, when it comes to using correspondences with moon magick, these are universal throughout all moon phases. When you are preparing your rituals or spellwork, the best way to figure out which correspondence would be best is to look at each of them individually to see how well they match or compliment your intentions for your magickal workings.

Lunar Herbal and Plant Correspondences

CABBAGE - *Fertility, good luck, money magick, profit.*
CACTUS - *Banishing, chastity, protection.*
CAMELLIA - *Riches*
CAMPHOR - *Divination, gives strength to any mixture, hopes, psychic awareness, ritual cleansing.*
CHICKWEED - *Attract a lover, love & fertility, maintain current relationship.*
CUCUMBER - *Chastity, fertility, healing.*
GARDENIA - *Attract love or friendship, promoting peace, protection from outside influences.*
GRAPE - *Fertility, garden magick, mental powers, money.*
JASMINE - *Attract money & wealth, charging quartz crystals, draw in love & attract a soulmate.*
LEMON - *Cleansing, getting rid of blockages, getting rid of negative energy, purifying, spiritual opening.*
LEMON BALM - *Healing, love, spiritual & psychic development, success.*
PASSION FLOWER - *Attracting friendship & prosperity, brings peace, diminishes arguments & stress.*
PEA - *Love, money.*
PEACH - *Fertility, keeps away evil if you carry a peach pit, love, wisdom.*
PEAR - *Love & lust. Eating a pear will induce love.*
POPPY - *Abundance, fertility, love, prosperity.*
POTATO - *Healing, image magick, luck, money.*
ROWAN - *Anti-haunting, healing, magickal power, promotes psychic powers, protection, success.*
TURNIP - *Ending relationships.*
VERVAIN - *Healing, money, peace, protection, purification, sleep.*
WILLOW - *Attracting or solidifying love, foretelling the future, healing, pushing sadness out.*

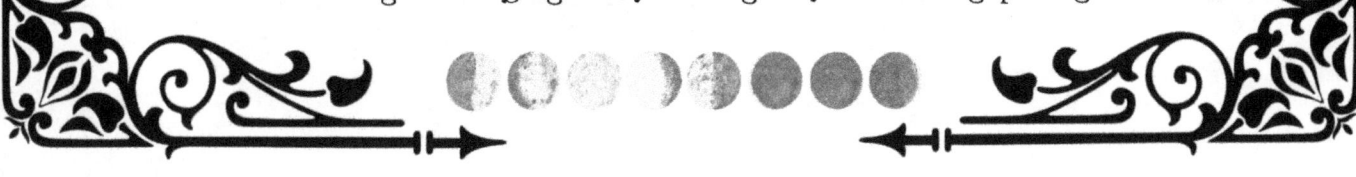

Moon Magick Correspondences

Witches do not utilize actual animals or creatures in our rituals or workings since it is against our laws, yet many witches do because animals have specific powers. They are open to the magickal because, like children, they are not bound by science or opinion. Many witches report that their cat or dog is drawn to the power of the circle, or that they know when their humans are coming home. It's well-known that pets can detect unseen beings, gazing at them with a heightened anxiety level, just like a newborn may detect something in the air and giggle.

Many witches are in touch with animal spirits, just like witches who have a spirit guide. This is especially true for witches who like animals more than people. Just like everything else in witchcraft, many animals have distinct correspondences and may be conjured for a variety of purposes. Below, you will find a selection of animal correspondences for moon magick. As with learning and growing your craft, it is encouraged that you research and record your own findings as well.

Lunar Animal Correspondences

BAT - *A messenger. The bat could bring a message from another world or from your own mind.*

CAT - *In confrontations, the cat is a fierce defender. As a prowler, is a great guardian of inner powers.*

COW - *Prosperity, sacred to Hathor, the goddess aspect.*

CRAB - *Adapting, connection to the ancient world that has been untouched by humans, dreams, intuition, protection, shielding from negative influences.*

DEER - *Charm, kindness and promptness.*

DOG - *Underworld hounds have white bodies and red ears, which mean they are good at tracking, are friendly, and will protect you.*

FROG - *Magick, shamanism, something beautiful hidden behind an illusion.*

MOTH - *Change, moon magick, omens, signs.*

OPOSSUM - *Go with the flow, teaches us to deal with things as they come.*

OWL - *Teaches us to witness life quietly and gather information to understand it.*

RABBIT - *Banishing phobias, faery magic, quick thinking.*

RACCOON - *Adaptability, curiosity, resourcefulness.*

SPIDER - *Guardians of the ancient languages and alphabet. Artistic endeavors, teacher.*

WOLF - *Loyalty, perseverance, ruled by the moon, solitary, thirst for knowledge.*

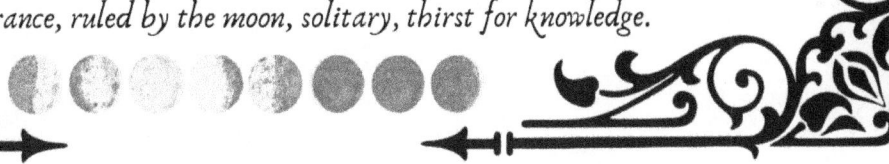

Moon Magick
Correspondences

Working with crystals, as well as comprehending their therapeutic powers, requires a thorough awareness of which crystals correspond to certain intentions. For example, if you are working on abundance magick, it makes sense to include crystals that are associated with money, wealth and well-being. Below is a small selection of the crystals that will work well with your intentions when doing moon magick.

Understanding the unique features of the crystals we deal with, especially their meanings and correspondences, may be quite valuable to your magickal practice. While working with crystals superficially is simple and in no way incorrect, with a little more information, we can begin to tap into a far deeper understanding of the energies present in the material and mineral world.

Lunar Crystal Correspondences

AQUAMARINE - Banishing, cleansing, communication, creativity, encourages joy, grief, healing, independence, inspiration, loss, love, mental clarity, peace, rejuvenation, relationships, travel.

CLEAR QUARTZ - Protection, purification, shamanic practice. Helps with decision-making and energy. Purifies the aura, raises consciousness, and enhances family relationships.

EMERALD - Helps uncover inner truth, improves psychic powers, strong protection. Ensures travel safety. Attracts love and wealth.

MOONSTONE - Abundance, calms, divination, dreamwork. Heals, fertility, integrates body and spirit, spirit communication, strengthens psychic powers, wisdom.

MOTHER-OF-PEARL - Heightens intuition, imagination, love, psychic sensitivity, soothing protection from negative energies.

OBSIDIAN - Binding, brings luck and calm, clarity to divination, communication, connection, protection, provides equilibrium at times of change.

PEARLS - Attracts both love and money, emotional equilibrium, fertility, knowledge, spirituality, tranquility.

SELENITE - Clarity, draws on the energy of renewal, harmony, justice, love spells, new beginnings, purification, wards of negativity.

TOPAZ - Blessings, encourages knowledge, energizes, good luck and wealth, linked to love and sex, protects, rejuvenation.

Moon Magick
Crystals & Gemstones

Moon Magick
Gods & Goddesses

People have gazed up at the moon for thousands of years, pondering its celestial meaning. It's not surprising that many cultures throughout history have had lunar deities, or gods or goddesses who are connected to the moon's power and life. If you are doing a moon-related ritual, you may want to call on one of these deities to help make your wishes and goals come true, however, please be mindful of the different cultures and traditions. Be respectful and research to see if a certain pantheon has a closed practice before calling upon their deities so that we are not appropriating.

When we see the moon, we pay attention. It doesn't matter if it's dark, new, waxing, waning, or full. Lunar energy pulls us to look at the night sky, no matter what phase it is at that specific moment. For many witches, the moon is known as "The Bright Lady." Many people, on the other hand, see the moon as a male and has a masculine energy. We may also see the moons energy in a non-binary understanding as well.

On the wiccan altar, the god and goddess can be shown in different ways, depending on the tradition or even your own personal tastes. Candles in gold, red, orange, or yellow are often used to show the wiccan god, as well as horns, spears, swords, wands, or arrows, which are phallic and projective. The colors green, silver, white, and black are frequently associated with the wiccan goddess, as are receptive symbols like as the chalice and cauldron, as well as symbols for abundance such as flowers and other greenery. If you're new to the craft and want to establish a connection with the goddess and god, you can include some of these representations onto your altar. However, the most effective approach to begin is to spend some time alone in nature, communicating to the celestial couple that you are ready to begin your relationship with them.

Many witches only worship moon deities, and the popular triad of Maiden, Mother, and Crone is often linked to the moon's phases. While western tradition frequently depicts the moon as female, masculine lunar deities are revered around the world. The earlier wiccan practitioners worshipped two deities, one male and one female: "the Mother Goddess; the birth giver, who brings all life into being," and a male hunter who perished each year and was resurrected, known as the "Horned God."

There are several gods and goddesses who have something to do with the moon or moon energies. Below is a list of the top 11 gods and goddesses that are most closely related to the moon and her divine power. There are many other pantheons and hundreds of different deities that can be used when practicing your magick. It is encouraged that you do more research on gods and goddesses, the different pantheons and their associations and correspondences.

Moon Magick
Gods & Goddesses

Lunar Deity Correspondences

ALIGNAK

PANTHEON: Inuit (God / Male)

According to Inuit myth, Alignak is a very powerful god of weather and the moon. He is in charge of the tides, earthquakes, water, eclipses, and comets. In some stories, he also brings the souls of the dead back to earth so that they can be born again. Alignak may show up in harbors to protect fishermen from the sea goddess Sedna, who is very angry and full of wrath.

MAGICKAL ASSOCIATIONS: Manifesting, personal change, protection, weather magick.

ARTEMIS (*also DIANA in Roman Mythology*)

PANTHEON: Greek (Goddess / Female) [THE MAIDEN]

Artemis, the Greek huntress. Since her twin brother Apollo was linked to the Sun, Artemis became linked to the Moon instead. Although Artemis was a lunar goddess in ancient Greece, she was never depicted as the moon. Post-classical art usually depicts her with a crescent moon. She is also linked to the Roman Diana, the Roman Luna, and the Greek Selene.

MAGICKAL ASSOCIATIONS: Fertility, healing, nature magick, protection for children and women.

CERRIDWEN

PANTHEON: Celtic (Goddess / Female)

Cerridwen is the Celtic guardian of the cauldron of knowledge. She is related with the moon and the intuitive process because she gives insight and inspiration. A white sow signifies both Cerridwen's abundance and fertility, as well as her power as a mother. Cerridwen is respected by many modern Pagans because she is linked to the full moon.

MAGICKAL ASSOCIATIONS: Creativity, fertility, harvest, inspiration, knowledge, luck.

Moon Magick
Gods & Goddesses

Lunar Deity Correspondences

CHANG'E (also CH'ANG-O or HENG'O)

PANTHEON: Chinese (Goddess / Female)

Chang'e was the queen of Hou Yi in Chinese legend. Known as a skilled archer, Hou Yi subsequently became a tyrant who inflicted death and ruin wherever he went. Hou Yi dreaded death, so a healer offered him an elixir that would make him immortal. Chang'e stole the potion one night as Hou Yi slept. When he spotted her and demanded the potion back, she drank it and sailed up into the sky as the moon. In some Chinese tales, this is the perfect illustration of selfless sacrifice.

MAGICKAL ASSOCIATIONS: Fertility, love, luck, manifesting, protection, sexual energy.

COYOLZAUHQUI

PANTHEON: Aztec (Goddess / Female)

Coyolxauhqui was the Aztec god Huitzilopochtli's sister. Her sibling sprang from his mother's womb, massacred his siblings, severed Coyolxauhqui's head, and threw it into the sky, where it stays as the moon. She is usually shown as a youthful, lovely woman with bells and lunar symbols.

MAGICKAL ASSOCIATIONS: Death, fertility, life, magickal energy, rebirth.

DIANA (Identifies with Artemis)

PANTHEON: Roman (Goddess / Female)

Diana, like Artemis in Greek mythology, began as a huntress before becoming a lunar goddess. Diana was Jupiter's daughter and Apollo's twin. While the Greek Artemis and the Roman Diana have many similarities, Diana grew into a distinct figure in Italy. Many feminist Wiccan organizations, notably the Dianic Wiccan tradition, worship Diana as the divine feminine manifestation. She is typically connected with the moon's powers and is seen wearing a crown with a crescent moon.

MAGICKAL ASSOCIATIONS: Abundance, fertility, harvest, protection for children, providence.

Moon Magick
Gods & Goddesses

Lunar Deity Correspondences

HECATE
PANTHEON: *Greek (Goddess / Female)* [THE CRONE]

Hecate was initially a mother goddess, but became the Ptolemaic Alexandrian goddess of spirits and the spirit realm. Because of her relationship to both childbirth and maidenhood, many contemporary pagans and wiccans regard Hecate as a dark goddess, rather than an aspect of the Crone. Her "dark goddess" status presumably stems from her relationship to the spirit realm, ghosts, the dark moon, and magick.

MAGICKAL ASSOCIATIONS: *Crossroads, entrances, ghosts, goddess of witchcraft, knowledge of herbs and poisonous plants, magick, necromancy, sorcery. Additionally, she is regarded as the protector of flocks, seafarers, and witches.*

SELENE (also LUNA, PHOEBE; associated with ARTEMIS)
PANTHEON: *Greek (Goddess / Female)* [THE MOTHER]

Selene was Helios's sister. Her honor was paid on full moon days. Like many Greek deities, she had several facets. She was worshipped as Phoebe, the huntress, and then as Artemis.

MAGICKAL ASSOCIATIONS: *Agriculture, fertility, inspiration, intuition, long life, travel, visions.*

SINA
PANTHEON: *Polynesian (Goddess / Female)*

Sina is a well-known Polynesian deity. She sits within the moon and guards people who travel at night. She used to live on Earth, but she became weary of the treatment she received from her husband and family. So, according to Hawaiian folklore, she packed her bags and went to dwell on the moon. In Tahiti, Sina, or Hina, simply wanted to see what it was like on the moon, so she took her magickal boat there. She arrived and was captivated by the moon's serene beauty and so decided to stay.

MAGICKAL ASSOCIATIONS: *Any body of water, moon water, protection when travelling at night, water magick.*

Moon Magick
Gods & Goddesses

Lunar Deity Correspondences

THOTH (*Represents the* FULL MOON)

PANTHEON: Egyptian (God / Male)

According to certain legends, Thoth is the deity who weighs the souls of the dead, although Anubis usually does it. As a moon deity, Thoth is typically shown with a crescent moon on his head. He is linked to Seshat, the heavenly scribe and goddess of writing and learning. Thoth is sometimes invoked for knowledge, magick, and fate. Invoke him if you're working on a Book of Shadows or a spell, saying words of healing or meditation, or settling a conflict.

MAGICKAL ASSOCIATIONS: *Balance, communication, creativity, destiny, divination, general magick, guidance, healing, honesty, intelligence, justice, mental power, messages/omens, peace, prophecy/secrets, success, truth, wisdom.*

KHONSU (*Represents the* NEW MOON)

PANTHEON: Egyptian (God / Male)

Khonsu is the Egyptian moon deity. His name means "traveler", maybe referring to the moon's nightly travels. He, like Thoth, measured time. Khonsu aided in the creation of all living beings by bringing new life. At Thebes, he was part of a trio with Mut and Amun (the "Theban Triad").

MAGICKAL ASSOCIATIONS: *Protection from wild animals, Cattle, Passage of Time, Male verility, Healing*

In magickal practice, the energy of the moon, depending on its phase, may be extremely beneficial in a range of spells. While an effective spell can be cast at any time, using correspondences such as the moon phase, the day of the week, plants and herbs, crystals, deities, as well as seeking out nature or spiritual allies with the equivalent energy of the spell's intention, can help you focus on your main objective or goal. Although a witch can instinctively choose the moon phase that is most appropriate for their needs, there are some standard recommendations. Therefore, let us examine the energy accessible throughout various moon phases and the varieties of magick that you can use as a focal point in your spellwork and rituals.

MOON MAGICK
Gods & Goddesses

Moon Phases & the Zodiac

The Magickal associations with the 12 Astrological Signs and how you can benefit from their power

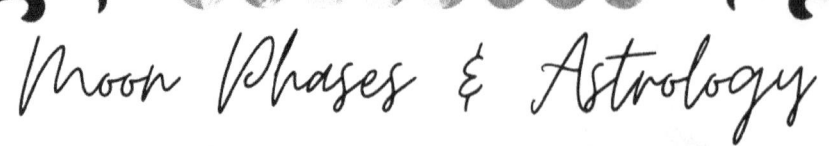

Moon Phases & Astrology

When the 'moon is in' a specific zodiac sign, this could signify an additional boost of magick depending on the astrological significance and meaning of each sign. The moon can be seen in various portions of the sky because of its rotation and orbit around the earth. This causes the moon to move continuously through the many constellations of the Zodiac, changing signs every two and a half days as a result of its rotation.

Even if you don't personally pay attention to astrology or believe in astrology, incorporating astrological associations into your magickal work with the phases of the moon will considerably increase your results. Below is a list of the 12 moon signs, or zodiac, with connected meanings and words that you may use in your moon spellwork and practice.

Lunar Astrological Influences

- Aries – ♈ (Fire): Taking initiative, start new projects, putting yourself out there.
- Taurus – ♉ (Earth): Security, pleasure, getting things done.
- Gemini – ♊ (Air): Communication.
- Cancer – ♋ (Water): Connect with feelings, home and domestic life.
- Leo – ♌ (Fire): Leadership, confidence.
- Virgo – ♍ (Earth): Service, well-being, self-care.
- Libra – ♎ (Air): Balance, harmony, compromise.
- Scorpio – ♏ (Water): Healing, rebirth. Fresh start.
- Sagittarius – ♐ (Fire): Adventure, risk, try something new, change your routine.
- Capricorn – ♑ (Earth): Structure, long-term goals.
- Aquarius – ♒ (Air): Passion/love, unconventional ideas & approaches.
- Pisces – ♓ (Water): Creativity, passion, reflection.

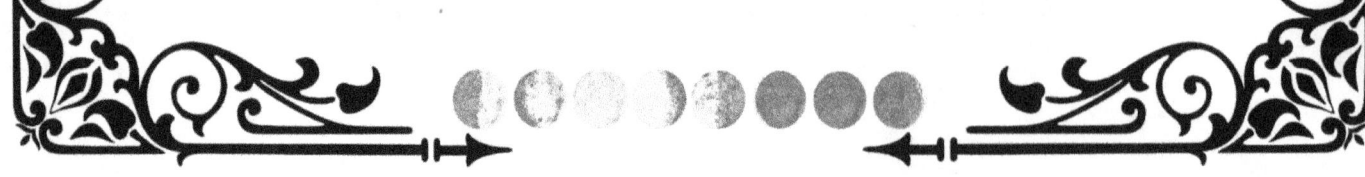

MOON
PHASES

Moon Magick
Moon Phases

New Moon (Dark Moon)

As the sky darkens when the moon and sun align, the new moon has risen. This represents the merging of the feminine and masculine. During the new moon, connect with your inner wisdom and reflect. It's a moment to let go of what no longer serves you in order to create room for the new. When we slow down, we have access to our true desires and needs on a soul level, from which we may create fresh intentions for the upcoming moon phase and beyond.

This is an ideal moment to embark on a new endeavor, develop a new habit, or challenge yourself to do something unusual. It's also an excellent opportunity to assess whatever elements of your life are now out of balance and to breathe fresh vitality into them. The new moon is similar to a blank canvas, and as it develops toward the full moon, you may focus on areas of your life that could use more abundance - health, wealth, relationships, and creativity. If you've been thinking about starting something new, now is the time to put those plans into motion. This is an ideal time to start a business, go on a new diet, or even embark on a 14 to 30-day personal development challenge.

If this is your first time working with the moon phases, I recommend beginning with the new and full moons. Once you've established a connection with these two moon phases, you may determine whether working with four phases works for you and then progressively increase to eight. However, do not attempt to complete all eight moon phases if you are a complete beginner, since this would most certainly be overwhelming.

Rituals for the New Moon

- Take a cleansing bath to symbolize the removal of the old.
- Meditate to generate calm in order to hear your soul's greatest wishes.
- Reorganize and redecorate your altar.
- Light a candle, grab your notebook, and be very precise about what you want to materialize in the following 30 days.
- Create new, unique intentions from the heart.

Moon Magick
Moon Phases

New Moon (Dark Moon)

- **RISES:** Dawn   **SETS:** Sunset   (Best magick between these times)
- **PURPOSE:** Beginnings
- **WITCHES HOLIDAY:** Yule - Winter Solstice
- **OFFERINGS:** Milk and honey
- **THEME:** Abundance
- **TAROT ASSOCIATION:** The Fool
- **MAGICKAL WORKINGS:** Beauty, creative ventures, farms/gardens, health, job hunting, letting go, love/romance, networking, new beginnings, reboot, self-improvement, setting intentions, soul-searching, taking time for yourself.

Questions to ask yourself during a New Moon Ritual

Should I let go of something in my life?
What is it that I don't need in my life anymore?
Does I need to release anything?
In what ways could I be out-of-balance?
Has there been any constant thoughts?
Right now, how am I feeling?
What would I like to manifest in the next 30 days?
What exciting new experiences would I love to happen?

Moon Magick
New Moon (Dark Moon)

Moon Magick
New Moon (Dark Moon)

MOON MAGICK
Moon Phases

Waxing Crescent

A sliver of the moon appears in the sky, symbolizing the beginning of our new intentions or objectives. Make a list of one or two objectives that you'd want to work on and bring to completion this cycle. Which direction do you wish to direct your energy?

It's a nice sight to see the Waxing Crescent as the moon begins to fill in after disappearing during the New Moon. You must put in the necessary effort to bring about the manifestation of your objective or purpose that you established during the New Moon.

During this moon phase, visualizations and affirmations will be beneficial. Make your aspirations a reality by visualizing them. Take note of what you are able to see, hear, and feel. Additionally, create affirmations to assist you in walking your path forward, changing any limiting thoughts into empowering ones.

Rituals for the Waxing Crescent

- Practice a guided meditation or visualization.
- Think of new and exciting affirmations.
- Each evening, set aside 5 minutes to reflect on your accomplishments. It makes no difference how minor or how far off track you have strayed. Celebrate the fact that you can begin again tomorrow.
- Celebrate that you made a green smoothie instead of eating a donut.
- Celebrate that you completed day 3 of your 30-day challenge.
- Always, always, celebrate your wins – every single day! No matter how small.
- Have an 'Attitude of Gratitude' everyday, for everything.

Moon Magick
Moon Phases

Waxing Crescent

- RISES: Mid-morning   SETS: After sunset   (Best magick between these times)
- PURPOSE: The movement or building of something.
- WITCHES HOLIDAY: Imbolc
- OFFERINGS: Candles
- THEME: Manifestation
- TAROT ASSOCIATION: The Magician
- MAGICKAL WORKINGS: Affirmations, hustle, manifesting, take action, visualizations.

Waxing Crescent Cleanse & Protection Bath

Spiritual baths protect us when we feel vulnerable. This spell bath requires Dandelion, Bay Leaf, Rosemary, and one white candle. Then, follow these instructions:

- To a cup of boiling water, add a teaspoon of each herb and simmer for 20 minutes.
- Take a normal shower, this will ensure you are clean and prepared for the bath.
- Prepare the tub. This phase is completely customizable. For instance, you may light a candle or listen to relaxing music.
- Add your herbal water to your bath water after removing or straining out the herbs.
- Scoop after scoop, pour the bath water over you.
- Simply take a moment to breathe and feel at ease. Reconnect with your inner power.
- When you're done, it is ideal if you air dry.

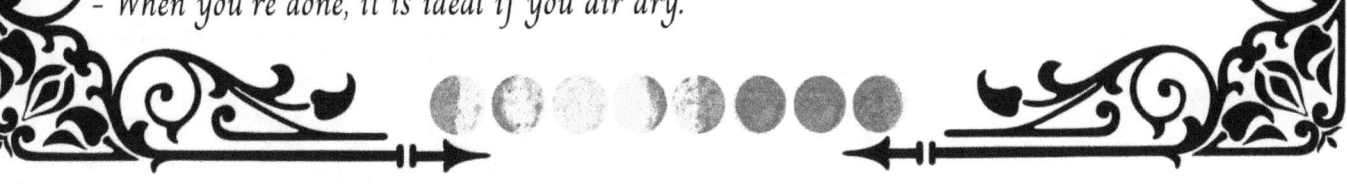

Moon Magick
Waxing Crescent

Moon Magick
Waxing Crescent

Moon Magick
Moon Phases

First Quarter

The first quarter is when the road might get a little bumpy. The initial exhilaration of beginning a new endeavor or habit will have worn off, and you will almost certainly encounter internal opposition and roadblocks to overcome. Now is the moment to go into your soul and discover your motivation. If you find yourself delaying or self-sabotaging, investigate why. Make an attempt to ascertain the root problem so that you can move on.

Never surrender at the first indication of difficulty. This lunar phase is all about altering your goals (or thinking), devising workarounds, and accepting obstacles. Recognize that the difficulties you confront will serve as some of your greatest instructors, and that you are always greater than any obstacle. Often, all that is required is a slight adjustment of perspective.

Your willpower may be tested. Beginning a new endeavor or habit is exciting, but hard work follows. Faced with resistance and hurdles, the First Quarter is a time to focus on solutions and growth opportunities. The First Quarter Moon is a good time to concentrate on motivation, overcoming procrastination, and stopping self-sabotaging behaviors.

Rituals for the First Quarter

- Re-establish contact with your dreams and visions.
- Allow yourself to be free of any judgements that may occur.
- Just be imperfect for a change.
- Extend the scope of your intentions and be more detailed.
- Create a timetable or plan for yourself.
- Engage in something encouraging to watch, read, or listen to.

Moon Magick
Moon Phases

First Quarter

- RISES: Noon   SETS: Midnight   (Best magick between these times)
- PURPOSE: The shaping of something.
- WITCHES HOLIDAY: Ostara - Spring Equinox
- OFFERINGS: Feathers
- THEME: Luck
- TAROT ASSOCIATION: Strength or the Star
- MAGICKAL WORKINGS: Courage, creativity, elemental magick, friends, luck, motivation, moving forward, navigating obstacles, resistance.

First Quarter Ritual

A white candle should be lit and a piece of clear quartz should be held in your hand. This is an opportune moment to examine what is truly happening. Get in touch with the vision you have for your life. Additionally, this is a time for forgiveness.

Excuse yourself for reverting to old habits. Avoid self-judgment and self-condemnation. Simply identify your current state and then make a commitment to re-commit!

Re-read your diary entry from the New Moon to reacquaint yourself with your vision. Are you being specific with your desires and intentions? If not, dig deep and fill in any spaces or blanks. Organize your thoughts into a vision board. Establish a schedule. Read a book about personal growth. Watch an inspiring or motivational video. Make this a daily habit and always be grateful.

Moon Magick
First Quarter

Moon Magick
First Quarter

Moon Magick
Moon Phases

Waxing Gibbous

As we approach the full moon, the moment has come to harness the strong energy associated with this phase and leap into action. Everything should begin to feel more in sync with you and your goals. Have faith that the cosmos is assisting you. Keep your mind focused on maintaining a laser-like concentration on your intended goal and to invest your entire heart in it.

Now is the moment to give oneself a boost in order to progress and actualize your inner aspirations. If necessary, revise your intentions or plan. Bear in mind that your original objectives are likely to shift slightly as you immerse yourself in this journey, so take the time now to become clear on what is calling you. If something isn't working, shift course or abandon it. If something is effective, replicate it. Allow yourself sufficient time and space to accomplish your goals. It may take several moon phases to finish, which is OK.

Consider how you may better support yourself on this path, or seek outside assistance.

Rituals for the Waxing Gibbous

- Daily, read your affirmations.
- Consider how you can contribute more to your projects/goals.
- Welcome, appreciate, and be grateful for assistance.
(from yourself & others)
- Ask yourself: What is working? What's not working?
- Is your timeline realistic?
- What obstacles are currently in your way?

Moon Magick
Moon Phases

Waxing Gibbous

- **RISES:** Mid-afternoon   **SETS:** Around 3 am   (Best magick between these times)
- **PURPOSE:** Details
- **WITCHES HOLIDAY:** Beltane - Beginning of Summer
- **OFFERINGS:** Ribbons
- **THEME:** Perfection
- **TAROT ASSOCIATION:** The Wheel of Fortune
- **MAGICKAL WORKINGS:** Action, alignment, celebration, courage, endurance, harmony, high energy, patience, peace, perspective, refinement, trust.

The Energy of a Waxing Gibbous

Cast a spell during this moon phase to assist you in attracting what you desire in your life. This is an excellent moment for long-term or material gain intentions such as job, business, or education.

While the Moon is growing and getting brighter every day, you may focus on self-development and healing. Additionally, self-esteem, beauty, family, and fertility spells could be successful at this time. This lunar phase also enhances love spells.

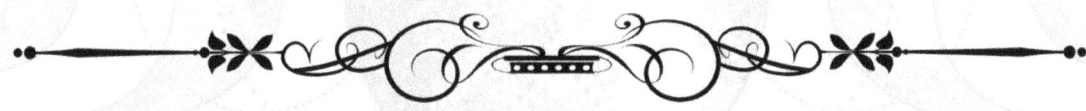

Moon Magick
Waxing Gibbous

Moon Magick
Waxing Gibbous

Moon Magick
Moon Phases
Full Moon

In the sky, the sun is now directly opposite the moon. Through the night, she receives his light and reflects it back to us. The moon is symbolic of the collective feminine, which indicates that now is an especially potent moment to connect with other women and respect the divine feminine inside you and us all.

A full moon is both nourishing and energizing, but it also shines a light on our shadows. We are invited to reflect on our own darkness, to feel our most deepest feelings, and to use the information we get to transcend. This is also a moment to rejoice. Celebrate your progress and cultivate an attitude of thankfulness for what you have. What we value will grow even more.

The full moon is a time to enjoy and reap the rewards of your new moon intentions. You may not have reached your target in two weeks. Perhaps your 30-day challenge is half-finished. Maybe you strayed from your new moon goals. It's fine. It's not time to judge or criticize yourself. It is time to enjoy your recent victories, regardless the size.

Be thankful for where you are now and how far you have gone since the new moon. If you've strayed, utilize the full moon to recommit and restart.

Rituals for the Full Moon

- Write a gratitude list.
- Bathe in the moonlight, meditate and just breathe.
- Celebrate your wins from the past two weeks (big & small).
- Write a Thank-You letter to the moon.
- Do some shadow work, and journal on your feelings.
- Attend a moon circle with other women (or host your own).

Moon Magick
Moon Phases
Full Moon

- RISES: Sunset   SETS: Dawn   (Best magick between these times)
- PURPOSE: Completion of a project
- WITCHES HOLIDAY: Litha - Summer Solstice
- OFFERINGS: Flowers
- THEME: Power
- TAROT ASSOCIATION: The Sun
- MAGICKAL WORKINGS: Artistic endeavors, beauty, change, children, competition, decisions, dreams, families, fitness, health, knowledge, legal undertakings, love, money, motivation, protection, psychic power, romance, self-improvement.

Full Moon Gratitude Ritual

While I highly encourage thinking of five things you are grateful for each day, the Full Moon is a terrific opportunity to completely appreciate your blessings.
Light a candle, light your favorite incense (or diffuser),
and treat yourself to some self-care.
Then celebrate your victories over the last two weeks.
Visualize your goal or dream becoming realized and be grateful that it is happening and coming to fruition.
Record your thoughts and emotions in a notebook. You can even thank the Moon for her support and encouragement.

Moon Magick
Full Moon

Moon Magick
Full Moon

Moon Magick
Moon Phases

Waning Gibbous

To achieve our dreams and intentions, we must constantly let go of or give up something else. This is what keeps you from your soul's desires. The moment has come for introspection.

What's holding you back? What is stifling the fruition of your goals? Negative thoughts, procrastination, self-sabotaging behavior, fear, laziness, unbalanced life, toxic relationship or devoting too much energy to others? Allow yourself to feel this until you find the source of your obstructions. Remind yourself of your achievements, but don't grow complacent. There's more to do. Be open to accepting these teachings and performing the hard work. Make time for self-care.

Well, put on your adulting pants, because it's time to commit to your personal and spiritual growth. It's time to identify at least one aspect of your life that is impeding your goal or intention fulfilment and work toward resolving it.

Whatever it is, use this time to reflect and pinpoint one issue in your life that is preventing you from moving forward.

The Waning Gibbous Moon serves as a reminder that, while progress has been achieved, there is still work to be done.

Rituals for the Waning Gibbous

- Eliminate bad and negative energy from your life with a burning ritual.
- Practice self-care & kindness. Take ritual cleansing baths and pamper yourself at this time.
- Meditate as a way of opening yourself to receive from the universe.

Moon Magick
Moon Phases

Waning Gibbous

- RISES: Mid-evening   SETS: Mid-morning   (Best magick between these times)
- PURPOSE: Initial destruction
- WITCHES HOLIDAY: Lammas or Lughnasadh
- OFFERINGS: Grain or rice
- THEME: Reassessment
- TAROT ASSOCIATION: The Tower
- MAGICKAL WORKINGS: Abundance, addictions, appreciate, decisions, divorce, emotions, protection, receive, release, removal, stress.

Waning Gibbous Quick Banishing Ritual

To utilize the magickal quality of 'removal' from the Waning Gibbous moon, this is a simple ritual that can be done to release any negative aspect in your life.

WHAT YOU WILL NEED:
- Pen & a piece of paper
- White tea light candle

- Write down what is now upsetting you or what you wish to eliminate from your life on the paper. A poor habit, a symptom, a person, a scenario, or an emotion might all be considered.
- In a safe location (always practice candle safety), light the white candle and recite aloud what you have written.
- Keep the paper next to the candle. After the candle has extinguished itself, rip the paper into pieces and discard it together with the candle's remnants.

Moon Magick
Waning Gibbous

Moon Magick
Waning Gibbous

Moon Magick
Moon Phases
Last Quarter

As the moon's brightness dims, our energy is drawn within ourselves once again. Whatever direction and answers you seek are contained inside. Create calmness and room in which to receive and act on these messages, regardless of how they are conveyed to you.

It's also a chance to consider balance (or what's out of balance) and where limits should be established. During the Waning Gibbous Moon, you've found a facet of your life that you desire to give up.

When removing something from your life, you must replace it with something else. This week, you're going to purge that space and reserve it for something more beneficial. For instance, if you've terminated a bad relationship, make room for a wonderful, inspiring companion. If your objective is to lose weight, purge your kitchen of any unhealthy, junk foods. If your objective is to be more creative, eliminate an hour of television watching (or Facebook, or whatever) and reserve that time for creative endeavors.

Rituals for the Last Quarter

- De-clutter. Do it slowly and in steps. Practice clearing out a small space each day, it doesn't have to be a full house cleaning in one day.
- Create a schedule or a budget for yourself. Be careful not to overwhelm yourself as this can sometimes be no small task.
- Engage in breathing exercises to calm your nervous system.

Moon Magick
Moon Phases

Last Quarter

- RISES: Midnight   SETS: Noon   (Best magick between these times)
- PURPOSE: Absolute destruction
- WITCHES HOLIDAY: Mabon - Fall Equinox
- OFFERINGS: Incense
- THEME: Banishing
- TAROT ASSOCIATIONS: Judgement
- MAGICKAL WORKINGS: Addictions, ancestors, banishing, breath, divorce, endings, health and healing, make space, protection, set boundaries, stress.

Last Quarter House Detox Spell

WHAT YOU WILL NEED:
- Sage smudge and a Palo Santo stick
- White candle
- Cauldron

- Place your cauldron next to the white candle. Light your sage and Palo Santo separately, and when burning, place them in the cauldron.
- As the smoke rises, light your white candle and chant:

Mother Earth and Goddess of the cosmic sphere,

My heart is pure, bring your power of cleansing here.

- Chant as many times as you feel is necessary, and if needed, re-light the sage and Palo Santo so that the smoke fills your home with protective energy.

Moon Magick
Last Quarter

Moon Magick
Last Quarter

Moon Magick
Moon Phases

Waning Crescent

This is the final lunar phase of the cycle, just before the sky totally darkens in preparation for the new moon. While your physical vitality may be depleted during the waning crescent, your emotional and spiritual intelligence will be at an all-time high. Surrender to this. Slow down and schedule time for self-care; this will assist you in achieving your goals and aspirations and provide much-needed space for introspection and reflection.

You've accomplished and endured a great deal during the last three weeks. Be aware and mindful of this. Allow time for self-recharging in preparation for the next moon cycle.

Questions to ask yourself during this moon phase:

What have I learned this cycle?
How can I use this to help me manifest my intentions?
Where am I holding back/where can I be more present and in the moment more?
How have I grown?

Rituals for the Waning Crescent

- Practice self-care every day during this phase. Making changes requires a lot of energy, so go ahead and pamper yourself. You deserve it.
- Make time for deep reflection by journaling about your experiences, thoughts and feelings over the past three weeks.
- Complete and tie up loose ends before the new moon.

Moon Magick
Moon Phases
Waning Crescent

- RISES: 3 am   SETS: Mid-afternoon   (Best magick between these times)
- PURPOSE: Rest
- WITCHES HOLIDAY: Samhain - Witches New Year
- OFFERINGS: Honesty
- THEME: Justice
- TAROT ASSOCIATION: Justice
- MAGICKAL WORKINGS: Addictions, barriers, breakups, equality, fights, foes, removal, separation, stopping stalkers and theft, transformation.

Rest & Relax Rockstar - You deserve it

Since the moon cycle is almost over, now is a good time to rest and take it easy. You have done a lot of personal work over these past weeks. The best thing you can do for yourself right now is to enjoy some quiet time, be in a comfortable space, and just practice some great self-care. Below is a list of self-care ideas. Feel free to choose which ones stand out to you, or go through and do them all, it is completely up to you.

- PRACTICE GRATITUDE
- READ A POSITIVE BOOK
- TAKE A WALK IN NATURE
- DRINK A GREEN SMOOTHIE
- TAKE 3 DEEP BREATHS
- DO A FULL BODY STRETCH
- HAVE A CUP OF TEA (OR COFFEE)
- AROMATHERAPY
- LAUGH
- SAY SOMETHING KIND TO YOURSELF
- DECLUTTER A SMALL SPACE
- LIGHT SOME CANDLES
- DIGITAL DETOX (PUT ELECTRONICS AWAY AND BE PRESENT)

Moon Magick
Waning Crescent

Moon Magick
Waning Crescent

Moon Phase Calendar

When working with your Moon Phase Calendar, you can plan ahead for your spellwork, rituals, and magick associated with each phase of the moon. Use these charts as your personal magickal planner to know what phases are approaching, and to better organize and help you with your spellwork and rituals.

If you wish to fill in all the upcoming moon phases before you start planning, a great website to find all of the information needed is: **https://mooncalendar.astro-seek.com/**
With this site, you can select your desired month and year, and it will also show you the exact dates in every month for each of the 8 moon phases, along with the Astrological Zodiac association that each individual phase falls into.

HOW TO USE YOUR MOON PHASE CALENDAR

You can fill in your Moon Phase Calendar however you wish. Do whatever works best for you and your practice. There is no right or wrong. Using the website mentioned above, you can fill in all of these sections:

- **MONTH:** You can start at the beginning of the Year, or you can start at the current month.
- **DATE:** The exact date or dates that the moon phase falls on, or the time the moon will be in that phase.
- **MOON PHASE:** This is the specific moon phase for that time period.
- **MOON IS IN ZODIAC:** This is the zodiac sign that the moon is currently in to help you better plan ahead for your spellwork and rituals.
- **RITUALS, SPELLS & MAGICK PLANNED:** This section is where you can plan out your spellwork and rituals for the desired moon phases to help you plan ahead. There is enough space in the calendar to input a full year of information.

MONTH	DATE	MOON PHASE	MOON IS IN: ZODIAC	RITUALS, SPELLS & MAGICK PLANNED

SAMPLE CALENDAR

Remember to utilize the information in this section when planning out your spellwork & rituals. Consider all the correspondences and other information provided.

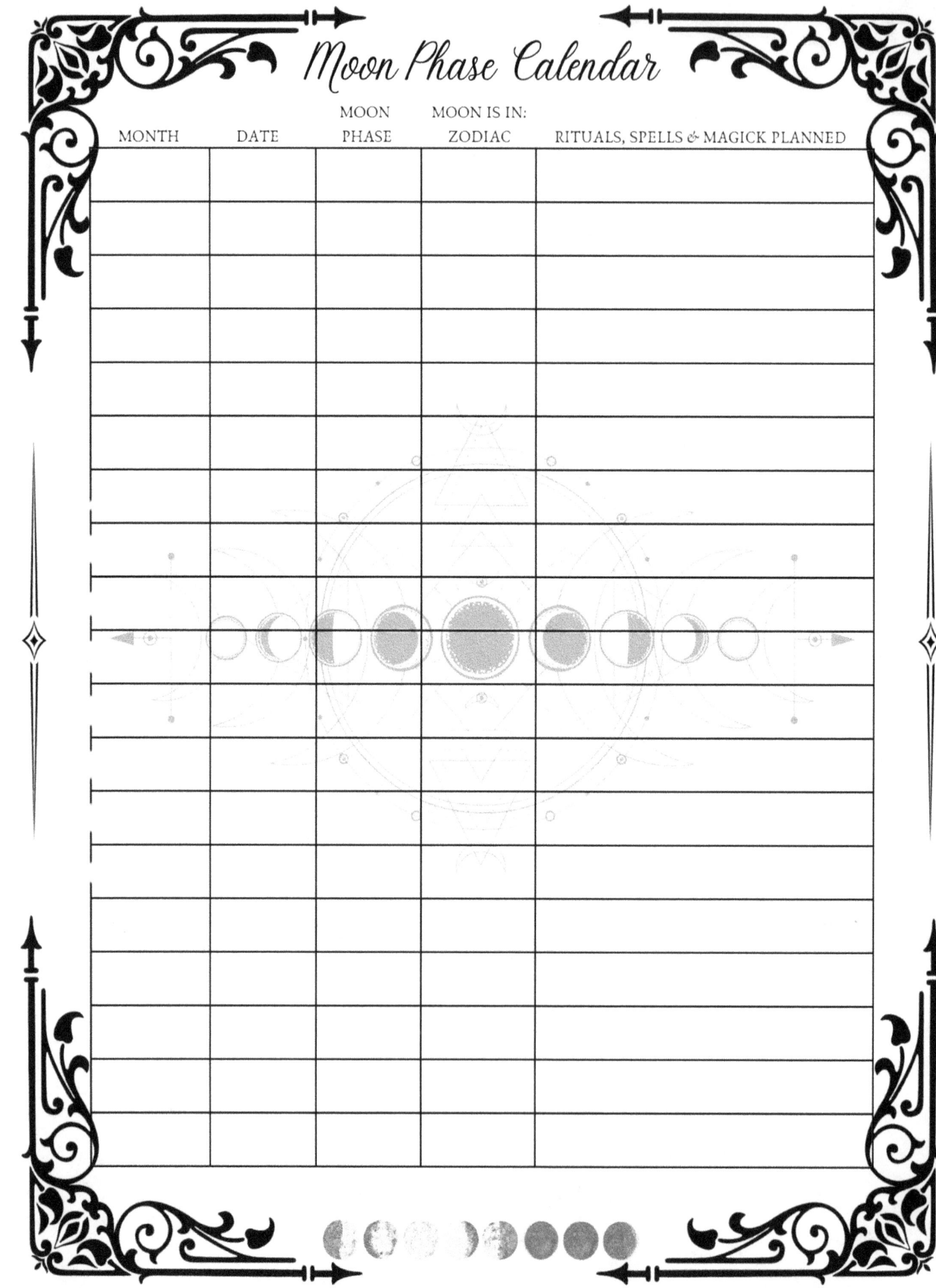

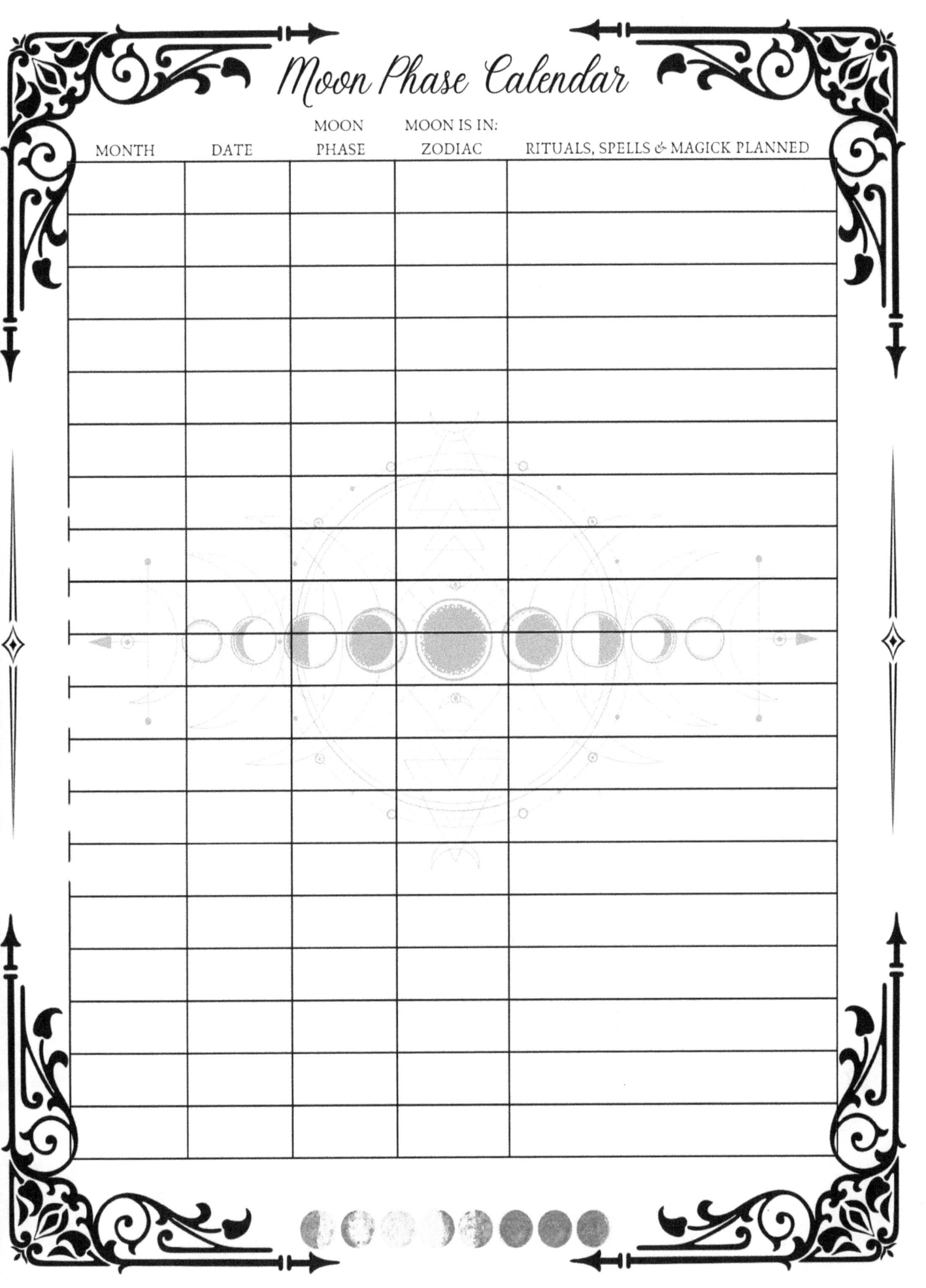

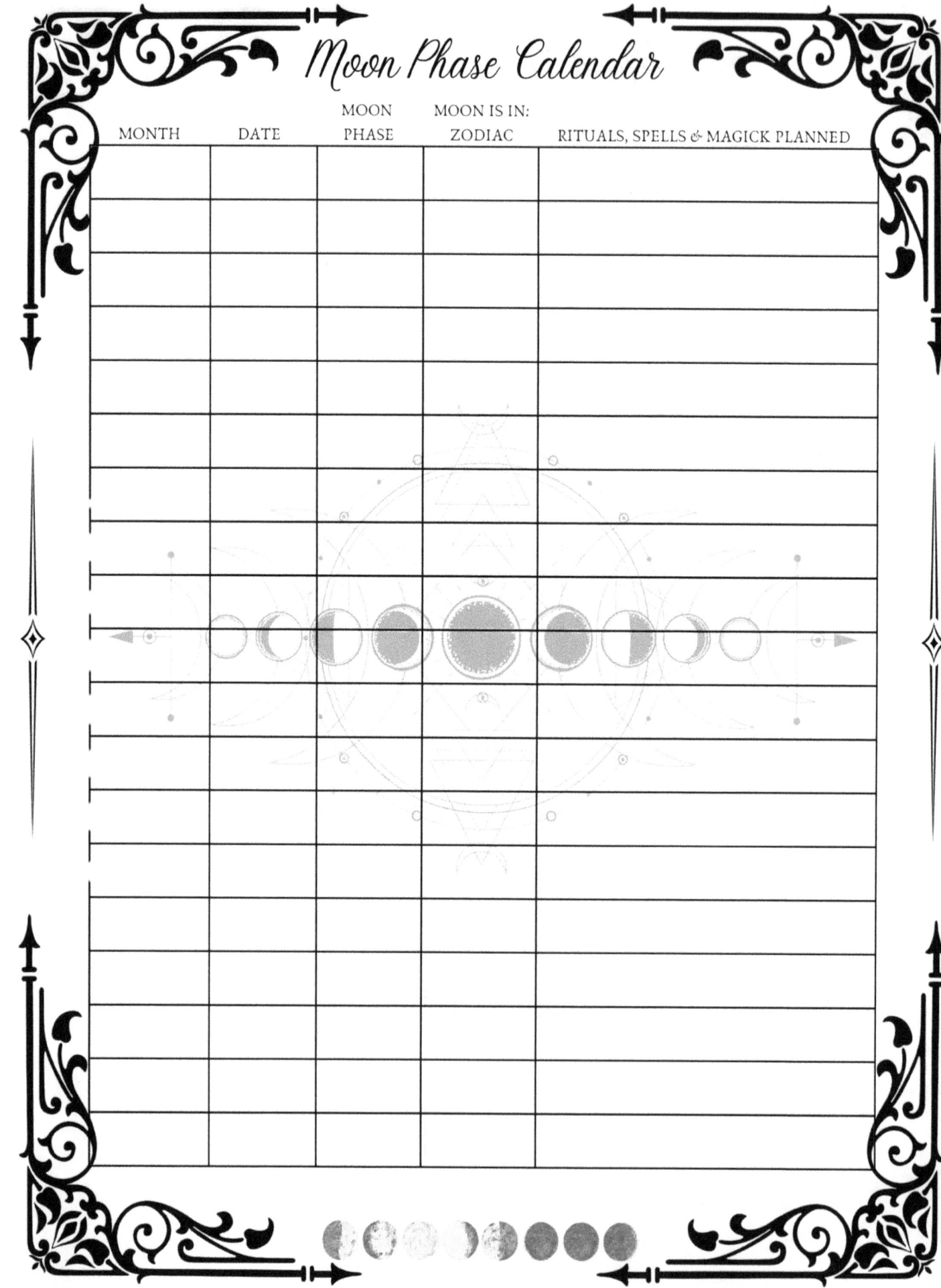

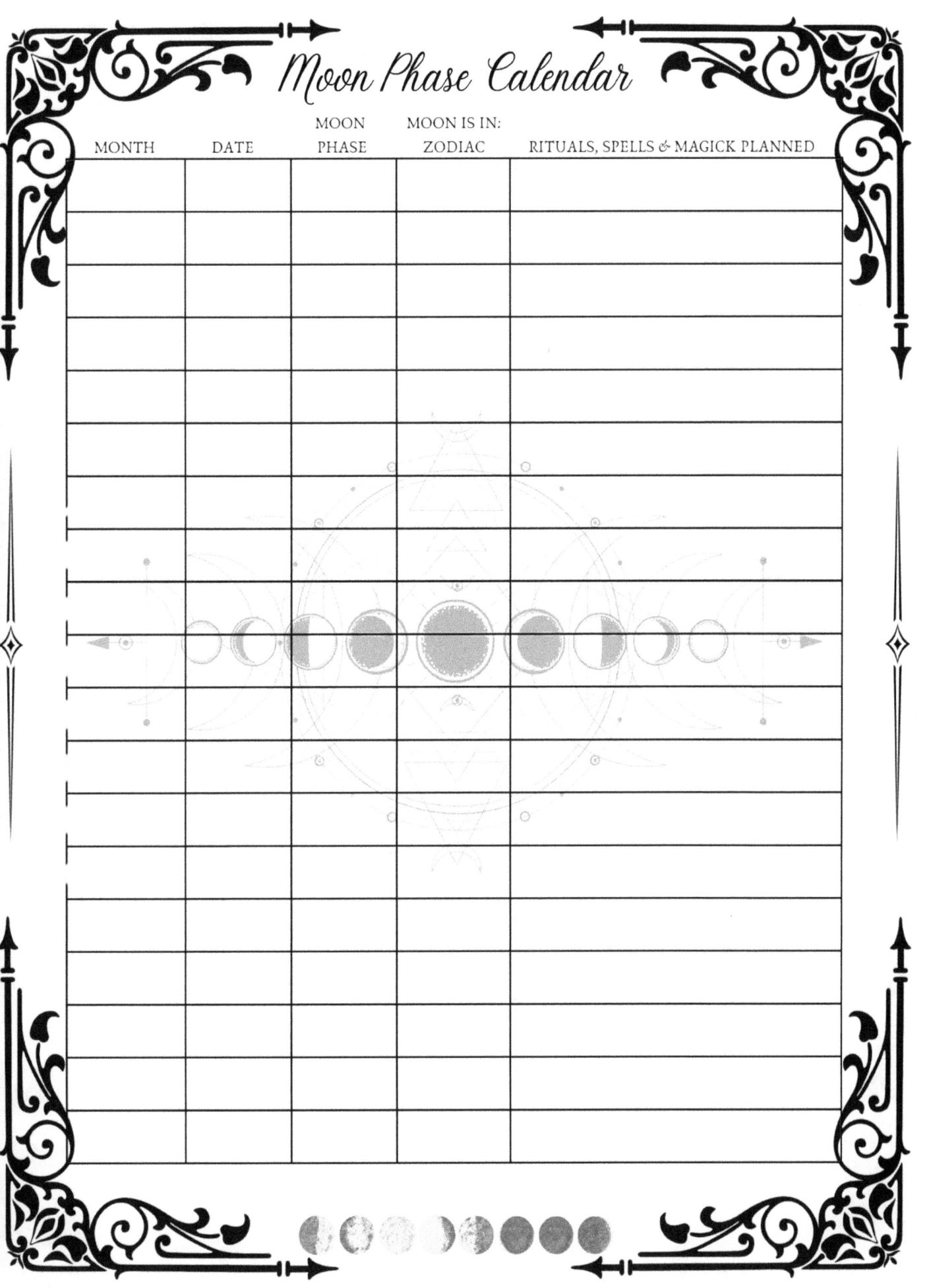

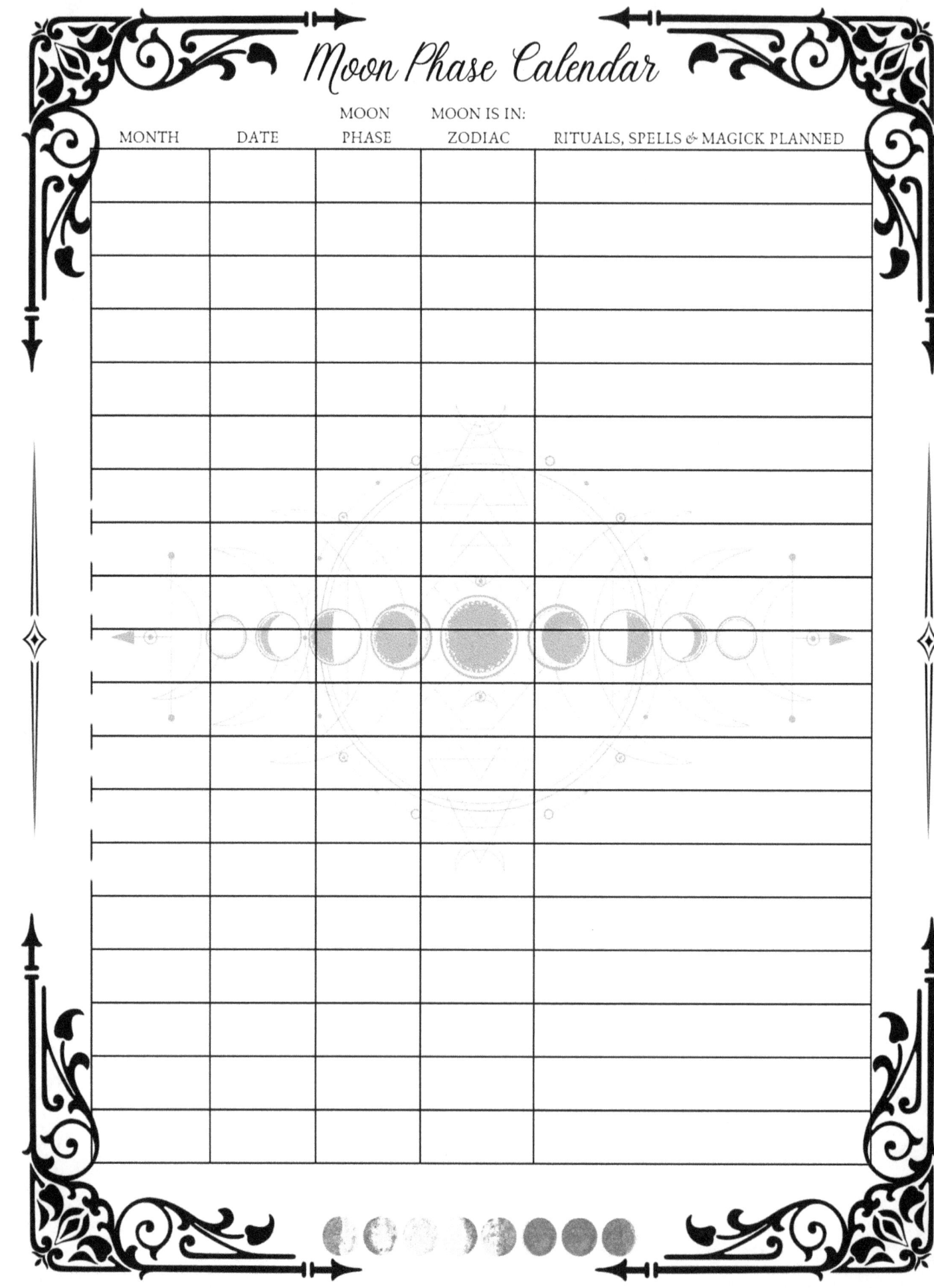

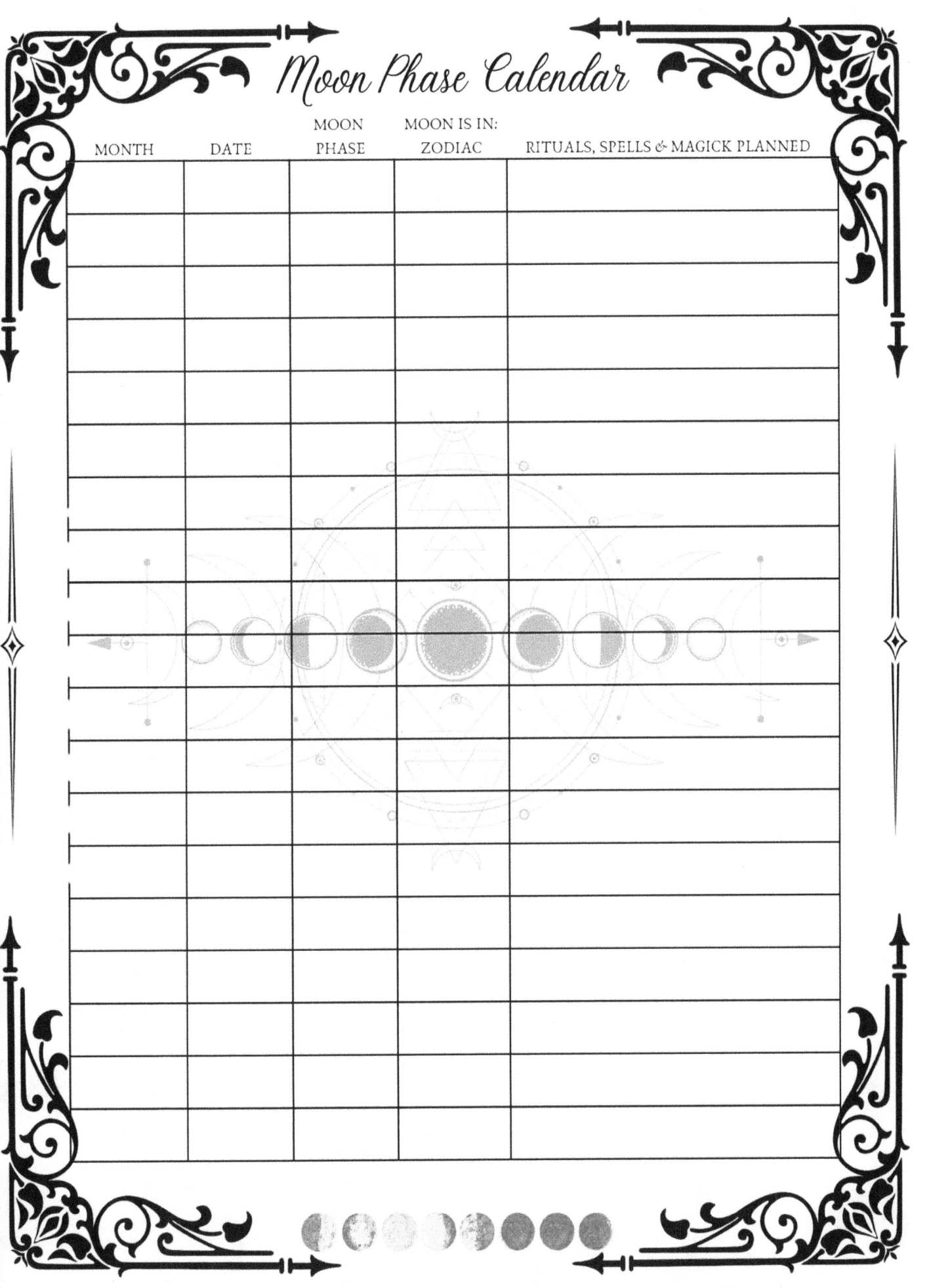

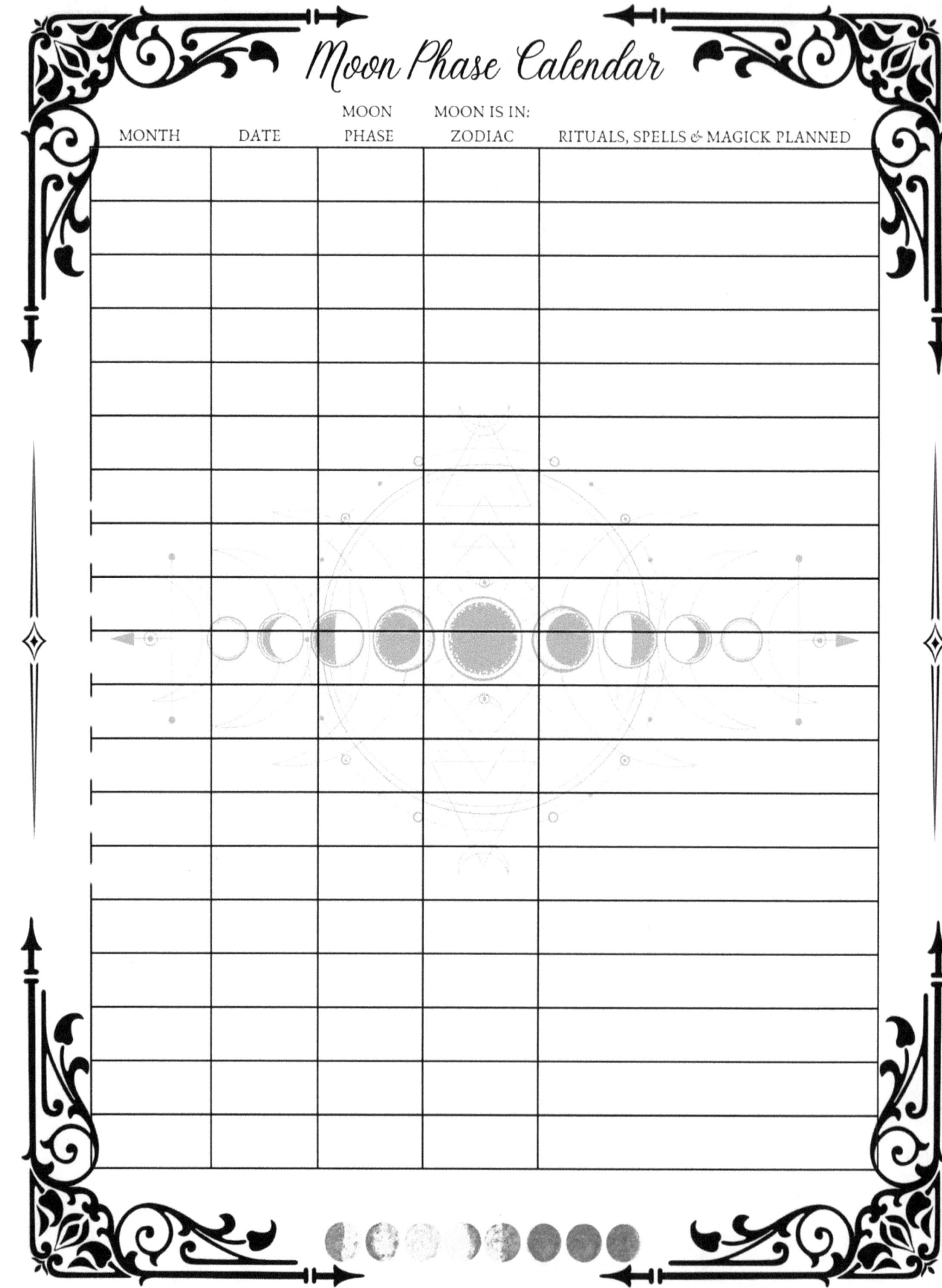

Moon Water

What is Moon Water?

Throughout history, several spiritual traditions have placed importance on the moon, thinking that its varied cycles have an effect on our moods and physical well-being. For generations, rituals for harnessing the moon's energy have existed. One of these is moon water collection. According to some, this water is imbued with lunar energy, which may be utilized to cleanse bad energies and facilitate spiritual change.

It is not available in supermarkets. Moon water is made at home during a specific lunar phase. Usually, it is made when the moon is full, when its energy is at its highest. Following that, it is used as a drink, applied topically, or sprayed throughout the home. While witches traditionally charge their water on a full moon, new moon, or other notable lunar event, moon water may be made at any time.

It is believed that energy can be stored in water, but there is no proof. Water is an incredibly programmable substance, which means it readily absorbs the energy qualities of the objects it comes into contact with. Moon water infused with lunar energy may assist us in integrating, connecting with, and manifesting our intentions and goals, since we are made of 60% water.

WHAT CAN MOON WATER BE USED FOR?

According to some, you can harness the moons energy to promote in cleansing, rejuvenation, renewal and intention setting. Moon water is frequently used to amplify intentions. The new moon is an excellent time to materialize your goals and bring opportunities to you. You can then use that water in a number of ways to help your manifestations come true.

Moon Water is generally used in spellwork, rituals such as spiritual & healing rituals, manifesting your intentions and goals, and also in your daily beauty routine as a refreshing facial spray and toner (when using only water with no additional herbs, essential oils or crystals).

CLEANING: *Add to cleaning to deepen house and altar energy purification.*
WATERING PLANTS: *Plants love to be misted with moon water.*
FULL MOON BATH: *A full moon bath connects you to lunar energy. Bathe in moon water to connect on a deeper level.*
IN YOUR TEA: *To re-align with the moons energy, boil your moon water for tea.*
CLEANSING CRYSTALS: *The full moon, like moon water, may recharge and cleanse your crystals. Some crystals don't like water, so be cautious.*
WATER-SAFE OPTIONS: *Agate, Amethyst, Citrine and Moonstone.*

How to make Moon Water

Moon water may be quite restorative, both energetically and physically, and it is a great cleansing tool for the home and body, as well as a multitude of other uses within your magickal practice.

1. Choosing your container

Fill a glass jar with water, preferably fresh rainwater, and set it aside. If you want to use the moon to help you reach a certain goal or intention, you could also have some fun and choose a container that fits with your goal. If you're going to drink your moon water, make sure it is safe to do so. You can leave your jar open, but if you put a lid on it, the water will stay cleaner. (The moonlight is still capable of reaching it!) Some witches like to brew their moon water in a silver bowl, as this reflects the light of the moon and energizes the water more powerfully. How you make moon water is up to you.

2. Find a location with full direct moonlight

This can be as easy as simply setting your jar or bowl of water outside at night during the moon phase you wish to charge your water with. If it is going to be cold outside, and there is a chance that your water can freeze, you can also set your jar on a windowsill that will also receive the majority of the moons light. As long as your jar or bowl can be in direct moonlight, there is no right or wrong location. Let your intuition guide you on the process.

3. Say an affirmation and/or set your intentions

Consider how your overall intention for the moon water. Over the jar, say an affirmation or chant to set an intention for the full moon. When setting goals, it's also a good idea to think about what zodiac sign the full moon is in so that you can use the energy of the current cycle. For example, if your goals are related to love, a Taurus or Libra full moon could help you achieve them.

4. Use crystals to empower your moon water

To increase the amplification, you may add your favorite crystals on top of the jar to charge and enhance the water. Clear quartz, moonstone, and selenite are all great crystals for clearing energy and making intuition stronger.

5. Leave out overnight

Once everything is set up and your goal is clear, leave the jar in the moonlight overnight. You can start using your moon water the next morning. Some witches prefer to retrieve their moon water from its location prior to the sun coming up. Some believe that if the suns morning rays touch the water, it will deplete the moon energy, but this belief is completely your choosing. Some witches also like to transfer their moon water into ornate jugs or labelled flasks for future use as well.

Moon Water
LOG - RECORD - USES

DATE & TIME	MOON PHASE	ZODIAC	INTENTIONS - AFFIRMATIONS

Moon Magick

Moon Magick

Deities & Spirit Guides

Deities & Spirit Guides

Deities and spirit guides, although quite similar, have some differences between them. Deities can take on a variety of shapes and are frequently worshipped as such. They are a form of the divine. If you want to be a witch, you don't have to believe in or even worship any deities. This is your choice completely, which is why we have secular or non-religious witches.

Spirit guides are spirits who help us or show us the way through our lives on Earth. These beings can also come in many different forms, but most people think of them as ancestors, spirit animals, or divine beings such as gods and goddesses. They can be related to a deity or even become a familiar.

Which gods and goddesses you revere depends on your spiritual path's pantheon. Modern pagans and wiccans are mostly eclectic. This implies people can worship gods from different traditions. We may ask a god or goddess for aid with a spell or a challenge we are currently facing, and those deities can come from many different pantheons. You'll have to start organizing them eventually, so doing research and learning about all the different pantheons and their associated deities would be beneficial. Keeping a record of your workings with different gods and goddesses is also a great practice to start implementing. This way, you can start to see patterns, notice changes, or begin to see how differing deities help you.

When we start to think about deities that we would like to work with, we have to consider the multitude of pantheons that are available to us. How do you know which god or goddess, and from which pantheon would benefit our purpose and goal? Consider your own particular interests as a means of narrowing down the options. For starters, I feel drawn to Egyptian, Celtic, Norse and Greek culture, art and mythology, so naturally, I would also be interested in the deities of those pantheons.

Alternatively, if you are seeing an abundance of a certain type of spirit guide in your life, it may also be associated with a specific god or goddess. For example, if you are constantly seeing crows in your presence, this could be your spirit guide and a welcome sign from the god Odin, wishing to communicate with you.

So how do we know which deities would care enough about our situation to pay attention and help? Worshipping appropriately is ideal here. It is also important to mention that if we cannot take the time to get to know our chosen gods or goddesses, make offerings, and worship them consistently, then we really should not be asking them for help. It is also imperative that we choose the appropriate deity for the purpose we are striving for. For example, if we are celebrating the end of a successful harvest season, with the coming of winter, then we would not be making offerings of milk and flowers to a spring goddess. Just be mindful of that when selecting, which is why it is important to understand what each of the gods and goddesses correspond to, and how it fits with your ritual or spellwork.

Deities & Spirit Guides

When we are making offerings or praying to a god or goddess, think carefully about the reason you are doing so. Similarly to crystals, familiars and herbs, each of the gods and goddesses corresponds to distinct emotions, traits, desires, or dreams that you may require assistance resolving or manifesting.

What is a Patron Deity?

A *patron deity* is a god or goddess of your choice or one to whom you feel connected. This god or goddess is important to you and is considered your 'main' deity to work with. They will guide you on your spiritual journey and throughout your life. You are not required to have a dedicated patron deity, although many individuals find them beneficial.

How to find your Patron Deity

- Doing research of as many gods and goddesses as you can.
- Watch for signs from spirit guides associated with gods or goddesses (Seeing crows, which is associated with the God Odin)
- Think about different cultural or mythological stories, do you feel drawn to any specific god or goddess from history?
- Your patron deity should make you feel happy, joyful, safe, excited and powerful. You should almost have a sense of oneness and connection with your patron god or goddess.

Deities & Spirit Guides

Finding your Spirit Guide

- Find somewhere quiet to sit, think and meditate.
- Make sure you are at ease, relaxed and comfortable.
- Say or think out loud that you would like your spirit guide to come into your space.
- Make it apparent that you want an open and straightforward dialogue with them.
- Have confidence and believe that your spirit guide will contact you at the appropriate moment.
- Do not try to force anything with your spirit guides. Let messages and advice come to you effortlessly and naturally.

How to communicate with your Spirit Guide

- Simply asking for help and guidance.
- Show them gratitude and meditate daily.
- Be mindful of subtle signs and messages that can often be overlooked.
- You can utilize tarot cards, pendulums or other divination methods to get direct answers.
- Follow their instructions. Ignoring their counsel might damage the connection between you and your spirit guide.

Deities & Spirit Guides

How to communicate with a Deity

- Do something relating to their source of power. Sit in the sun to feel the God Apollo, or conduct a water ritual for intuition to sense Poseidon.
- Use your pendulum, tarot cards or another form of divination to get direct answers.
- Create a connection through meditation, prayer and ritual dedicated to their power and divinity.
- Leave suitable offerings on your altar, and create a shrine or dedicated space for them.
- Have statues or pictures of your chosen god or goddess to have a visual connection when working with them.

Pantheons

A pantheon is the group of divine beings (gods and goddesses) in a polytheistic religion, folklore, mythology or tradition. A culture's pantheon reflects its ideals and sense of self. A pantheon led by a thunderbolt-wielding ruler suggests patriarchy and fighting capabilities. A great-mother goddess-led pantheon suggests a village-based agricultural community. To face the Egyptian pantheon is to face a world view based on death and resurrection and nature's cycles. The Greek pantheon represents a pragmatic vision of life that values artistry, beauty, and individual strength but is suspect of human nature. Next we are going to look at the different pantheons, and go over the top five most popular pantheons and their associated deities.

Deities & Spirit Guides

Pantheons

(These are some of the most popular and well-known. This list is non-exhaustive)

- AFRICAN
- ARMENIAN
- AZTEC
- BUDDHIST
- BERBER
- BURMESE
- CANAANITE
- CELTIC
- CHINESE
- EGYPTIAN
- GERMANIC
- GREEK
- GAUNCHE
- HINDU
- INCAN
- IRISH
- JAIN
- JAPANESE
- JAPANESE-BUDDHIST
- MAYA
- NATIVE AMERICAN
- NORSE
- RIGVEDIC
- ROMAN
- SLAVIC
- SUMERIAN
- YORUBA

When looking at different Pantheons, we need to be mindful of cultural appropriation. It is recommended that you research, study, learn and understand each cultures traditions and practices before incorporating them into your personal magickal practice to be respectful. It is also important to note that some cultures have 'closed' practices, so unless you are from that tradition or ancestry, it may not be appropriate to call upon those deities.

Polytheistic

Relating to, believing in, or worshipping more than one god or goddess. A pantheon with multiple deities.

PANTHEONS

PLEASE NOTE: *This is a small list of the more popular deities. There are hundreds, if not thousands more.*

Celtic Gods

- **ALATOR:** God of protection and war.
- **BELENUS:** The 'Bright One,' God of healing.
- **CERNUNNOS:** Horned god representing nature, fertility, wealth, fruit and the underworld.
- **HERNE:** God of the wild hunt, Autumn, vegetation.
- **LUGH:** 'Master of Skills,' God of craftsmanship, blacksmiths, artisans. Justice, rulership, the Sun.
- **THE DAGDA:** 'The good God,' fertility, knowledge, Father God of Ireland.

Celtic Goddesses

- **BRIGANTIA:** Goddess of crafts, poetry, rivers and water.
- **BRIGHID (BRIGIT):** Goddess of fertility, poetry, cattle, healing, fire.
- **CAILLEACH:** 'Dark Mother,' Goddess of storms and creation.
- **CERRIDWEN:** Goddess of magick, rebirth, prophecy, wisdom. Also known as a sorceress.
- **THE MORRIGHAN (MORRIGAN):** Goddess of war, death, sovereignty, fate, battle. Crows and ravens are closely connected.
- **RHIANNON:** Goddess of horses, kinship of Wales.

CELTIC PANTHEON

PANTHEONS

PLEASE NOTE: *This is a small list of the more popular deities. There are hundreds, if not thousands more.*

Egyptian Gods

- **ANUBIS:** Has the head of a jackal. God of the deceased and embalming. He led the souls of the dead to the realm of the afterlife.
- **HORUS:** God of healing, the sky, sun, air, protection and kinship.
- **OSIRIS:** God of the dead, rebirth, resurrection, fertility, eternal life. His name translates to 'powerful' or 'mighty.'
- **RA:** God of creation, afterlife, sun and ruler of all Egyptian gods.
- **SET:** God of disorder, violence, storms and the desert.
- **THOTH:** God of the law, truth, the moon, writing, knowledge and wisdom.

Egyptian Goddesses

- **BASTET:** Goddess of protection. Takes the form of a lioness or cat.
- **HATHOR:** Goddess of the afterlife, music, dance, motherhood, sexuality, love, the sky and sun.
- **ISIS:** Goddess of magick, motherhood and protection.
- **MA'AT:** Goddess of balance, justice and truth. She used her feather to determine if the acts of the deceased were worthy of the afterlife.
- **SESHET:** Goddess of architecture, astronomy, mathematics and historical records.
- **TEFNET:** Lunar goddess of fertility and water.

EGYPTIAN PANTHEON

PANTHEONS

**PLEASE NOTE: This is a small list of the more popular deities. There are hundreds, if not thousands more.

Greek Gods

- **AETHER:** God of light. The 'spark of life' for every creature on earth.
- **APOLLO:** God of verse, singing, enlightenment, healing, and prophecy.
- **ARES:** God of courage, order and war.
- **EROS:** God of love, fertility, procreation and sexuality.
- **HADES:** Ruler of the underworld, grants prosperity and wealth.
- **HERMES:** God of business and commerce, messenger for the gods.
- **POSEIDON:** The god of the seas, oceans, rivers, intuition, earthquakes, floods, drought and horses.
- **ZEUS:** God of the sky, father to all Greek gods and humans. 'Lord of Justice.'

Greek Goddesses

- **APHRODITE:** Goddess of beauty and love.
- **ARTEMIS:** Goddess of wild animals, hunting, the wilderness, protector of young girls, childbirth and the moon.
- **ATHENA:** Goddess of strategic warfare, wisdom and protection. Considered among the most powerful of the Greek gods.
- **GAIA:** Mother of all and goddess of Mother Earth.
- **HECATE:** Goddess of witchcraft, magick and protectress of witches.
- **HERA:** Goddess of marriage, motherhood, childbearing, feminine power, defense and protection.

GREEK PANTHEON

PANTHEONS

PLEASE NOTE: *This is a small list of the more popular deities. There are hundreds, if not thousands more.*

Norse Gods

- **BALDUR:** God of peace, innocence, rebirth and beauty.
- **FREY:** God of the sun, rain, fertility and peace.
- **KVASIR:** God of wisdom and inspiration.
- **LOKI:** God of trickery and mischief.
- **ODIN:** God of war, the All-father, magick, poetry and wisdom.
- **THOR:** God of thunder, battle and protection for all mankind.
- **TYR:** God of the skies, war and justice.
- **VALI:** God of vengeance and revenge.

Norse Goddesses

- **EOSTRE:** Goddess of the dawn and spring. The sabbat Ostara is derived from her name.
- **FREYJA:** Goddess of magick, combat, fertility, love and witchcraft.
- **FRIGG:** Goddess of marriage, motherhood, maternity as well as Queen of the Norse gods.
- **GEFJUN:** Goddess of abundance, prosperity and fertility.
- **GULLVEIG:** Goddess of sorcery, magick, seer-ship and healing.
- **IDUNNA:** Goddess of youth, beauty, immortality, long life and responsibility.
- **NANNA:** Goddess of prosperity, wealth, love, romance and fertility.

NORSE PANTHEON

PANTHEONS

**PLEASE NOTE: *This is a small list of the more popular deities. There are hundreds, if not thousands more.*

Roman Gods

- **APOLLO:** God of poetry, sun, music, archery, truth and healing. He is also known by the same name in the Greek pantheon.
- **CUPID:** God of love, sexual desire, affection, attraction, companion to Aphrodite.
- **HERCULES:** God of bravery, adventure, courage, power and strength.
- **MARS:** God of military and war, protector of farming and agriculture.
- **MERCURY:** Bearer of the souls into the underworld, messenger to the gods.
- **NEPTUNE:** God of divination, mysteries, water, oceans, intuition, and imagination.
- **SATURN:** God of seeds, sowing, agriculture and harvest.

Roman Goddesses

- **AURORA:** Goddess of dawn, the morning red, light within the dark, new beginnings, and intuition. The 'Northern Lights' dance in her honor.
- **CERES:** Goddess of agriculture and harvest.
- **DIANA:** Goddess of childbirth, virginity, the moon and the hunt. Often seen depicted with a stag by her side.
- **LUNA:** Goddess of femininity, miracles, luck, creativity and instinct. Also known as Selene.
- **VENUS:** Goddess of gardens, beauty, love and sexuality.
- **VESTA:** Goddess of hearth and home, the sacred fire and protection for family members.

ROMAN PANTHEON

Deities & Spirit Guides

Divination

To "divine" is to establish a connection with a higher force. Throughout thousands of years, several civilizations have used this term in a variety of ways. Additionally, it has developed to mirror modern witchcraft.

Divination is the process of attempting to uncover a pattern or symbol in the natural world in order to communicate with gods, spirits, or the cosmos in order to get guidance, gain insight, or make predictions. There are several hundreds of methods to accomplish this, however, we will cover the most popular methods here. Feel free to research and learn more about all the different methods available.

In your magickal practice, you might employ a variety of divinatory methods. Some individuals like experimenting with a variety of techniques, but you may discover that you are more adept at one than the others. Determine which of the several divination techniques works best for you and your skills. Remember that, as with any other ability, the more you practice, the better you get.

Divination Methods

- Cartomancy
- Astrology
- Norse Runes
- Palmistry
- Pendulum
- Tasseomancy
- Pyromancy
- Dowsing
- Osteomancy
- Automatic Writing

- Tea Leaves
- Numerology
- Dreams
- I Ching
- Scrying
- Dice
- Libanomancy
- Celtic Ogham
- Lithomancy
- Intuition

Please note that this list is just a small fraction of available divination methods. There are hundreds more to explore.

Cartomancy
Tarot Card Divination

Cartomancy is commonly referred to as tarot, however its origin is unknown. Some think that the present tarot originated with the ancient Egyptians and later with the Italians.

Cartomancy is a simple strategy that involves arranging cards relating to a given topic or enquiry. The cards then convey information or a prediction on the question. Cartomancy was historically used to predict the future. Modern witches, on the other hand, typically use it to connect with their intuition in order to create positive life changes and make their dreams come true.

THE CHARIOT.

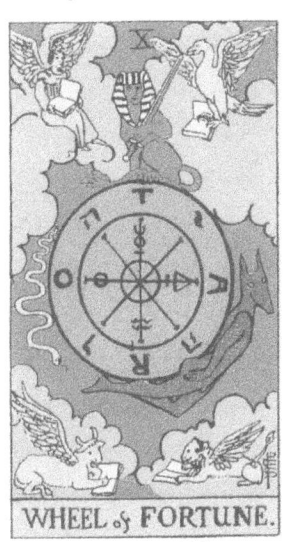
WHEEL of FORTUNE.

THE HIGH PRIESTESS

Numerous varieties of tarot card decks are available. The most popular would be the Rider-Waite tarot deck, which was first printed in 1909 and is still widely loved and used today by many divination practitioners.

Tarot decks typically contain 78 cards, each with its unique significance and image. The 22 Major Arcana cards, depict how humans learn, grow and evolve. The 56 cards of the Minor Arcana are split into four houses: Cups, Swords, Pentacles and Wands. There are various techniques to do a tarot reading, but the shuffle method and the fan approach are the most frequently used. After selecting the cards, they are placed in a layout, and the reader examines what the cards represent in regard to the question or topic. Cartomancy or Tarot is by far the most popular form of divination in the world.

TAROT TIP:

Some witches believe that a Tarot Deck has to be gifted to you by someone else in order to bond and connect with your cards. Although some strongly believe this, it is not necessary. If you are pulled to a certain deck, just purchase it. You were destined to discover them.

Cartomancy
Tarot Card Divination

Pendulum Divination

With simple yes or no queries, the pendulum is likely one of the easiest forms of divination. Most individuals like to use a crystal that they are connected with, but you can use anything that is heavy, with a string or chain attached.

Charge & Calibrate your Pendulum

Charge your pendulum by soaking it in water or salt overnight. Remember that certain crystals will disintegrate in water, so double-check. Another alternative is to leave it out in the moonlight overnight.

Calibrating your pendulum simply means to test it. To do so, hold it by the chain's free end with the weighted end dangling loosely. Do not move it at all, and try to be still. Ask a simple yes/no question, like "Am I a man or a woman?" or "Do I live in _____?"

Keep a watch on the pendulum, and observe whether it moves sideways, forwards, or backwards. This is your "Yes" sign.

Next, pose a question you know the answer to is No. This will be your "No" direction. Do this a few times with different queries to get a sense for your pendulum's response. Some swing horizontally or vertically, others in little or huge circles, while others do nothing unless the response is significant. If you are using a Pendulum Chart, keep an eye on which way your pendulum swings according to the chart when calibrating as well.

Using your Pendulum for Divinaton

You'd be astonished what a pendulum can tell you with "yes" and "no" replies. It's all about asking the correct questions. Here are some methods to use your pendulum to find out what you want to know: Using a divination board or chart. The pendulum board or chart, has the phrases Yes, No, Maybe and Rephrase. A pendulum chart is provided on the next page.

Like a dowsing rod, the pendulum may be used to point in the direction of misplaced objects. Lay out a Tarot card spread with the various answers if you have a particular yet complicated query. The pendulum might help you find the correct card to answer your question.

Using a pendulum to find magickal places: if you're outside, bring it with you. A pendulum may be useful in locating ley lines; if you chance to find a spot that causes your pendulum to go wild, you might want to perform a ceremony or ritual there.

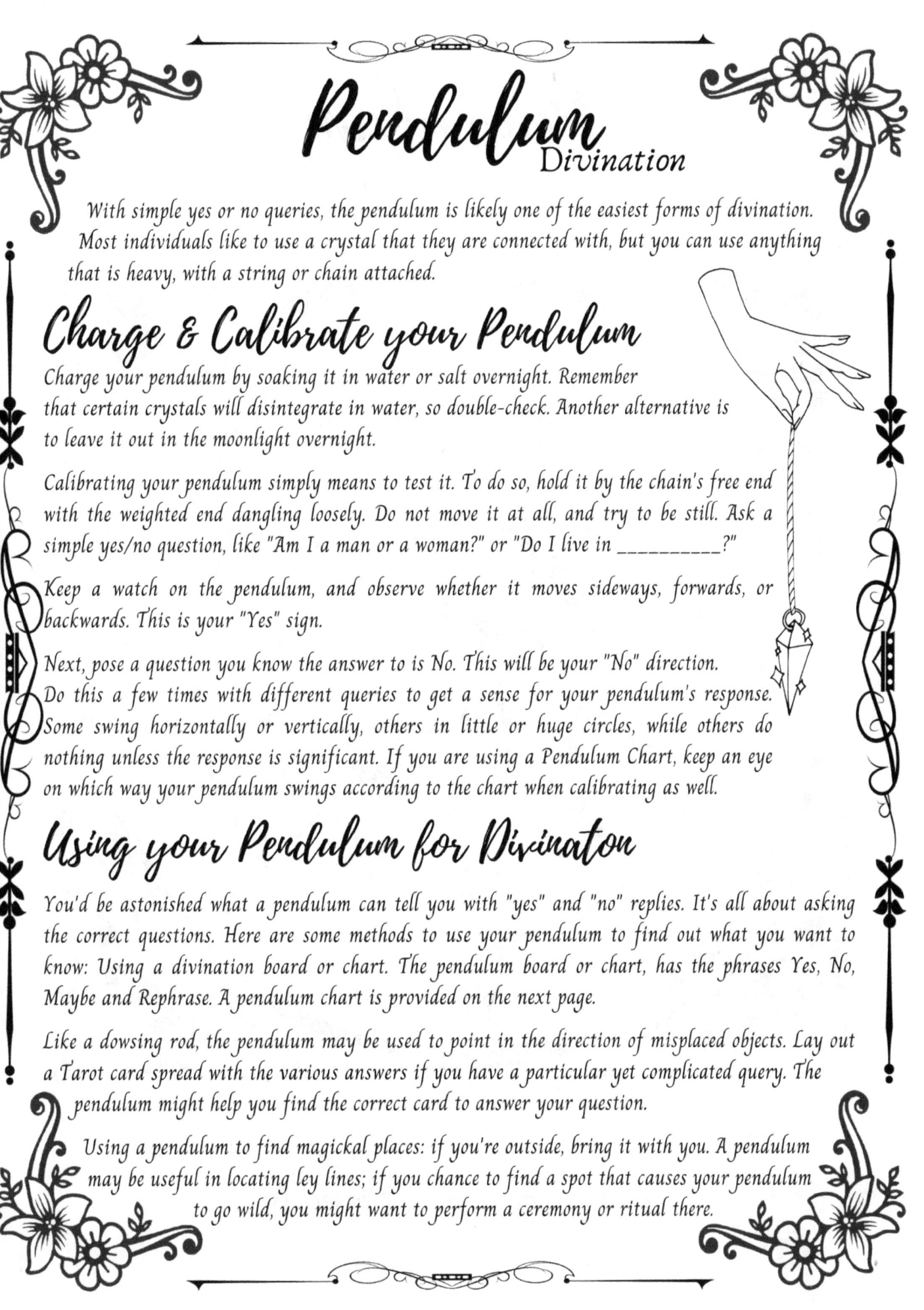

Pendulum Divination

Palmistry

In palmistry, the palm of a person's hand is looked at to figure out what will happen to them. Chiromancy and chirognomy are the two forms of palmistry. Chirognomy looks at the colors and shapes of the fingers, thumb, and palm. Chiromancy looks at the lines on the palm.

People look at three major lines on the palm: the life line, which runs just around the fat part of the thumb, the heart line, which runs just under the fingers starting just under the pinky, and the head line, which runs just under the heart line.

The Heart line describes the person's emotional condition as well as other relationships.

The head line describes the psychological and mental characteristics, in addition to the intuitive ability. Contrary to the misinformation of the mainstream media, the life line gives information about the individual's health, physical and emotional strength, as well as experiences in his or her life relating to those aspects.

In addition to these lines, the reader analyzes smaller, more delicate lines, such as the Bracelet Lines, which can indicate a person's lifespan, prosperity, imbalance, and destiny. Four bracelet lines, for instance, may imply that the querent will live close to 100 years.

In addition to the lines of the palm, the mounts or lumps of fatty tissue are examined because they reveal how the planets impact the individual and may reveal a great deal about their physical and emotional condition. The Sun, Moon, Mars, Mercury, Jupiter, Venus, and Saturn make up these seven groups.

Palm readers also look at the shape of a person's hand to figure out what kind of person they are. There are six main hand shapes that are studied: the conical, the spatulate, the square, the intellectual, and the mixed hand. But in Western palmistry, the most common way to group hand shapes is by the four elements: earth, air, fire, and water.

In the end, palmistry can tell a person a lot about who they are and what will happen to them in this life, similar to how astrology can.

Palmistry

Scrying

Scrying is the ability to look into water to find answers to questions. This can be done in a bowl at your altar, or under the full moon as mentioned here.

Are you the type of person who feels more sensitive and aware when the moon is full?

Try this simple yet powerful water scrying ritual to channel that energy into something helpful. This is best done outdoors.

What you need:
- Clear sky and a Full Moon
- A dark bowl
- Pitcher of water to fill the bowl
- Paper or Journal, and a pen
- Meditative music if you prefer

Depending on your custom, cast a circle. Start playing your music. Work comfortably. Close your eyes and tune into the surrounding energies. The ground is soft. Hear the woods rustling. Inhale the grass and earthy scents. Feel the moon's energy by raising your arms, palms up.

Gather your energy. We can sense a pull if we search for it. Recognize your connection to that silvery force and the Divine.

Open your eyes once you are ready to start scrying. The lunar energies are working if you experience clarity and attentiveness. Lift your pitcher over the bowl and visualize that wisdom and guidance imbue the water as you do so. Consider the water becoming imbued with the moon's vitality as you pour the water into the dark bowl. Consider that this water will reveal the secrets of the moon.

When the bowl is filled, stand or sit so the moonlight reflects in the water. Look for patterns, signals, or pictures in the water. Images may appear or words may form. Write down everything. You can stare at the water for as long as you need. Stop when you start to feel restless or when simple mundane thoughts start to pull your attention away, such as "did I feed that cat?"

After scrying, record all that you saw, thought, and felt. We regularly miss messages from other realms. If something doesn't make sense, let your unconscious mind digest it for a few days. It'll probably make sense. If you receive a message that doesn't appear to pertain to you, consider your friends. HINT: If you live near a body of water like a lake or pond, you can most certainly use this larger 'bowl' of water for scrying as well.

Scrying

Pyromancy
Candle Flame Divination

Have you ever gazed into a candles flame for a period of time and watched it dance? Pyromancy is the skill of gazing into a candle flame and interpreting the way that it 'dances.' The flowing movement of the flame can signify different meanings and messages. This practice was deeply routed in Greek Mythology as fire was a very important part of life.

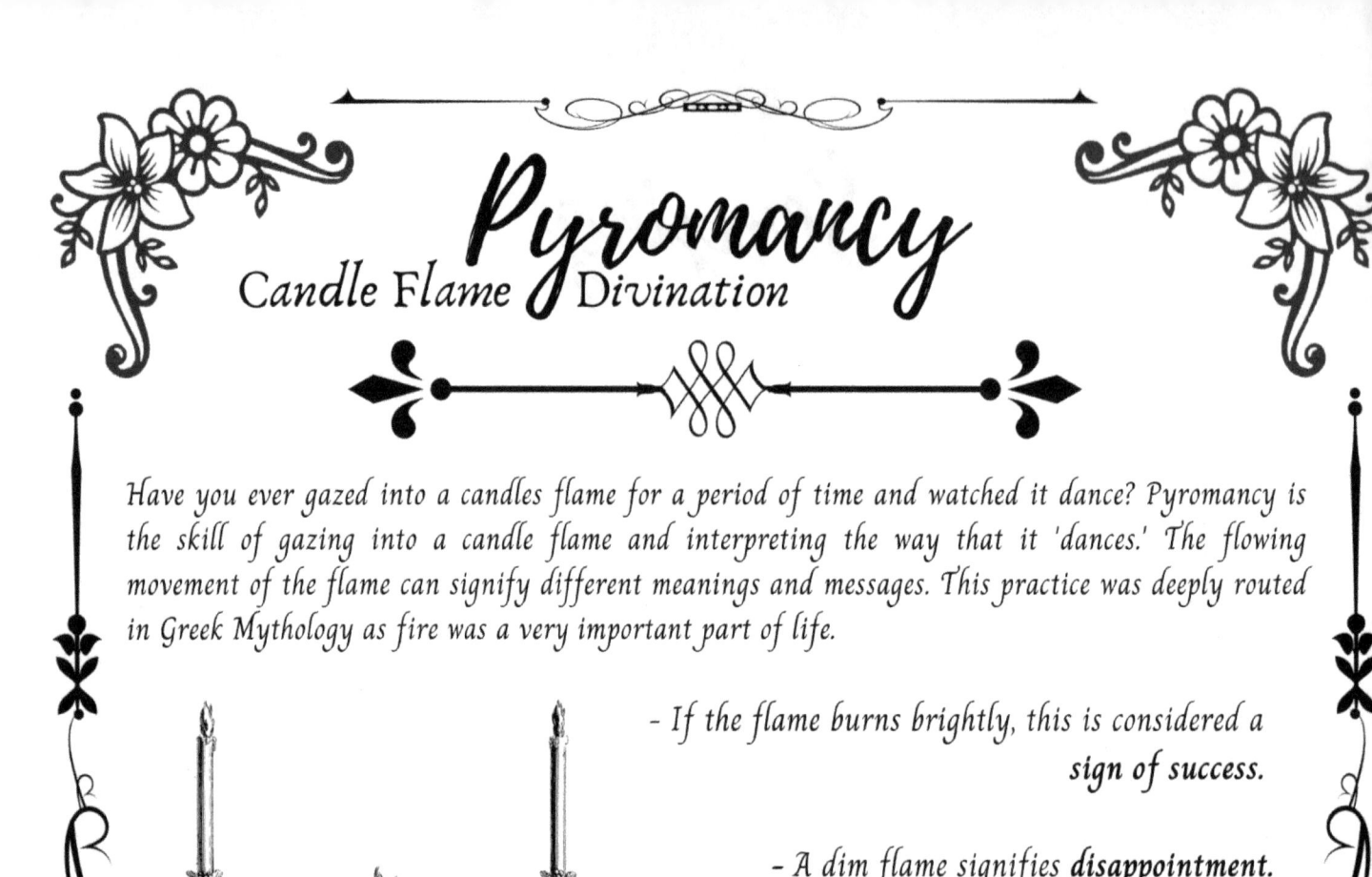

- If the flame burns brightly, this is considered a **sign of success**.

- A dim flame signifies **disappointment**.

- A flickering flame shows **wavering fortunes**.

- A spark means that an **important message** will be delivered to you shortly.

- Jumping candle flames represent there is **a lot of energy**.

- Dancing flames indicate **change**.

- A spiral-like effect is a **warning**.

- When candles are hard to light, then burn with a weak flame, it is a sign that **the time is not right** for the magick.

- If the candle goes out for no apparent reason (Ex: breeze) stop the ritual and **conduct it again at a later time**.

Pyromancy

Libanomancy
Smoke Divination

Incense burning is a centuries-old tradition. Healers, yogis, witches and religious leaders utilize incense for meditation, focus, rituals, and cleansing. Not everyone realizes that incense smoke might provide more significant information than they know.

Libanomancy, also known as Capnomancy, Livanomancy and Knissomancy, is a form of divination in which the smoke and ash from burning incense are interpreted. Typically, you have to ask a specific question, just like any other divination methods. The answer to the question must be correctly interpreted in the smoke from the incense.

In order to interpret the smoke from the incense, you will need to find your favorite incense, light it, and watch how the smoke behaves. It would be a good idea to have a notepad or journal with you to record your findings.

The most important thing to keep in mind when reading smoke is to have a clear question and an open mind. If you've never tried to read smoke before, the first time can be hard. Sometimes it's hard to see the different symbols that the smoke makes.

But the more you use incense smoke readings, the clearer you'll be able to see all the signs and symbols that the smoke shows you, and the better you'll be able to follow your intuition.

Libanomancy
Smoke Divination
INTERPRETATIONS CHEAT SHEET

CLEANSING A ROOM:
- Thin line of smoke straight up means dense thick energy.
- Cloud of smoke moving around signifies a cleansed and purified space.

YES | NO ANSWERS:
- If the smoke goes straight up without deviating left or right, this is a YES.
- Smoke breaks up into uneven pieces, NO.
- If the smoke has branching rings, this indicates a YES, however, the situation may not go as intended.
- Rings can also mean and incredible rise and success in all areas of your life.
- Ask the smoke to show you a YES or NO answer. Simply state, "If it is YES, smoke rise towards me," and, "If it is NO, smoke rise away from me."

WHEN TALKING ABOUT SUCCESS:
- Smoke goes right, you will succeed and be lucky.
- Smoke moving left signifies that you may lose something or someone, and/or failure is imminent.
- If smoke clots, you will succeed, enjoy the profits, and luck is by your side.
- Cut-off upper portion of smoke signifies difficulties.

GOOD OR BAD OMENS:
- If the smoke gathers at the top like a date palm remaining thin at the bottom; foreshadows trouble.
- If the smoke has divided into two even or uneven strips, you will face conflict or disease.
- Smoke flowing upwards in two or more smooth flows signifies the amount of people that could be involved in your situation. If the same separate flows are broken or scattered, then there will be conflict between these people.
- Smoke drifts to the right - a positive indication.
- Smoke drifts to the left - a negative or bad indication.
- Broken-edged shapes represent impending danger.
- Numbers can symbolize dates of events happening, or how many days left until an event happens.
- Any type of face that appears should be interpreted by your intuition.
- A trident, knife or fork means that danger is coming.
- The infinity symbol shows when you are going to undergo or experience significant life changes.

Libanomancy
Smoke Divination

NEED MORE SPACE TO RECORD YOUR THOUGHTS AND NOTES?

You will be happy to know that there is a Book of Shadows Companion Journal that compliments this book. It is available on Amazon, and has over 200 blank pages for you to record more notes, thoughts, spells, rituals and any other information you desire. It also has all the same templates and charts.

GET YOUR MAGICKAL COMPANION TODAY

On Amazon:

Book of Shadows Companion Journal
by J.C. Marco

How to write your own Spells

There are a lot of spells that look and sound great out there that have been used by other witches. I mean, you can just Google 'spells' and you would get a myriad of options. There is no harm in using a pre-written spell or something that you find online. These spells typically worked for someone else, which is why they wanted to share it with the world. However, using a spell that was successful for someone else, doesn't necessarily mean that it will be successful for you.

There is no harm in trying the ones that you find, which is a great way to discover what works and what doesn't for your practice. If you feel drawn to a pre-written spell, even better. Just be mindful that the witch behind the spell put in a lot of effort to make sure that their energy, correspondences, candles, tools and wording worked for what they had at their disposal. If you find that you have everything you need and the incantations resonate with you, then give it a whirl. You never know until you try right? That's half the fun anyway. Each of us must get our hands dirty and attempt new things in order to grow and learn.

Spell writing is a huge part of who we are as witches, pagans, wiccans or practitioners. Spells take the essence of our intentions, focus our energies, and send out our desires to the cosmos in a concentrated wave. We use spells to manifest what we truly desire in our lives, change something, help someone or just give thanks to this world and it's beautiful aura. You intention is the single most important factor when writing your own spells. Please refer to the Intention section for more details.

Before we get into the mechanics behind spell construction, we are going to briefly touch on a few 'misconceptions' regarding spell crafting.

- Spells do not need to be written in Latin or some form of dead language. English (or your official language) is just fine.
- Spells do not need to rhyme like a poem. I mean, it sounds nice yes, but you can write them any way you please. Plus it takes three times longer trying to find rhyming words when we can be magicking instead.
- Spells do not need to be written in blood. First of all, that's super messy and would probably hurt, and second, it's easier with an ordinary pen & paper.

How to write your own Spells

Writing spells is something that every witch should learn. It is a great skill to have in your witchy 'toolbox' to have at your disposal. If you are going to write a spell, it needs to be specific to each and every individual. Understanding the fundamentals of spell composition will enable you to create customized, effective spells for any purpose.

Spell Crafting Essentials

- **STATE YOUR INTENTION/PURPOSE:** Decide on the result you want to accomplish. Meditate if you need help seeing your intention in your mind before going forward with the rest of the spell. Utilize the Intention section to articulate precisely what you want to manifest. Take your time, it's no race by any means. It should be a comfortable and relaxing discovery process.

- **TIMING YOUR SPELL / WHEN TO CAST:** Timing can be very important when casting spells. This could include time of day, day of the week or the moon phase to consider. Some witch's simply just wait for a moment that feels 'right' to them. Considering the time of year and the seasons is also crucial. There is a natural season for beginnings (Spring), maturing (Summer), harvesting (Autumn), as well as a time for relaxation and preparation (Winter).

- **GATHER YOUR TOOLS / INGREDIENTS:** Decide on which tools you will use to help you cast your spell effectively. This could be your cauldron, wand, or athame. Or, this could also be your crystals and herbs. Sometimes just your spoken word is enough, but using correspondences can help boost your spell immensely. There is a ton of information in this book about all the different kinds of correspondences, so utilize the knowledge provided. Whatever is most comfortable, go with that.

- **UNDERSTAND THE MAGICK / HOW TO PERFORM:** Remember that magick is the manipulation of energy. Your thoughts, emotions and desires are energy, and you must funnel this energy into your spell. Do you want to cleanse, clear, charge, ground, etc. before you start? Be sure to write down the step-by-step details of how you are going to proceed from start to finish. It's a great way to keep a record of what you did so you can change or enhance the spell for better results later.

- **WRITE YOUR SPELL, CHANT OR INCANTATION:** Writing your spell in a rhyme will make it stronger when spoken aloud, but it is not necessary at all. You can formulate your spell as a poem, a chant or a simple phrase or paragraph stating your desired goal for the spell

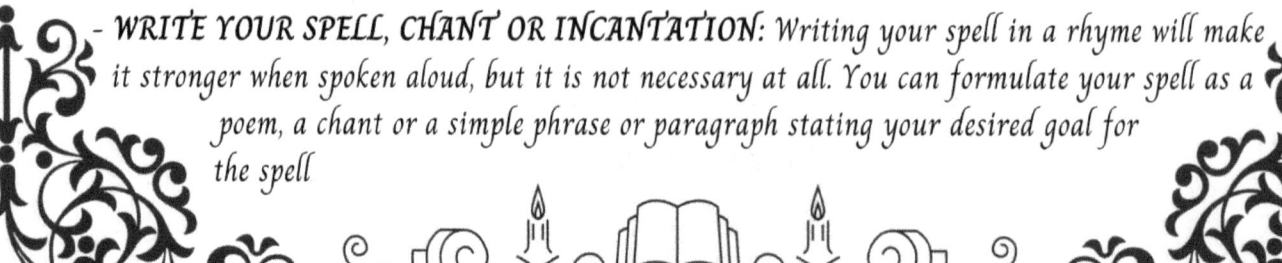

How to write your own Spells

VARIATIONS: Is your spell going to have different variations to the outcome? Maybe there is multiple different ways to 'cast' your spell to achieve a desired goal. If your spell has variations, be sure to record them so you know that you can try it a different way next time, or look back to see what worked and what didn't. This way, you can improve your spell via revisions.

- REMEMBER THE LAWS OF MAGICK: Read over your spell, and be sure that it abides by your personal ethics and morals, and brings no harm to human, nature or animal. If you follow the Rule of Three, this should also be considered. Put down any notes you have before, during and after you have conducted your spell so you can check the progress, the success rate and make any changes or alterations.

These are the main parts to constructing your spell for maximum power and effectiveness. Please jot down any other tips or tricks you may have to building your spells below to help you in the future. On the following pages you will find spell templates to help you organize and write your very own spells. Have fun, good luck, and let the magick flow.

SPELL TITLE / NAME

SPELL PURPOSE / INTENTION:

TIMING / MOON PHASE:

HOW TO PERFORM:

INGREDIENTS & CORRESPONDENCES

SPELL / WRITTEN WORDS, INCANTATION OR CHANT:

VARIATIONS:

SPELL TITLE / NAME

SPELL PURPOSE / INTENTION:

TIMING / MOON PHASE:

HOW TO PERFORM:

INGREDIENTS & CORRESPONDENCES

SPELL / WRITTEN WORDS, INCANTATION OR CHANT:

VARIATIONS:

SPELL TITLE / NAME

SPELL NOTES - THOUGHTS

SPELL TITLE / NAME

SPELL PURPOSE / INTENTION:

TIMING / MOON PHASE:

HOW TO PERFORM:

INGREDIENTS & CORRESPONDENCES

SPELL / WRITTEN WORDS, INCANTATION OR CHANT:

VARIATIONS:

SPELL TITLE / NAME

SPELL PURPOSE / INTENTION:

TIMING / MOON PHASE:

HOW TO PERFORM:

INGREDIENTS & CORRESPONDENCES

SPELL / WRITTEN WORDS, INCANTATION OR CHANT:

VARIATIONS:

SPELL TITLE / NAME

SPELL NOTES - THOUGHTS

SPELL TITLE / NAME

SPELL PURPOSE / INTENTION:

TIMING / MOON PHASE:

HOW TO PERFORM:

INGREDIENTS & CORRESPONDENCES

SPELL / WRITTEN WORDS, INCANTATION OR CHANT:

VARIATIONS:

SPELL TITLE / NAME

SPELL PURPOSE / INTENTION:

TIMING / MOON PHASE:

HOW TO PERFORM:

INGREDIENTS & CORRESPONDENCES

SPELL / WRITTEN WORDS, INCANTATION OR CHANT:

VARIATIONS:

Sources

3 Simple Yule Rituals to Perform this Year. (2020, December 19). The Wholesome Witch. Retrieved 2021, from https://www.thewholesomewitch.com/simple-yule-rituals/

8 Phases Of The Moon. (n.d.). The Hoodwitch. Retrieved 2022, from https://www.thehoodwitch.com/8-phases-of-the-moon

123RF. (n.d.-a). End User Licensing Agreement And Legal Matters - 123RF. 123RF Stock Photos. Retrieved 2022, from ttps://www.123rf.com/license.php?type=standard

123RF. (n.d.-b). License Summary For Commercial And Editorial Usages - 123RF. 123RF Stock Photos. Retrieved 2022, from https://www.123rf.com/license_summary.php

A. (2022a, February 11). Sigil Magic: How to Create Symbols That Manifest Your Destiny. LonerWolf. Retrieved 2022, from https://lonerwolf.com/sigil-magic/

Aboriginal Sacred Plants: Sage. (n.d.). Indigenous Corporate Training Inc. Retrieved July 6, 2022, from https://www.ictinc.ca/blog/aboriginal-sacred-plants-sage

Alignak | Myths and Folklore Wiki | Fandom. (n.d.). Myths and Folklore Wiki. Retrieved 2022, from https://mythus.fandom.com/wiki/Alignak

Allen, C. (2001, January 1). The Scholars and the Goddess. The Atlantic. Retrieved 2022, from https://www.theatlantic.com/magazine/archive/2001/01/the-scholars-and-the-goddess/305910/

Amethyst, A. (2020, June 13). Animal Correspondences. Wiccan | Aminoapps.Com. Retrieved 2022, from https://aminoapps.com/c/wiccanss/page/item/animal-correspondences/wK6X_WwhpIWKkMNXGRGaEvKlW4Vqxr5qpX

Animal Correspondences. (n.d.). Sacred Wicca. Retrieved 2022, from https://sacredwicca.com/animal-correspondences

Baghadia, N. (2021, January 24). Here's How to Perform a Burning Ceremony In 4 Simple Steps. YogiApprovedTM. Retrieved 2022, from https://www.yogiapproved.com/how-to-burning-ceremony/

Barton, N., HDipCT (VTCT), LCHE, MFHT, MBA. (2021, May 25). Essential oils for cleansing negative energy. Baseformula.Com. Retrieved 2022, from https://www.baseformula.com/blog/essential-oils-negative-energy

Basics of Magic: Clearing and Charging Ritual Tools —. (2017, November 6). Wicca Living. Retrieved 2022, from https://wiccaliving.com/clearing-charging-ritual-tools/

The Best Timing for Spells, Charms, Rituals & Magical Operations. (2020, August 3). Wise Witches and Witchcraft. Retrieved July 15, 2022, from https://witchcraftandwitches.com/spells/the-best-timing-for-spells-charms-rituals-and-magical-operations/

Beyer, C. (2019, June 5). What to Know About the Five Classical Elements. Learn Religions. Retrieved 2021, from https://www.learnreligions.com/elemental-symbols-4122788

Black Salt: How to Make and Use It for Protection. (2019, November 24). Moody Moons. Retrieved July 6, 2022, from https://www.moodymoons.com/2019/11/24/black-salt-how-to-make-and-use-it-for-protection/

Brethauer, A. (2021, June 17). Theban Alphabet: Ultimate Guide to the Witches Alphabet for Beginners. The Peculiar Brunette. Retrieved 2022, from https://www.thepeculiarbrunette.com/theban-alphabet-ultimate-guide-to-the-witches-alphabet-for-beginners/

Brethauer, A. (2022a, May 9). Norse Rune Meanings in the Awesome Elder Futhark Alphabet. The Peculiar Brunette. Retrieved 2022, from https://www.thepeculiarbrunette.com/rune-symbols-meanings-and-uses/

Brethauer, A. (2022b, May 31). Magic Elements of Fire, Water, Air, Earth, Spirit and Powerful Ways To Use These Symbols. The Peculiar Brunette. Retrieved 2022, from https://www.thepeculiarbrunette.com/element-symbols-of-fire-water-air-earth-spirit-and-powerful-ways-to-use them/#Spirit_Element_Magic_Symbol

Bruce, E. (2022, January 19). Simple Solo Rituals to Celebrate Imbolc. The Seasonal Soul. Retrieved 2021, from https://www.theseasonalsoul.com/imbolc-rituals/

Building Beautiful Souls, Inc. (2021, July 9). Numerology Numbers and Meanings | Numerology. Retrieved 2022, from https://www.buildingbeautifulsouls.com/symbols-meanings/numerology-meanings/

Burton, N., & Polish, J. (2022, February 24). Is Burning Sage Cultural Appropriation? What You Should Know. Bustle. Retrieved July 30, 2022, from https://www.bustle.com/wellness/is-burning-sage-cultural-appropriation-heres-how-to-smoke-cleanse-in-sensitive-ways-18208360

C. (2014a, August 15). Cumin (Cuminum cyminu). Unleash Your Inner Witch. Retrieved 2022, from https://cladinscarlet.tumblr.com/post/94765850056/cumin-cuminum-cyminu-folk-names-cumino-cumino

C. (2020a, October 19). 25 Witchcraft Symbols Everyone Should Know About. Thought Catalog. Retrieved 2022, from https://thoughtcatalog.com/christine-stockton/2018/05/witchcraft-symbols-and-meanings/

Carding, E. (2012, October 22). The Septagram: Seven Directions and Seven Qualities. Llewellyn. Retrieved 2022, from https://www.llewellyn.com/journal/article/2320

Sources

Celtic Deities. (2021, November 21). Lunvrwitch. Retrieved 2022, from https://lunvrwitch.tumblr.com/post/668478207061819392/you-do-not-need-to-work-with-a-deity-to-be-a

Centering and Grounding. (2014, July 22). Cladinscarlet. Retrieved 2022, from https://cladinscarlet.tumblr.com/post/92468560509/centering-and-grounding

Chamberlain, L. (n.d.). Wicca Candle Magic: A Beginner's Guide to Practicing Wiccan Candle Magic, with Simple Candle Spells (Hardcover) | A Room Of One's Own Books & Gifts. Roomofonesown.Com. Retrieved 2022, from https://www.roomofonesown.com/book/9781912715596

Chamberlain, L. (2022). Wicca Elemental Magic: A Guide to the Elements, Witchcraft, and Magic Spells (Hardcover) | RJ Julia Booksellers. RJ Julia Booksellers. Retrieved 2022, from https://www.rjjulia.com/book/9781912715664

Collings English Dictionary. (n.d.). Definition of Wicca. Www.Dictionary.Com. Retrieved 2021, from https://www.dictionary.com/browse/wicca

Collins English Dictionary. (n.d.-a). Definition of pagan. Www.Dictionary.Com. Retrieved 2021, from https://www.dictionary.com/browse/pagan

Collins English Dictionary. (n.d.-b). Definition of witchcraft. Www.Dictionary.Com. Retrieved 2021, from https://www.dictionary.com/browse/witchcraft

Common Animal Associations in Witchcraft. (2019, August 25). Witches' Collection. Retrieved 2022, from https://witchescollection.tumblr.com/post/187263814398/common-animal-associations-in-witchcraft

Content License Agreement. (2022). Canva. Retrieved July 18, 2022, from https://www.canva.com/policies/content-license-agreement/

Crawford, C. (2022, February 4). Moon Phases and Their Meanings. The Self-Care Emporium. Retrieved 2022, from https://theselfcareemporium.com/blog/moon-phases-and-their-meanings

Crystal, A. (n.d.). Lapis Lazuli: Meaning, Healing Properties and Powers. Mycrystals.Com. Retrieved 2022, from https://www.mycrystals.com/meaning/lapis-lazuli-meaning-and-healing-properties

CrystalAge. (2022). History of Crystals and Healing. Crystalage.Com. Retrieved 2022, from https://www.crystalage.com/crystal_information/crystal_history/

Devash, M. (2018, March 30). How to Harness the Blue Moon's Magickal Energy to Cast Spells. Allure. Retrieved 2022, from https://www.allure.com/story/blue-moon-energy-spell-ritual

Draconian Witch. (2015, October 29). The Witch Is In. Retrieved 2021, from https://imawitchywitch.tumblr.com/post/132151358063/draconian-witch-witches-who-call-upon-dragons

Dugan, E. (2004, November 8). Magic, Seven Days a Week. Llewellyn. Retrieved 2022, from https://www.llewellyn.com/journal/article/710

Easy Spells for the Waning Moon: Magick and Ritual Ideas. (2021, August 8). Spells8. Retrieved 2022, from https://spells8.com/waning-moon-magic/

The Egyptian Goddess List. (n.d.). Goddess-Guide. Retrieved 2022, from https://www.goddess-guide.com/egyptian-goddess-list.html

Eileen, S. (2020, September 29). 25 Forms of Banishing — A Versatile Tool in Witchcraft. The Balancing Path. Retrieved 2022, from https://www.patheos.com/blogs/thebalancingpath/2020/09/25-forms-of-banishing-a-versatile-tool-in-witchcraft/

Eller-Five, M. (2019, September 10). The Seven Magical Weekdays. Mystic Elements. Retrieved 2022, from https://mysticelements.com/the-seven-magical-weekdays/

Elliot, A. (n.d.). Magical Properties Of - Dill | Magic herbs, Dill magical properties, Herbs. Pinterest. Retrieved 2022, from https://www.pinterest.ca/pin/828099450208936959/

EnergyMuse. (2018, January 13). Lapis Lazuli Crystal Meaning & Healing Properties. Retrieved 2022, from https://www.energymuse.com/lapis-lazuli-meaning

Enodian, R. (2018, March 23). More Than Just Intention: What Makes Magic Work. Patheos - Tea Addicted Witch. Retrieved 2022, from https://www.patheos.com/blogs/teaaddictedwitch/2018/03/more-than-just-intention-magic/

Estrada, J. (2022, June 29). How To Set Intentions For Manifestation, According To Experts Who Vouch For The Practice. The Zoe Report. Retrieved 2022, from https://www.thezoereport.com/wellness/how-to-set-intentions-for-manifestation

Fields, K. (2020, April 22). Magical Days of the Week: Correspondences & Daily Energy. Otherworldly Oracle. Retrieved 2022, from https://otherworldlyoracle.com/magical-days-of-the-week/

Fields, K. (2021, May 31). Lunar Magick for Beginners: Moon Phases, Correspondences, & More. Otherworldly Oracle. Retrieved 2022, from https://otherworldlyoracle.com/lunar-magick-beginners/

Fosu, K. (2021, December 16). Shadow Work: A Simple Guide to Transcending The Darker Aspects of Yourself. Medium. Retrieved 2022, from https://medium.com/big-self-society/shadow-work-a-simple-guide-to-transcending-the-darker-aspects-of-the-self-e948ee285723

Friedman, H. (n.d.). Malachite: The mineral malachite information and pictures. Minerals.Net. Retrieved 2022, from https://www.minerals.net/mineral/malachite.aspx

Sources

Gill, C. (2021, May 10). An Introduction to Crystal Grids. Crystal Visions Store. Retrieved July 5, 2022, from https://crystalvisions.net.au/blogs/an-introduction-to-crystal-grids/an-introduction-to-crystal-grids

Gill, N. S. (2019, August 13). 12 Ancient Lunar Luminaries. ThoughtCo. Retrieved 2022, from https://www.thoughtco.com/moon-gods-and-moon-goddesses-120395

Goddess Cerridwen. (2013, June 7). Journeying to the Goddess. Retrieved 2022, from https://journeyingtothegoddess.wordpress.com/2012/07/03/goddess-cerridwen/

Gonzo, W. (2022, May 27). The Different Types Of Witches Creating Magic All Around You. Vondechii's Vault. Retrieved 2021, from https://www.vondechii.com/post/the-different-types-of-witches-creating-magic-all-around-you

Grant, E. (2013). The Book of Crystal Spells: Magical Uses for Stones, Crystals, Minerals . . . and Even Sand. Llewellyn Publications.

The Greek Gods: Full List and Background. (2020, October 31). Greek Travel Tellers. Retrieved 2022, from https://greektraveltellers.com/blog/the-greek-gods#:%7E:text=Zeus%2C%20Poseidon%2C%20Hera%2C%20Hestia,%E2%80%9Cthe%2012%20Olympian%20Gods%E2%80%9D.

Haduch, G. (n.d.). A Guide to Waxing Moon Rituals. KelleeMaize. Retrieved 2022, from https://www.kelleemaize.com/post/a-guide-to-waxing-moon-rituals

Hancock, P. (n.d.). Black Obsidian - Properties - Associations - Uses. Psychic Revelation. Retrieved 2022, from https://www.psychic-revelation.com/reference/a_d/crystals/obsidian_black.html

Haseman, M. (2021, February 18). How to Create and Use Sigils. Mumbles & Things. Retrieved 2022, from https://www.mumblesandthings.com/blog/create-use-sigils

Hearn, S. (2021, June 18). How to Cast a Circle. Letters to Lilith. Retrieved 2022, from https://www.letterstolilith.com/blog/howtocastacircle

Heavenly Crystals Online. (2022). A - Z Crystal Dictionary. Retrieved 2022, from https://heavenlycrystalsonline.com.au/pages/a-z-crystal-dictionary

Hecate: Goddess Symbols, Correspondences, Myth & Offerings. (2022a, February 20). Spells8. Retrieved 2022, from https://spells8.com/lessons/hecate-goddess-symbols/#hecate-correspondences

Hecate: Goddess Symbols, Correspondences, Myth & Offerings. (2022b, February 20). Spells8. Retrieved 2022, from https://spells8.com/lessons/hecate-goddess-symbols/

Heketa. (n.d.). Crystal Correspondence A to Z / Alles over Edelstenen / Blog. Retrieved 2022, from https://www.heketa.nl/blog/alles-over-edelstenen/crystal-correspondence-a-to-z

Herstik, G. (2017, May 24). Ask A Witch: Moon Magick 101. Nylon. Retrieved 2022, from https://www.nylon.com/articles/ask-a-witch-all-about-moon-magick

Houlis, A. (2021, December 16). The Power of Setting Intentions — and How to Do It Correctly. Shape. Retrieved 2022, from https://www.shape.com/lifestyle/mind-and-body/mental-health/how-to-set-intentions

Houston, D. (2020, November 16). Jade Stone: Meanings, Properties and Uses. CrystalsandJewelry.Com. Retrieved 2022, from https://meanings.crystalsandjewelry.com/jade/

Ishler, J. (2021, June 16). 7 Simple and Joyous Rituals to Celebrate the Summer Solstice. Apartment Therapy. Retrieved 2021, from https://www.apartmenttherapy.com/summer-solstice-rituals-36932962

J. (2012, August 21). Khonsu - God of youth and the moon. - Egyptian God. The White Goddess. Retrieved 2022, from http://www.thewhitegoddess.co.uk/divinity_of_the_day/egyptian/khonsu.asp

J. (2022b, April 22). The History and Symbolism of the Pentagram. DualCrossroads. Retrieved 2021, from https://www.dualcrossroads.com/post/the-history-and-symbolism-of-the-pentagram

J. (2022c, April 26). The White Goddess - Divinity of the Day - Coatlicue - Urcuchillay. The White Goddess. Retrieved 2022, from http://www.thewhitegoddess.co.uk/divinity_of_the_day/index.asp?DOY=115

Jay, N. (2020, September 14). Spiral Goddess — What This Symbol Really Means. Symbol Sage. Retrieved 2022, from https://symbolsage.com/spiral-goddess-symbolism/

Jay, N. (2021, September 5). Unicursal Hexagram — What Does it Symbolize? Symbol Sage. Retrieved 2022, from https://symbolsage.com/unicursal-hexagram-symbolism-and-meaning/

Jay, S. (2022a, March 10). New Moon Ritual To Reset & Manifest Magic. She Rose Revolution. Retrieved 2022, from https://sheroserevolution.com/shanijay/new-moon-ritual/

Jay, S. (2022b, March 10). The Eight Phases Of The Moon Cycle & How To Flow With Them | SRR. She Rose Revolution. Retrieved 2022, from https://sheroserevolution.com/shanijay/the-8-moon-phases-of-the-moon-cycle/

Sources

Johnson, S. (2020, March 25). HOW TO MAKE A SIGIL || Witchcraft 101. ARCANE ALCHEMY. Retrieved 2022, from http://www.arcanealchemy.com/blog/2020/3/25/how-to-make-a-sigil-witchcraft-101

Kelly, A. (2021, December 24). A Guide to Angel Numbers and What They Mean. Allure. Retrieved 2022, from https://www.allure.com/story/what-are-angel-numbers

Kelly, A. (2022, April 15). What Master Numbers 11, 22 & 33 Mean In Numerology. YourTango. Retrieved 2022, from https://www.yourtango.com/2018311236/astrology-what-does-master-numbers-mean-personality-traits-numerology-zodiac-signs

Khonsu. (n.d.). WikiPagan. Retrieved 2022, from https://pagan.fandom.com/wiki/Khonsu

Kyteler, E. (2021, October 3). What Is The Theban Alphabet? Eclectic Witchcraft. Retrieved 2022, from https://eclecticwitchcraft.com/what-is-the-theban-alphabet/

L. (2017a, April 21). Magickal Correspondences ~ Tree, Herb & Flower. MoonChild Spiritual Emporium. Retrieved 2022, from https://www.moonchildspiritual-emporium.co.uk/blogs/news/tree-herb-flower-correspondences

L. (2017b, April 21). Magickal Correspondences ~ Tree, Herb & Flower. MoonChild Spiritual Emporium. Retrieved 2022, from https://www.moonchildspiritual-emporium.co.uk/blogs/news/tree-herb-flower-correspondences

LLEWELLYN WESCHCKE, C. (2017, May 10). Norse Gods & Goddesses. LLEWELLYN. Retrieved 2022, from https://www.llewellyn.com/encyclopedia/article/26366

Lucas, C. (2020, June 19). Howlite: Meaning, Properties, Powers and Uses. CrystalsandJewelry.Com. Retrieved 2022, from https://meanings.crystalsandjewelry.com/howlite/

Lunar Deities - Witchipedia. (n.d.). Witchipedia. Retrieved 2022, from http://witchipedia.wikidot.com/arch:god-dess-of-the-moon

M. (2019a, October 16). Artemis. The Witchipedia. Retrieved 2022, from https://witchipedia.com/deity/artemis/

M. (2019b, October 30). Boline. The Witchipedia. Retrieved 2021, from https://witchipedia.com/glossary/boline/

M., L. (n.d.). Black Tourmaline: Meaning, Healing Correspondences, and Uses. Gemstone Well. Retrieved 2022, from https://gemstonewell.com/blogs/news/black-tourmaline

The Magic of Numerology: Numbers with Their Symbolism and Meaning. (2020, August 3). Wise Witches and Witchcraft. Retrieved 2022, from https://witchcraftandwitches.com/witch/the-magic-of-numerology-numbers-with-their-symbolism-and-meaning/

Magic or Magick? (2021). World of Magick. Retrieved 2021, from https://www.worldofmagick.com/post/magic-or-magick

Magical Properties of Colors —. (2017, November 6). Wicca Living. Retrieved 2022, from https://wiccaliving.com/magical-properties-colors/

Marco, J. C. (2021). Elder Futhark Bindrunes: A Beginners Guide to Creating Bindrunes + Manifesting & Intention-Setting with Purpose. Independently published.

Mark, J. J. (2022a, June 28). Egyptian Gods - The Complete List. World History Encyclopedia. Retrieved 2022, from https://www.worldhistory.org/article/885/egyptian-gods---the-complete-list/

Mark, J. J. (2022b, June 29). The Ankh. World History Encyclopedia. Retrieved 2022, from https://www.worldhistory.org/Ankh/

Marks-McMahan, K. (2020, December 12). Methods of Divination For Your Magical Practice. Lunar Spell. Retrieved 2022, from https://lunarspell.com/blog/methods-of-divination/

Mastin, L. (2009). Incense - Witchcraft Terms and Tools - Witchcraft. LukeMastin. Retrieved 2021, from http://www.lukemastin.com/witchcraft/terms_incense.html

May, A. (2020a, May 20). Crystal Correspondences — The Most Comprehensive Guide Ever. Welcome To Wicca Now. Retrieved 2022, from https://wiccanow.com/crystal-correspondences/

May, A. (2020b, May 20). Crystal Correspondences — The Most Comprehensive Guide Ever. Welcome To Wicca Now. Retrieved 2022, from https://wiccanow.com/crystal-correspondences/

Merriam-Webster Dictionary. (n.d.-a). pagan. The Merriam-Webster.Com Dictionary. Retrieved 2021, from https://www.merriamwebster.com/dictionary/pagan

Merriam-Webster Dictionary. (n.d.-b). Wicca. The Merriam-Webster.Com Dictionary. Retrieved 2021, from https://www.merriamwebster.com/dictionary/Wicca

Merriam-Webster Dictionary. (n.d.-c). witchcraft. The Merriam-Webster.Com Dictionary. Retrieved 2021, from https://www.merriamwebster.com/dictionary/witchcraft?src=search-dict-hed

Sources

Mulhern, K., PhD. (2021, March 31). What Are the Sabbats? Patheos. Retrieved 2021, from https://www.patheos.com/answers/what-are-the-sabbats

Mystic Sisters Gallery. (n.d.). Flax seed correspondences #kitchenwitch #kitchenwitchery #spells #rituals #money #protection #healing | Flax seed, Magickal herbs, Magical herbs. Pinterest. Retrieved 2022, from https://www.pinterest.ca/pin/38351034313913954/

Netzer, J. (2021, September 17). What is a Green Witch? The Beginner Guide & 4 Tips to Embrace Earthly Magick. Cratejoy. Retrieved 2021, from https://www.cratejoy.com/box-insider/green-witch-primer/

Nightphilly, I. (2017, November 15). Difference Between Cleansing and Banishing. Pagans & Witches | Aminoapps.Com. Retrieved 2022, from https://aminoapps.com/c/pagans-witches/page/blog/difference-between-cleansing-and-banishing/g0zj_3WMI6uVoGBEg0L4vLL6RVbVroJpwkv

Numerology.com Staff. (2022, June 2). Number 1 Meaning. Numerology.Com. Retrieved 2022, from https://www.numerology.com/articles/about-numerology/single-digit-number-1-meaning/

O, N. (2021, January 7). Agate. InJewels Healing Jewelry. Retrieved 2022, from https://injewels.net/blogs/healing-properties-meanings/agate

OMalley, N. (2021a, January 7). Amazonite. InJewels Healing Jewelry. Retrieved 2022, from https://injewels.net/blogs/healing-properties-meanings/amazonite

OMalley, N. (2021b, January 7). Amethyst. InJewels Healing Jewelry. Retrieved 2022, from https://injewels.net/blogs/healing-properties-meanings/amethyst

OMalley, N. (2021c, January 7). Aventurine. InJewels Healing Jewelry. Retrieved 2022, from https://injewels.net/blogs/healing-properties-meanings/aventurine

Peters, R. (2018, May 16). A ritual guide to the days of the week. Rylandpeters. Retrieved 2022, from https://rylandpeters.com/blogs/health-mind-body-and-spirit/a-ritual-guide-to-the-days-of-the-week

Pham, M. (2021, February 21). What Is Smudging? What Are The Different Types Of Smudges? Pure Chakra. Retrieved July 6, 2022, from https://purechakra.com/blogs/a-hippie-spirituality-blog/what-is-smudging-what-are-the-different-types-of-smudges

Pixabay - Terms of Service. (2021, December 13). Pixabay. Retrieved 2021, from https://pixabay.com/service/terms/#license

The Premium License. (n.d.). DesignBundles. Retrieved 2021, from https://designbundles.net/license-explorer/index.php

P.W. (2019c, May 8). The Wheel of the Year: Celebrating the 8 Pagan Sabbats. Learn Religions. Retrieved 2021, from https://www.learnreligions.com/eight-pagan-sabbats-2562833

Regan, S. (2021, February 24). How (And Why) To Make Moon Water & 5 Ways To Use It. Mindbodygreen.Com. Retrieved 2022, from https://www.mindbodygreen.com/articles/moon-water/

Rex, E. (2021, December 7). The Pentagram, Symbol of What Exactly? - Modern Mythology. ModernMythology. Retrieved 2021, from https://modernmythology.net/realpentagramhistory-64fdc64866a5

Royal Museums Greenwich. (2022). What are the names of full moons throughout the year? Retrieved 2022, from https://www.rmg.co.uk/stories/topics/what-are-names-full-moons-throughout-year

Russell, D. (2022a, February 2). 25 Simple, Powerful Self-Care Ideas (That Take Less Than 10 Minutes). DavyandTracy.Com. Retrieved 2022, from https://davyandtracy.com/spirituality/simple-self-care-ideas/

Russell, D. (2022b, May 16). The Ultimate Guide To Working With Moon Phases. DavyandTracy.Com. Retrieved 2022, from https://davyandtracy.com/spirituality/working-with-moon-phases/

S. (2020b, March 19). God Studies: Thoth. Sabrina's Grimoire. Retrieved 2022, from https://sabrinasgrimoire.tumblr.com/post/612999275244388352/god-studies-thoth

Sebastiaan, D. (2019, November 18). Simple Cleansing Spells. Tragic Beautiful. Retrieved 2022, from https://www.tragicbeautiful.com/blogs/style-blog/simple-cleansing-spells

Selenite Meaning: Healing Properties & Everyday Uses. (n.d.). Tiny Rituals. Retrieved 2022, from https://tinyrituals.co/blogs/tiny-rituals/selenite-meaning-healing-properties-everyday-uses

Shutterstock Terms of Service & License Agreements. (n.d.). Shutterstock. Retrieved 2021, from https://www.shutterstock.com/license

Smith, D. (2016, March 26). Wiccan Holidays Celebrating the Moon on the Esbats. Dummies. Retrieved 2022, from https://www.dummies.com/article/body-mind-spirit/religion-spirituality/wicca/wiccan-holidays-celebrating-the-moon-on-the-esbats-192770/

Smoky Quartz Meaning: Healing Properties & Everyday Uses. (n.d.). Tiny Rituals. Retrieved 2022, from https://tinyrituals.co/blogs/tiny-rituals/smoky-quartz-meaning-healing-properties-everyday-uses

Spiral Goddess. (2020, October 22). Pagans & Witches | Aminoapps.Com. Retrieved 2022, from https://aminoapps.com/c/pagans-witches/page/item/spiral-goddess/MQdW_bnET0IeEPR78xYQ4Lrq1G7GX5dvPaV

Staff, S. (2019, September 22). *How To Read Incense Smoke? Libanomancy Knows The Answer.* SOLANCHA. Retrieved 2022, from https://solancha.com/how-to-read-incense-smoke-libanomancy-knows-the-answer/

Stokes, V. (2021, July 30). *Moon Water: Add This Lunar Infusion to Your Spiritual Toolkit.* Healthline. Retrieved 2022, from https://www.healthline.com/health/moon-water#uses

The Sun Cross. (2018, September 4). Ancient Symbols. Retrieved 2022, from https://www.ancient-symbols.com/symbols-directory/the-sun-cross.html

Syrdal, K. (2021, April 13). *Here's Everything You Need To Know About Setting Up Your Witch Altar For Spells, Meditation, And More.* Thought Catalog. Retrieved 2021, from https://thoughtcatalog.com/kendra-syrdal/2018/08/heres-everything-you-need-to-know-about-setting-up-your-altar-for-spells-meditation-and-more/

Tallent, E. (n.d.). *swamp witch characteristics | Witch, Hedge witch, Hedge witchcraft.* Pinterest. Retrieved 2021, from https://www.pinterest.ca/pin/821836631989529060/

Terms of Use. (2022). Canva. Retrieved July 18, 2022, from https://www.canva.com/policies/terms-of-use/

The Irish Times. (2018, October 27). *Smudge and sweep out negative vibes.* Retrieved 2022, from https://www.irishtimes.com/life-and-style/homes-and-property/smudge-and-sweep-out-negative-vibes-1.3675601

The Lady Of The Forest. (2019a, June 30). *Beginner's Guide to Spell Candle Magick and Colour Correspondences.* ForestofWisdom. Retrieved 2022, from https://forestofwisdom.com.au/blogs/into-the-forest/beginner-s-guide-to-spell-candle-magick-and-colour-correspondences

The Lady Of The Forest. (2019b, June 30). *Beginner's Guide to Spell Candle Magick and Colour Correspondences.* ForestofWisdom. Retrieved 2022, from https://forestofwisdom.com.au/blogs/into-the-forest/beginner-s-guide-to-spell-candle-magick-and-colour-correspondences

The Thrifty Witch School. (2022). *A Complete List of Herbs and Their Magickal Uses.* Retrieved 2022, from https://coven.thethriftywitch.com/pages/magickal-uses-of-herbs

Thomas, S. S. (2018, July 3). *How Moon Phases Affect Your Magical Spells.* Allure. Retrieved 2022, from https://www.allure.com/story/moon-phases-magic-spells

Tiny Rituals. (n.d.-a). *Jade Meaning: Healing Properties & Everyday Uses.* Retrieved 2022, from https://tinyrituals.co/blogs/tiny-rituals/jade-meaning-healing-properties-everyday-uses

Tiny Rituals. (n.d.-b). *Moonstone Meaning: Healing Properties & Everyday Uses.* Retrieved 2022, from https://tinyrituals.co/blogs/tiny-rituals/moonstone-meaning-healing-properties-everyday-uses

Tiny Rituals. (n.d.-c). *Obsidian Meaning: Healing Properties & Everyday Uses.* Retrieved 2022, from https://tinyrituals.co/blogs/tiny-rituals/obsidian-meaning-healing-properties-everyday-uses

Tiny Rituals. (n.d.-d). *Pyrite Meaning: Healing Properties & Everyday Uses.* Retrieved 2022, from https://tinyrituals.co/blogs/tiny-rituals/pyrite-meaning-healing-properties-everyday-uses

Tiny Rituals. (n.d.-e). *Rose Quartz Meaning: Healing Properties And Everyday Uses.* Retrieved 2022, from https://tinyrituals.co/blogs/tiny-rituals/rose-quartz-meaning-healing-properties-and-everyday-uses

V. (n.d.-a). *Bay Leaves (Bay Laurel).* Vayas Witchcraft. Retrieved 2022, from https://vayas-witchcraft-and-spiritual.tumblr.com/search/bay+leaf

V. (n.d.-b). *Herb - Basil.* Vayas Witchcraft. Retrieved 2022, from https://vayas-witchcraft-and-spiritual.tumblr.com/search/basil

V. (n.d.-c). *Herb - Cinnamon.* Vayas Witchcraft. Retrieved 2022, from https://vayas-witchcraft-and-spiritual.tumblr.com/search/cinnamon

V. (n.d.-d). *Herb - Garlic.* Vayas Witchcraft. Retrieved 2022, from https://vayas-witchcraft-and-spiritual.tumblr.com/search/garlic

V. (n.d.-e). *Herb - Oregano.* Vayas Witchcraft. Retrieved 2022, from https://vayas-witchcraft-and-spiritual.tumblr.com/search/oregano

V. (n.d.-f). *Herb - Rosemary.* Vayas Witchcraft. Retrieved 2022, from https://vayas-witchcraft-and-spiritual.tumblr.com/search/rosemary

V. (n.d.-g). *Herb - Sage.* Vayas Witchcraft. Retrieved 2022, from https://vayas-witchcraft-and-spiritual.tumblr.com/search/sage

V. (n.d.-h). *Herb - Thyme.* Vayas Witchcraft. Retrieved 2022, from https://vayas-witchcraft-and-spiritual.tumblr.com/search/thyme

V. (2014b, December 15). *Herb - Cloves.* Vayas Witchcraft. Retrieved 2022, from https://vayas-witchcraft-and-spiritual.tumblr.com/post/105265409390/herb-cloves

Ward, K. (2021, September 22). *FYI: There Are Many Types of Witches.* Cosmopolitan. Retrieved 2021, from https://www.cosmopolitan.com/lifestyle/a37681530/types-of-witches/

Wiccan Esbats: The Magic of the Full Moon —. (2017, November 6). Wicca Living. Retrieved 2022, from https://wiccaliving.com/wiccan-esbats-full-moon/

The Wiccan Goddess and God — Wiccan Deities —. (n.d.). Wicca Living. Retrieved 2022, from https://wiccaliving.com/wiccan-goddess-god/

Sources

Wiccan Symbols and Their Meanings - Mythologian. (2019, May 20). Mythologian. Retrieved 2022, from https://mythologian.net/wiccan-symbols-meanings/

Wigington, P. (2018a, January 5). 13 Magical Colors to Use. Learn Religions. Retrieved 2022, from https://www.learnreligions.com/color-magic-magical-correspondences-4105405

Wigington, P. (2018b, January 5). Create a God or Goddess Altar to the Deities of Your Tradition. Learn Religions. Retrieved 2021, from https://www.learnreligions.com/create-a-god-altar-2561555

Wigington, P. (2018c, February 19). Rites, Rituals and Ways to Celebrate Mabon, the Autumn Equinox. Learn Religions. Retrieved 2021, from https://www.learnreligions.com/mabon-rites-and-rituals-2562284

Wigington, P. (2018d, March 31). 5 Ways to Cleanse or Purify a Sacred Space. Learn Religions. Retrieved 2022, from https://www.learnreligions.com/cleanse-or-purify-a-sacred-space-2562876

Wigington, P. (2018e, April 23). Pagan Rituals to Celebrate Litha, the Summer Solstice. Learn Religions. Retrieved 2021, from https://www.learnreligions.com/litha-rites-and-rituals-2561483

Wigington, P. (2018f, May 24). How to Make Four Thieves Vinegar. Learn Religions. Retrieved 2022, from https://www.learnreligions.com/four-thieves-vinegar-2562515

Wigington, P. (2018g, August 2). 10 Lunar Gods & Goddesses You Should Know. Learn Religions. Retrieved 2022, from https://www.learnreligions.com/lunar-deities-2562404

Wigington, P. (2018h, December 11). What is an Altar, and How Do You Set One Up, Anyway? Learn Religions. Retrieved 2021, from https://www.learnreligions.com/setting-up-your-magical-altar-2561940

Wigington, P. (2018i, December 24). 10 Celtic Deities You Should Know. Learn Religions. Retrieved 2022, from https://www.learnreligions.com/gods-of-the-celts-2561711

Wigington, P. (2018j, December 31). Wiccan and Paganism: Do You Have a Magical Animal Familiar? Learn Religions. Retrieved 2022, from https://www.learnreligions.com/what-is-an-animal-familiar-2562343

Wigington, P. (2019a, January 1). Does the Moon Phase Matter When it Comes to Magic? Learn Religions. Retrieved 2022, from https://www.learnreligions.com/moon-phases-and-magical-workings-2562405

Wigington, P. (2019b, January 3). Perform a Balance Meditation for Mabon. Learn Religions. Retrieved 2021, from https://www.learnreligions.com/mabon-balance-meditation-2562287

Wigington, P. (2019c, January 6). Try This Ritual To Consecrate Your Magical Tools. Learn Religions. Retrieved 2021, from https://www.learnreligions.com/consecrate-your-magical-tools-2562860

Wigington, P. (2019d, January 14). Learn to Use a Pendulum for Divination. Learn Religions. Retrieved 2022, from https://www.learnreligions.com/pendulum-divination-2561760

Wigington, P. (2019e, February 9). Celebrate the Full Moon with an Esbat Ritual. Learn Religions. Retrieved 2022, from https://www.learnreligions.com/esbat-rite-celebrate-the-full-moon-2562864

Wigington, P. (2019f, February 17). Here's How to Do Some Water Scrying at the Full Moon. Learn Religions. Retrieved 2022, from https://www.learnreligions.com/full-moon-water-scrying-divination-2561752

Wigington, P. (2019g, April 26). What to Put on a Beltane Altar. Learn Religions. Retrieved 2021, from https://www.learnreligions.com/setting-up-your-beltane-altar-2561656

Wigington, P. (2019h, April 28). Hold This Simple Harvest Ritual to Celebrate Lammas. Learn Religions. Retrieved 2021, from https://www.learnreligions.com/hold-a-lammas-harvest-ritual-2562166

Wigington, P. (2019i, April 28). Learn About the Basics of Numerology. Learn Religions. Retrieved 2022, from https://www.learnreligions.com/the-basics-of-numerology-2561761

Wigington, P. (2019j, May 6). What the Elements Are, and Why They Matter in Paganism and Wicca. Learn Religions. Retrieved 2022, from https://www.learnreligions.com/four-classical-elements-2562825

Wigington, P. (2019k, May 9). 14 Magical Tools for Pagan Practice. Learn Religions. Retrieved 2021, from https://www.learnreligions.com/magical-tools-for-pagan-practice-4064607

Wigington, P. (2019l, May 9). Magical Banishing Spells and Folklore. Learn Religions. Retrieved 2022, from https://www.learnreligions.com/about-magical-banishing-2562757

Wigington, P. (2019m, June 25). *Herbal Correspondences for Magic & Ritual*. Learn Religions. Retrieved 2022, from https://www.learnreligions.com/magical-herb-correspondences-4064512

Wigington, P. (2019n, June 25). *How to Magically Ground, Center, and Shield*. Learn Religions. Retrieved 2022, from https://www.learnreligions.com/grounding-centering-and-shielding-4122187

Wigington, P. (2019o, June 25). *How to Work With Pagan Gods & Goddesses*. Learn Religions. Retrieved 2022, from https://www.learnreligions.com/working-with-the-gods-and-goddesses-2561950

Wigington, P. (2019p, June 25). *Meet Artemis, the Greek Goddess of the Hunt*. Learn Religions. Retrieved 2022, from https://www.learnreligions.com/artemis-greek-goddess-of-the-hunt-2561956

Wigington, P. (2019q, July 11). *Do the Days of the Week Influence Magic?* Learn Religions. Retrieved 2022, from https://www.learnreligions.com/magical-days-of-the-week-2561697

Wigington, P. (2019r, July 31). *20 Magical Pagan and Wiccan Symbols*. Learn Religions. Retrieved 2022, from https://www.learnreligions.com/pagan-and-wiccan-symbols-4123036

Wigington, P. (2019s, September 25). *Magical Tools: Use a Mortar and Pestle For Your Herbs*. Learn Religions. Retrieved 2021, from https://www.learnreligions.com/mortar-and-pestle-uses-2561906

Wigington, P. (2019t, October 21). *What in the World is a Blue Moon?* Learn Religions. Retrieved 2022, from https://www.learnreligions.com/what-is-blue-moon-2561873

Wigington, P. (2019u, October 29). *7 Types of Witches Explained*. Learn Religions. Retrieved 2021, from https://www.learnreligions.com/types-of-witches-4774438

Wigington, P. (2019v, November 27). *10 Basic Divination Methods to Try*. Learn Religions. Retrieved 2022, from https://www.learnreligions.com/methods-of-divination-2561764

Wigington, P. (2020a, January 12). *Wicca, Witchcraft or Paganism - What's the Difference?* Learn Religions. Retrieved 2021, from https://www.learnreligions.com/wicca-witchcraft-or-paganism-2562823

Wigington, P. (2020b, February 3). *Rituals & Celebrations for the Beltane Sabbat*. Learn Religions. Retrieved 2021, from https://www.learnreligions.com/beltane-rites-and-rituals-2561678

Wiki Targeted (Entertainment). (n.d.). *The Salem Wiki*. Retrieved 2021, from https://salem.fandom.com/wiki/Divination

wikiHow. (2020, May 16). *How to Set up a Simple Pagan or Wiccan Altar: 8 Steps*. Retrieved 2021, from https://www.wikihow.com/Set-up-a-Simple-Pagan-or-Wiccan-Altar

wikiHow. (2021, June 30). *How to Cast a Circle: 10 Steps (with Pictures)*. Retrieved 2022, from https://www.wikihow.com/Cast-a-Circle

Wikipedia contributors. (2020, June 22). *Alignak*. Wikipedia. Retrieved 2022, from https://en.wikipedia.org/wiki/Alignak

Wikipedia contributors. (2022a, February 14). *Banishing*. Wikipedia. Retrieved 2022, from https://en.wikipedia.org/wiki/Banishing

Wikipedia contributors. (2022b, March 16). *List of pantheons*. Wikipedia. Retrieved 2022, from https://en.wikipedia.org/wiki/List_of_pantheons

Wikipedia contributors. (2022c, April 8). *Wikipedia:Text of Creative Commons Attribution-ShareAlike 3.0 Unported License - Wikipedia*. Wikipedia. Retrieved 2021, from https://en.wikipedia.org/wiki/Wikipedia:Text_of_Creative_Commons_Attribution-ShareAlike_3.0_Unported_License

Wikipedia contributors. (2022d, April 20). *Pantheon (religion)*. Wikipedia. Retrieved 2022, from https://en.wikipedia.org/wiki/Pantheon_(religion)

Wikipedia contributors. (2022e, May 20). *Hina (goddess)*. Wikipedia. Retrieved 2022, from https://en.wikipedia.org/wiki/Hina_(goddess)

Wikipedia contributors. (2022f, June 17). *List of lunar deities*. Wikipedia. Retrieved 2022, from https://en.wikipedia.org/wiki/List_of_lunar_deities

Wikipedia contributors. (2022g, June 20). *Methods of divination*. Wikipedia. Retrieved 2022, from https://en.wikipedia.org/wiki/Methods_of_divination

Willow. (2014, September 18). *Magical Correspondences of Crystals*. Flying the Hedge. Retrieved 2022, from https://www.flyingthehedge.com/2014/09/magical-correspondences-of-crystals.html

Willow. (2015, December 7). *Yule Correspondences*. Flying the Hedge. Retrieved 2021, from https://www.flyingthehedge.com/2015/12/yule-correspondences.html

Willow. (2016, January 18). *Imbolc Correspondences*. Flying the Hedge. Retrieved 2021, from https://www.flyingthehedge.com/2016/01/imbolc-correspondences.html

Willow. (2019, March 11). *Spirit Work for Ostara*. Flying the Hedge. Retrieved 2021, from https://www.flyingthehedge.com/2019/03/spirit-work-for-ostara.html

Sources

Willow. (2020a, February 24). Elemental Magic: A Complete Guide to Water Folklore & Correspondences. Flying the Hedge. Retrieved 2022, from https://www.flyingthehedge.com/2020/02/water-folklore-correspondences.html

Willow. (2020b, May 7). Elemental Magic: A Complete Guide to Earth Folklore & Correspondences. Flying the Hedge. Retrieved 2022, from https://www.flyingthehedge.com/2020/05/earth-folklore-correspondences.html

Willow. (2020c, June 18). Elemental Magic: A Complete Guide to Fire Folklore & Correspondences. Flying the Hedge. Retrieved 2022, from https://www.flyingthehedge.com/2020/06/fire-folklore-correspondences.html

Willow. (2020d, October 12). Elemental Magic: A Complete Guide to Air Folklore & Correspondences. Flying the Hedge. Retrieved 2022, from https://www.flyingthehedge.com/2020/10/air-folklore-and-correspondences.html

Willow. (2020e, December 8). Elemental Series: A Complete Guide to Spirit Folklore and Correspondences. Flying the Hedge. Retrieved 2022, from https://www.flyingthehedge.com/2020/12/spirit-folklore-and-correspondences.html

Wings in the Night. (2022). BLACK MUSTARD Magical SEEDS | Pagan & Wicca Supplies Shop. Retrieved 2022, from https://wings-in-the-night.co.uk/black-mustard-magical-seeds-6333-p.asp

WiseWitch, W. W. (2020, August 5). Elemental Witch | Learn about Elemental Witchcraft & 5 Elements Magick! Wise Witches and Witchcraft. Retrieved 2021, from https://witchcraftandwitches.com/types-of-witches/elemental-witch/

Witch Types. (n.d.). Wattpad. Retrieved 2021, from https://www.wattpad.com/555237340-witch-types-completed-spirit-working-and-draconian

Witchipedian, T. (2019a, September 10). Athame. The Witchipedia. Retrieved 2021, from https://witchipedia.com/glossary/athame/

Witchipedian, T. (2019b, November 24). Fennel. The Witchipedia. Retrieved 2022, from https://witchipedia.com/book-of-shadows/herblore/fennel/

Witchipedian, T. (2020, September 5). Western Elemental Correspondences. The Witchipedia. Retrieved 2022, from https://witchipedia.com/book-of-shadows/western-elemental-correspondences/

Witchwood, L. (2015, July 15). Salt Magick. Witchcraft & Pagan Lifestyle Blog, The Magick Kitchen. Retrieved 2022, from https://www.themagickkitchen.com/salt-magick/

Wood, C. (2022). 3 Types of simple Samhain rituals you can create at home. Corrina Wood. Retrieved 2022, from https://www.corinnawood.com/blog/samhain-rituals

Wooll, M. (2022, June 13). 8 Benefits of Shadow Work and How to Start Practicing It. Betterup. Retrieved 2022, from https://www.betterup.com/blog/shadow-work

Wright, J. (2015, August 1). Lughnasadh Correspondences. PaganPages.Org. Retrieved 2021, from https://paganpages.org/emagazine/2015/08/01/lughnasadh-correspondences-8/

Wright, J. (2018, September 1). Mabon Correspondences. PaganPages.Org. Retrieved 2021, from https://paganpages.org/emagazine/2018/09/01/mabon-correspondences-5/

Wright, J. (2020a, April 15). Beltane Correspondences. PaganPages.Org. Retrieved 2021, from https://paganpages.org/emagazine/2020/04/15/beltane-correspondences-11/

Wright, J. (2020b, December 1). Yule Correspondences. PaganPages.Org. Retrieved 2021, from https://paganpages.org/emagazine/2020/12/01/yule-correspondences-15/

Wright, J. (2021a, June 1). Summer Solstice/Litha Correspondences. PaganPages.Org. Retrieved 2021, from https://paganpages.org/emagazine/2021/06/01/summer-solstice-litha-correspondences-2/

Wright, J. (2021b, October 1). Samhain Correspondences. PaganPages.Org. Retrieved 2021, from https://paganpages.org/emagazine/2021/10/01/samhain-correspondences-13/

Wright, J. (2022a, February 1). Imbolc Correspondences. PaganPages.Org. Retrieved 2021, from https://paganpages.org/emagazine/2022/02/01/imbolc-correspondences-18/

Wright, J. (2022b, February 1). Ostara Correspondences. PaganPages.Org. Retrieved 2021, from https://paganpages.org/emagazine/2022/02/01/ostara-correspondences-12/

Wright, M. (2021, June 4). How to Cast a Wicca Ritual Magic Circle. The Not So Innocents Abroad. Retrieved 2022, from https://www.thenotsoinnocentsabroad.com/blog/how-to-cast-a-wicca-ritual-magic-circle

www.ingramcontent.com/pod-product-compliance
Lightning Source LLC
Chambersburg PA
CBHW080632170426
43209CB00008B/1558